The Legends Of The Jews

Vol. 2: Bible Times And Characters From Joseph To The Exodus

Your purchase helps us
to sponsor a new translation

The Legends Of The Jews

Vol. 2: Bible Times And Characters From Joseph To The Exodus

By Louis Ginzberg

Translated From The German Manuscript From Henrietta Szold

E-mail: info@everburninglight.org
WWW: http://www.everburninglight.org

Providence University, 2006
First edition, 2007
ISBN: 1-897352-12-3

For information:
ULC-ITALIA
Via C.A. Colombo 20/F, 34074 Monfalcone (GO)
Tel.: +39-(0)481-412574

Printed in USA.

Index of contents

Preface

The arrangement and presentation of the material in this volume are the same as in Volume I. In both my efforts have been directed to bringing together as full as possible a collection of Jewish legends that deal with Biblical personages and events. The sources of those legends and explanations of some of them will be given in the last volume of the entire work, and the numbers throughout the work refer to the notes in the concluding volume.

My original intention was to continue Volume II up to the death of Moses, but the legendary material clustering around the life and death of Moses is so abundant that practical considerations demanded the division of this material, in order not to make the second volume too bulky. The division chosen is a natural one. This volume closes with the Exodus, and contains the deeds of Moses in Egypt, while the following volume will deal with Moses in the desert.The fact that Job is placed between Jacob's sons and Moses may appear strange to some readers, since in the Bible Job is one of the last books; but "legend is above time and space", and I have, therefore, given Job the place which legend has ascribed to him.

Louis Ginzberg.

New York, March 28, 1910

I. Joseph

The Favorite Son

Jacob was not exempt from the lot that falls to the share of all the pious. Whenever they expect to enjoy life in tranquillity, Satan hinders them. He appears before God, and says: "Is it not enough that the future world is set apart for the pious? What right have they to enjoy this world, besides"? After the many hardships and conflicts that had beset the path of Jacob, he thought he would be at rest at last, and then came the loss of Joseph and inflicted the keenest suffering. Verily, few and evil had been the days of the years of Jacob's pilgrimage, for the time spent outside of the Holy Land had seemed joyless to him. Only the portion of his life passed in the land of his fathers, during which he was occupied with making proselytes, in accordance with the example set him by Abraham and Isaac, did he consider worth while having lived, and this happy time was of short duration. When Joseph was snatched away, but eight years had elapsed since his return to his father's house.

And yet it was only for the sake of Joseph that Jacob had been willing to undergo all the troubles and the adversity connected with his sojourn in the house of Laban. Indeed, Jacob's blessing in having his quiver full of children was due to the merits of Joseph, and likewise the dividing of the Red Sea and of the Jordan for the Israelites was the reward for his son's piety. For among the sons of Jacob Joseph was the one that resembled his father most closely in appearance, and, also, he was the one to whom Jacob transmitted the instruction and knowledge he had received from his teachers Shem and Eber. The whole course of the son's life is but a repetition of the father's. As the mother of Jacob remained childless for a long time after her marriage, so also the mother of Joseph. As Rebekah had undergone severe suffering in giving birth to Jacob, so Rachel in giving birth to Joseph. As Jacob's mother bore two sons, so also Joseph's mother. Like Jacob, Joseph was born circumcised. As the father was a shepherd, so the son. As the father served for the sake of a woman, so the son served under a woman. Like the father, the son appropriated his older brother's birthright. The father was hated by his brother, and the son was hated by his brethren. The father was the favorite son as compared with his brother, so was the son as compared with his brethren. Both the father and the son lived in the land of the stranger. The father became a servant to a master, also the son. The master whom the father served was blessed by God, so was the master whom the son served. The father and the son were both accompanied by angels, and both married their wives outside of the Holy Land. The father and the son were both blessed with wealth. Great things were announced to the father in a dream, so also to the son. As the father went to Egypt and put an end to famine, so the son. As the father exacted the promise from his sons to bury him in the Holy Land, so also the son. The father died in Egypt, there died also the son. The body of the father was embalmed, also the body of the son. As the father's remains were carried to the Holy Land for interment, so also the remains of the son. Jacob the father provided for the sustenance of his son Joseph during a period of seventeen years, so Joseph the son provided for his father Jacob during a period of seventeen years.

Until he was seventeen years old, Joseph frequented the Bet ha-Midrash, and he became so learned that he could impart to his brethren the Halakot he had heard from his father, and in this way he may be regarded as their teacher. He did not stop at formal instruction, he also tried to give them good counsel, and he became the favorite of the sons of the handmaids, who would kiss and embrace him.

In spite of his scholarship there was something boyish about Joseph. He painted his eyes, dressed his hair carefully, and walked with a mincing step. These foibles of youth were not so deplorable as his habit of bringing evil reports of his brethren to his father. He accused them of treating the beasts under their care with cruelty--he said that they ate flesh torn from a living animal--and he charged them with casting their eyes upon the daughters of the Canaanites, and giving contemptuous treatment to the sons of the handmaids Bilhah and Zilpah, whom they called slaves.

For these groundless accusations Joseph had to pay dearly. He was himself sold as a slave, because he had charged his brethren with having called the sons of the handmaids slaves, and Potiphar's wife cast her eyes upon Joseph, because he threw the suspicion upon his brethren that they had cast their eyes upon the Canaanitish women. And how little it was true that they were guilty of cruelty to animals, appears from the fact that at the very time when they were contemplating their crime against Joseph, they yet observed all the rules and prescriptions of the ritual in slaughtering the kid of the goats with the blood of which they besmeared his coat of many colors.

Joseph Hated by His Brethren

Joseph's talebearing against his brethren made them hate him. Among all of them Gad was particularly wrathful, and for good reason. Gad was a very brave man, and when a beast of prey attacked the herd, over which he kept guard at night, he would seize it by one of its legs, and whirl it around until it was stunned, and then he would fling it away to a distance of two stadia, and kill it thus. Once Jacob sent Joseph to tend the flock, but he remained away only thirty days, for he was a delicate lad and fell sick with the heat, and he hastened back to his father. On his return he told Jacob that the sons of the handmaids were in the habit of slaughtering the choice cattle of the herd and eating it, without obtaining permission from Judah and Reuben. But his report was not accurate. What he had seen was Gad slaughtering one lamb, which he had snatched from the very jaws of a bear, and he killed it because it could not be kept alive after its fright. Joseph's account sounded as though the sons of the handmaids were habitually inconsiderate and careless in wasting their father's substance.

To the resentment of the brethren was added their envy of Joseph, because their father loved him more than all of them. Joseph's beauty of person was equal to that of his mother Rachel, and Jacob had but to look at him to be consoled for the death of his beloved wife. Reason enough for distinguishing him among his children. As a token of his great love for him, Jacob gave Joseph a coat of many colors, so light and delicate that it could be crushed and concealed in the closed palm of one hand. The Hebrew name of the garment, Passim, conveys the story of the sale of Joseph. The first letter, Pe, stands for Potiphar, his Egyptian master; Samek stands for Soharim, the merchantmen that bought Joseph from the company of Ishmaelites to whom his brethren had sold him; Yod stands for these same Ishmaelites; and Mem, for the Midianites that obtained him from the merchantmen, and then disposed of him to Potiphar. But Passim. has yet another meaning, "clefts". His brethren knew that the Red Sea would be cleft in twain in days to come for Joseph's sake, and they were jealous of the glory to be conferred upon him. Although they were filled with hatred of him, it must be said in their favor that they were not of a sullen, spiteful nature. They did not hide their feelings, they proclaimed their enmity openly.

Once Joseph dreamed a dream, and he could not refrain from telling it to his brethren. He spoke, and said: "Hear, I pray you, this dream which I have dreamed. Behold, you gathered fruit, and so did I. Your fruit rotted, but mine remained sound. Your seed will set up dumb images of idols, but they will vanish at the appearance of my descendant, the Messiah of Joseph. You will keep the truth as to my fate from the knowledge of my father, but I will stand fast as a reward for the self-denial of my mother, and you will prostrate yourselves five times before me".

The brethren refused at first to listen to the dream, but when Joseph urged them again and again, they gave heed to him, and they said, "Shalt thou indeed reign over us? or shalt thou indeed have dominion over us"? God put an interpretation into their mouths that was to be verified in the posterity of Joseph. Jeroboam and Jehu, two kings, and Joshua and Gideon, two judges, have been among his descendants, corresponding to the double and emphatic expressions used by his brethren in interpreting the dream.

Then Joseph dreamed another dream, how the sun, the moon, and eleven stars bowed down before him, and Jacob, to whom he told it first, was rejoiced over it, for he understood its meaning properly. He knew that he himself was designated by the sun, the name by which God had called him when he lodged overnight on the holy site of the Temple. He had heard God say to the angels at that time, "The sun has come". The moon stood for Joseph's mother, and the stars for his brethren, for the righteous are as the stars. Jacob was so convinced of the truth of the dream that he was encouraged to believe that he would live to see the resurrection of the dead, for Rachel was dead, and her return to earth was clearly indicated by the dream. He went astray there, for not Joseph's own mother was referred to, but his foster-mother Bilhah, who had raised him.

Jacob wrote the dream in a book, recording all the circumstances, the day, the hour, and the place, for the holy spirit cautioned him, "Take heed, these things will surely come to pass". But when Joseph repeated his dream to his brethren, in the presence of his father, Jacob rebuked him, saying, "I and thy brethren, that has some sense, but I and thy mother, that is inconceivable, for thy mother is dead". These words of Jacob called forth a reproof from God. He said, "Thus thy descendants will in time to come seek to hinder Jeremiah in delivering his prophecies". Jacob may be excused, he had spoken in this way only in order to avert the envy and hate of his brethren from Joseph, but they envied and hated him because they knew that the interpretation put upon the dream by Jacob would be realized.

Joseph Cast into the Pit

Once the brethren of Joseph led their father's flocks to the pastures of Shechem, and they intended to take their ease and pleasure there. They stayed away a long time, and no tidings of them were heard. Jacob began to be anxious about the fate of his sons. He feared that a war had broken out between them and the people of Shechem, and he resolved to send Joseph to them and have him bring word again, whether it was well with his brethren. Jacob desired to know also about the flocks, for it is a duty to concern oneself about the welfare of anything from which one derives profit. Though he knew that the hatred of his brethren might bring on unpleasant adventures, yet Joseph, in filial reverence, declared himself ready to go on his father's errand. Later, whenever Jacob remembered his dear son's willing spirit, the recollection stabbed him to the heart. He would say to himself, "Thou didst know the hatred of thy brethren, and yet thou didst say, Here am

I".Jacob dismissed Joseph, with the injunction that he journey only by daylight, saying furthermore, "Go now, see whether it be well with thy brethren, and well with the flock; and send me word"--an unconscious prophecy. He did not say that he expected to see Joseph again, but only to have word from him. Since the covenant of the pieces, God had resolved, on account of Abraham's doubting question, that Jacob and his family should go down into Egypt to dwell there. The preference shown to Joseph by his father, and the envy it aroused, leading finally to the sale of Joseph and his establishment in Egypt, were but disguised means created by God, instead of executing His counsel directly by carrying Jacob down into Egypt as a captive.

Joseph reached Shechem, where he expected to find his brethren. Shechem was always a place of ill omen for Jacob and his seed--there Dinah was dishonored, there the Ten Tribes of Israel rebelled against the house of David while Rehoboam ruled in Jerusalem, and there Jeroboam was installed as king. Not finding his brethren and the herd in Shechem, Joseph continued his journey in the direction of the next pasturing place, not far from Shechem, but he lost his way in the wilderness. Gabriel in human shape appeared before him, and asked him, saying, "What seekest thou"? And he answered, "I seek my brethren". Whereto the angel replied, "Thy brethren have given up the Divine qualities of love and mercy. Through a prophetic revelation they learned that the Hivites were preparing to make war upon them, and therefore they departed hence to go to Dothan. And they had to leave this place for other reasons, too. I heard, while I was still standing behind the curtain that veils the Divine throne, that this day the Egyptian bondage would begin, and thou wouldst be the first to be subjected to it". Then Gabriel led Joseph to Dothan.

When his brethren saw him afar off, they conspired against him, to slay him. Their first plan was to set dogs on him. Simon then spoke to Levi, "Behold, the master of dreams cometh with a new dream, he whose descendant Jeroboam will introduce the worship of Baal. Come now, therefore, and let us slay him, that we may see what will become of his dreams". But God spoke: "Ye say, We shall see what will become of his dreams, and I say likewise, We shall see, and the future shall show whose word will stand, yours or Mine".

Simon and Gad set about slaying Joseph, and he fell upon his face, and entreated them: "Have mercy with me, my brethren, have pity on the heart of my father Jacob. Lay not your hands upon me, to spill innocent blood, for I have done no evil unto you. But if I have done evil unto you, then chastise me with a chastisement, but your hands lay not upon me, for the sake of our father Jacob". These words touched Zebulon, and he began to lament and weep, and the wailing of Joseph rose up together with his brother's, and when Simon and Gad raised their hands against him to execute their evil design, Joseph took refuge behind Zebulon, and supplicated his other brethren to have mercy upon him. Then Reuben arose, and he said, "Brethren, let us not slay him, but let us cast him into one of the dry pits, which our fathers dug without finding water". That was due to the providence of God; He had hindered the water from rising in them in order that Joseph's rescue might be accomplished, and the pits remained dry until Joseph was safe in the hands of the Ishmaelites.

Reuben had several reasons for interceding in behalf of Joseph. He knew that he as the oldest of the brethren would be held responsible by their father, if any evil befell him. Besides, Reuben was grateful to Joseph for having reckoned him among the eleven sons of Jacob in narrating his dream of the sun, moon, and stars. Since his disrespectful bearing toward Jacob, he had not thought himself worthy of being considered one of his sons. First Reuben tried to restrain his brethren from their purpose, and he addressed them in words full of love and compassion. But when he saw that neither words nor entreaties would change their intention, he begged them, saying: "My brethren, at least hearken unto me in respect of this, that ye be not so wicked and cruel as to slay him. Lay no hand upon your brother, shed no blood, cast him into this pit that is in the wilderness, and let him perish thus.

Then Reuben went away from his brethren, and he hid in the mountains, so that he might be able to hasten back in a favorable moment and draw Joseph forth from the pit and restore him to his father. He hoped his reward would be pardon for the transgression he had committed against Jacob. His good intention was frustrated, yet Reuben was rewarded by God, for God gives a recompense not only for good deeds, but for good intentions as well. As he was the first of the brethren of Joseph to make an attempt to save him, so the city of Bezer in the tribe of Reuben was the first of the cities of refuge appointed to safeguard the life of the innocent that seek help. Furthermore God spake to Reuben, saying: "As thou wast the first to endeavor to restore a child unto his father, so Hosea, one of thy descendants, shall be the first to endeavor to lead Israel back to his heavenly Father".

The brethren accepted Reuben's proposition, and Simon seized Joseph, and cast him into a pit swarming with snakes and scorpions, beside which was another unused pit, filled with offal. As though this were not enough torture, Simon bade his brethren fling great stones at Joseph. In his later dealings with this brother Simon, Joseph showed all the forgiving charitableness of his nature. When Simon was held in durance in Egypt as a hostage, Joseph, so far from bearing him a grudge, ordered crammed poultry to be set before him at all his meals.

Not satisfied with exposing Joseph to the snakes and scorpions, his brethren had stripped him bare before they flung him into the pit. They took off his coat of many colors, his upper garment, his breeches, and his shirt. However, the reptiles could do him no harm. God heard his cry of distress, and kept them in hiding in the clefts and the holes, and they could not come near him. From the depths of the pit Joseph appealed to his brethren, saying: "O my brethren, what have I done unto you, and what is my transgression? Why are you not afraid before God on account of your treatment of me? Am I not flesh of your flesh, and bone of your bone? Jacob your father, is he not also my father? Why do you act thus toward me? And how will you be able to lift up your countenance before Jacob? O Judah, Reuben, Simon, Levi, my brethren, deliver me, I pray you, from the dark place into which you have cast me. Though I committed a trespass against you, yet are ye children of Abraham, Isaac, and Jacob, who were compassionate with the orphan, gave food to the hungry, and clothed the naked. How, then, can ye withhold your pity from your own brother, your own flesh and bone? And though I sinned against you, yet you will hearken unto my petition for the sake of my father. O that my father knew what my brethren are doing unto me, and what they spake unto me"!

To avoid hearing Joseph's weeping and cries of distress, his brethren passed on from the pit, and stood at a bow- shot's distance. The only one among them that manifested pity was Zebulon. For two days and two nights no food passed his lips on account of his grief over the fate of Joseph, who had to spend three days and three nights in the pit before he was sold. During this period Zebulon was charged by his brethren to keep watch at the pit. He was chosen to stand guard because he took no part in the meals. Part of the time Judah also refrained from eating with the rest, and took turns at watching, because he feared Simon and Gad might jump down into the pit and put an end to Joseph's life.

While Joseph was languishing thus, his brethren determined to kill him. They would finish their meal first, they said, and then they would fetch him forth and slay him. When they had done eating, they attempted to say grace, but Judah remonstrated with them: "We are about to take the life of a human being, and yet would bless God? That is not a blessing, that is contemning the Lord. What profit is it if we slay our brother? Rather will the punishment of God descend upon us. I have good counsel to give you. Yonder passeth by a travelling company of Ishmaelites on their way to Egypt. Come and let us sell him to the Ishmaelites, and let not our hand be upon him. The Ishmaelites will take him with them upon their journeyings, and he will be lost among the peoples of the earth. Let us follow the custom of former days, for Canaan, too, the son of Ham, was made a slave for his evil deeds, and so will we do with our brother Joseph".

The Sale

While the brethren of Joseph were deliberating upon his fate, seven Midianitish merchantmen passed near the pit in which he lay. They noticed that many birds were circling above it, whence they assumed that there must be water therein, and, being thirsty, they made a halt in order to refresh themselves. When they came close, they heard Joseph screaming and wailing, and they looked down into the pit and saw a youth of beautiful figure and comely appearance. They called to him, saying: "Who art thou? Who brought thee hither, and who cast thee into this pit in the wilderness"? They all joined together and dragged him up, and took him along with them when they continued on their journey. They had to pass his brethren, who called out to the Midianites: "Why have you done such a thing, to steal our slave and carry him away with you? We threw the lad into the pit, because he was disobedient. Now, then, return our slave to us". The Midianites replied: "What, this lad, you say, is your slave, your servant? More likely is it that you all are slaves unto him, for in beauty of form, in pleasant looks, and fair appearance, he excelleth you all. Why, then, will you speak lies unto us? We will not give ear unto your words, nor believe you, for we found the lad in the wilderness, in a pit, and we took him out, and we will carry him away with us on our journey". But the sons of Jacob insisted, "Restore our slave to us, lest you meet death at the edge of the sword".

Unaffrighted, the Midianites drew their weapons, and, amid war whoops, they prepared to enter into a combat with the sons of Jacob. Then Simon rose up, and with bared sword he sprang upon the Midianites, at the same time uttering a cry that made the earth reverberate. The Midianites fell down in great consternation, and he said: "I am Simon, the son of the Hebrew Jacob, who destroyed the city of Shechem alone and unaided, and together with my brethren I destroyed the cities of the Amorites. God do so and more also, if it be not true that all the Midianites, your brethren, united with all the Canaanite kings to fight with me, cannot hold out against me. Now restore the boy you took from us, else will I give your flesh unto the fowls of the air and to the beasts of the field".

The Midianites were greatly afraid of Simon, and, terrified and abashed, they spake to the sons of Jacob with little courage: "Said ye not that ye cast this lad into the pit because he was of a rebellious spirit? What, now, will ye do with an insubordinate slave? Rather sell him to us, we are ready to pay any price you desire". This speech was part of the purpose of God. He had put it into the heart of the Midianites to insist upon possessing Joseph, that he might not remain with his brethren, and be slain by them. The brethren assented, and Joseph was sold as a slave while they sat over their meal. God spake, saying: "Over a meal did ye sell your brother, and thus shall Ahasuerus sell your descendants to Haman over a meal, and because ye have sold Joseph to be a slave, therefore shall ye say year after year, Slaves were we unto Pharaoh in Egypt".

The price paid for Joseph by the Midianites was twenty pieces of silver, enough for a pair of shoes for each of his brethren. Thus "they sold the righteous for silver, and the needy for a pair of shoes". For so handsome a youth as Joseph the sum paid was too low by far, but his appearance had been greatly changed by the horrible anguish he bad endured in the pit with the snakes and the scorpions. He had lost his ruddy complexion, and he looked sallow and sickly, and the Midianites were justified in paying a small sum for him.

The merchantmen had come upon Joseph naked in the pit, for his brethren had stripped him of all his clothes. That he might not appear before men in an unseemly condition, God sent Gabriel down to him, and the angel enlarged the amulet banging from Joseph's neck until it was a garment that covered him entirely. Joseph's brethren were looking after him as he departed with the Midianites, and when they saw him with clothes upon him, they cried after them, "Give us his raiment! We sold him naked, without clothes". His owners refused to yield to their demand, but they agreed to reimburse the brethren with four pairs of shoes, and Joseph kept his garment, the same in which he was arrayed when he arrived in Egypt and was sold to Potiphar, the same in which he was locked up in prison and appeared before Pharaoh, and the same he wore when he was ruler over Egypt.

As an atonement for the twenty pieces of silver taken by his brethren in exchange for Joseph, God commanded that every first-born son shall be redeemed by the priest with an equal amount, and, also, every Israelite must pay annually to the sanctuary as much as fell to each of the brethren as his share of the price.

The brethren of Joseph bought shoes for the money, for they said: "We will not eat it, because it is the price for the blood of our brother, but we will tread upon him, for that he spake, he would have dominion over us, and we will see what will become of his dreams". And for this reason the ordinance has been commanded, that he who refuseth to raise up a name in Israel unto his brother that hath died without having a son, shall have his shoe loosed from off his foot, and his face shall be spat upon. Joseph's brethren refused to do aught to preserve his life, and therefore the Lord loosed their shoes from off their feet, for, when they went down to Egypt, the slaves of Joseph took their shoes off their feet as they entered the gates, and they prostrated themselves before Joseph as before a Pharaoh, and, as they lay prostrate, they were spat upon, and put to shame before the Egyptians.

The Midianites pursued their journey to Gilead, but they soon regretted the purchase they had made. They feared that Joseph had been stolen in the land of the Hebrews, though sold to them as a slave, and if his kinsmen should find him with them, death would be inflicted upon them for the abduction of a free man. The high-handed manner of the sons of Jacob confirmed their suspicion, that they might be capable of man theft. Their wicked deed would explain, too, why they had accepted so small a sum in exchange for Joseph. While discussing these points, they saw, coming their way, the travelling company of Ishmaelites that had been observed earlier by the sons of Jacob, and they determined to dispose of Joseph to them, that they might at least not lose the price they had paid, and might escape the danger at the same time of being made captives for the crime of kidnapping a man. And the Ishmaelites bought Joseph from the Midianites, and they paid the same price as his former owners had given for him.

Joseph's Three Masters

As a rule the only merchandise with which the Ishmaelites loaded their camels was pitch and the skins of beasts. By a providential dispensation they carried bags of perfumery this time, instead of their usual ill-smelling freight, that sweet fragrance might be wafted to Joseph on his journey to Egypt. These aromatic substances were well suited to Joseph, whose body emitted a pleasant smell, so agreeable and pervasive that the road along which he travelled was redolent thereof, and on his arrival in Egypt the perfume from his body spread over the whole land, and the royal princesses, following the sweet scent to trace its source, reached the place in which Joseph was. Even after his death the same fragrance was spread abroad by his bones, enabling Moses to distinguish Joseph's remains from all others, and keep the oath of the children of Israel, to inter them in the Holy Land.

When Joseph learned that the Ishmaelites were carrying him to Egypt, he began to weep bitterly at the thought of being removed so far from Canaan and from his father. One of the Ishmaelites noticed Joseph's weeping and crying, and thinking that he found riding uncomfortable, he lifted him from the back of the camel, and permitted him to walk on foot. But Joseph continued to weep and sob, crying incessantly, "O father, father"! Another one of the caravan, tired of his lamentations, beat him, causing only the more tears and wails, until the youth, exhausted by his grief, was unable to move on. Now all the Ishmaelites in the company dealt out blows to him. They treated him with relentless cruelty, and tried to silence him by threats. God saw Joseph's distress, and He sent darkness and terror upon the Ishmaelites, and their hands grew rigid when they raised them to inflict a blow. Astonished, they asked themselves why God did thus unto them upon the road. They did not know that it was for the sake of Joseph.

The journey was continued until they came to Ephrath, the place of Rachel's sepulchre. Joseph hastened to his mother's grave, and throwing himself across it, he groaned and cried, saying: "O mother, mother, that didst bear me, arise, come forth and see how thy son hath been sold into slavery, with none to take pity upon him. Arise, see thy son, and weep with me over my misfortune, and observe the heartlessness of my brethren. Awake, O mother, rouse thyself from thy sleep, rise up and prepare for the conflict with my brethren, who stripped me even of my shirt, and sold me as a slave to merchantmen, who in turn sold me to others, and without mercy they tore me away from my father. Arise, accuse my brethren before God, and see whom He will justify in the judgment, and whom He will find guilty. Arise, O mother, awake from thy sleep, see how my father is with me in his soul and in his spirit, and comfort him and ease his heavy heart".

Joseph wept and cried upon the grave of his mother, until, weary from grief, he lay immovable as a stone. Then he heard a voice heavy with tears speak to him from the depths, saying: "My son Joseph, my son, I heard thy complaints and thy groans, I saw thy tears, and I knew thy misery, my son. I am grieved for thy sake, and thy affliction is added to the burden of my affliction. But, my son Joseph, put thy trust in God, and wait upon Him. Fear not, for the Lord is with thee, and He will deliver thee from all evil. Go down into Egypt with thy masters, my son; fear naught, for the Lord is with thee, O my son". This and much more like unto it did the voice utter, and then it was silent. Joseph listened in great amazement at first, and then he broke out in renewed tears. Angered thereby, one of the Ishmaelites drove him from his mother's grave with kicks and curses. Then Joseph entreated his masters to take him back to his father, who would give them great riches as a reward. But they said, "Why, thou art a slave! How canst thou know where thy father is? If thou hadst had a free man as father, thou wouldst not have been sold twice for a petty sum". And then their fury against him increased, they beat him and maltreated him, and he wept bitter tears.

Now God looked upon the distress of Joseph, and He sent darkness to enshroud the land once more. A storm raged, the lightning flashed, and from the thunderbolts the whole earth trembled, and the Ishmaelites lost their way in their terror. The beasts and the camels stood still, and, beat them as their drivers would, they refused to budge from the spot, but crouched down upon the ground. Then the Ishmaelites spake to one another, and said: "Why hath God brought this upon us? What are our sins, what our trespasses, that such things befall us"? One of them said to the others: "Peradventure this hath come upon us by reason of the sin which we have committed against this slave. Let us beg him earnestly to grant us forgiveness, and if then God will take pity, and let these storms pass away from us, we shall know that we suffered harm on account of the injury we inflicted upon this slave".

The Ishmaelites did according to these words, and they said unto Joseph: "We have sinned against God and against thee. Pray to thy God, and entreat Him to take this death plague from us, for we acknowledge that we have sinned against Him". Joseph fulfilled their wish, and God hearkened to his petition, and the storm was assuaged. All around became calm, the beasts arose from their recumbent position, and the caravan could proceed upon its way. Now the Ishmaelites saw plainly that all their trouble had come upon them for the sake of Joseph, and they spoke one to another, saying: "We know now that all this evil hath happened to us on account of this poor fellow, and wherefore should we bring death upon ourselves by our own doings? Let us take counsel together, what is to be done with the slave". One of them advised that Joseph's wish be fulfilled, and he be taken back to his father. Then they would be sure of receiving the money they had paid out for him. This plan was rejected, because they had accomplished a great part of their journey, and they were not inclined to retrace their steps. They therefore resolved upon carrying Joseph to Egypt and selling him there. They would rid themselves of him in this way, and also receive a great price for him.

They continued their journey as far as the borders of Egypt, and there they met four men, descendants of Medan, the son of Abraham, and to these they sold Joseph for five shekels. The two companies, the Ishmaelites and the Medanites, arrived in Egypt upon the same day. The latter, hearing that Potiphar, an officer of Pharaoh, the captain of the guard, was seeking a good slave, repaired to him at once, to try to dispose of Joseph to him. Potiphar was willing to pay as much as four hundred pieces of silver, for, high as the price was, it did not seem too great for a slave that pleased him as much as Joseph. However, he made a condition. He said to the Medanites: "I will pay you the price demanded, but you must bring me the person that sold the slave to you, that I may be in a position to find out all about him, for the youth seems to me to be neither a slave nor the son of a slave. He appears to be of noble blood. I must convince myself that he was not stolen". The Medanites brought the Ishmaelites to Potiphar, and they testified that Joseph was a slave, that they had owned him, and had sold him to the Medanites. Potiphar rested satisfied with this report, paid the price asked for Joseph, and the Medanites and the Ishmaelites went their way.

Joseph's Coat Brought to His Father

No sooner was the sale of Joseph an accomplished fact than the sons of Jacob repented of their deed. They even hastened after the Midianites to ransom Joseph, but their efforts to overtake them were vain, and they had to accept the inevitable. Meantime Reuben had rejoined his brethren. He had been so deeply absorbed in penances, in praying and studying the Torah, in expiation of his sin against his father, that he had not been able to remain with his brethren and tend the flocks, and thus it happened that he was not on the spot when Joseph was sold. His first errand was to go to the pit, in the hope of finding Joseph there. In that case he would have carried him off and restored him to his father clandestinely, without the knowledge of his brethren. He stood at the opening and called again and again, "Joseph, Joseph"! As he received no answer, he concluded that Joseph had perished, either by reason of terror or as the result of a snake bite, and he descended into the pit, only to find that he was not there, either living or dead. He mounted to the top again, and rent his clothes, and cried out, "The lad is not there, and what answer shall I give to my father, if he be dead"? Then Reuben returned unto his brethren, and told them that Joseph bad vanished from the pit, whereat he was deeply grieved, because he, being the oldest of the sons, was responsible to their father Jacob. The brethren made a clean breast of what they had done with Joseph, and they related to him how they had tried to make good their evil deed, and how their efforts had been vain.

Now there remained nothing to do but invent a plausible explanation for their brother's disappearance to give to Jacob. First of all, however, they took an oath not to betray to his father or any human being what they bad actually done with Joseph. He who violated the oath would be put to the sword by the rest. Then they took counsel together about what to say to Jacob. It was Issachar's advice to tear Joseph's coat of many colors, and dip it in the blood of a little kid of the goats, to make Jacob believe that his son had been torn by a wild beast. The reason he suggested a kid was because its blood looks like human blood. In expiation of this act of deception, it was ordained that a kid be used as an atonement sacrifice when the Tabernacle was dedicated.

Simon opposed this suggestion. He did not want to relinquish Joseph's coat, and he threatened to hew down any one that should attempt to wrest it from him by force. The reason for his vehemence was that he was very much enraged against his brethren for not having slain Joseph. But they threatened him in turn, saying, "If thou wilt not give up the coat, we shall say that thou didst execute the evil deed thyself". At that Simon surrendered it, and Naphtali brought it to Jacob, handing it to him with the words: "When we were driving our herds homeward, we found this garment covered with blood and dust on the highway, a little beyond Shechem. Know now whether it be thy son's coat or not". Jacob recognized Joseph's coat, and, overwhelmed by grief, he fell prostrate, and long lay on the ground motionless, like a stone. Then he arose, and set up a loud cry, and wept, saying, "It is my son's coat".

In great haste Jacob dispatched a slave to his sons, to bid them come to him, that he might learn more about what had happened. In the evening they all came, their garments rent, and dust strewn upon their heads. When they confirmed all that Naphtali had told him, Jacob broke out in mourning and lamentation: "It is my son's coat; an evil beast hath devoured him; Joseph is without doubt torn in pieces. I sent him to you to see whether it was well with you, and well with the flock. He went to do my errand, and while I thought him to be with you, the misfortune befell". Thereto the sons of Jacob made reply: "He came to us not at all. Since we left thee, we have not set eyes on him".

After these words, Jacob could doubt no longer that Joseph bad been torn by wild beasts, and he mourned for his son, saying: "O my son Joseph, my son, I sent thee to inquire after the welfare of thy brethren, and now thou art torn by wild beasts. It is my fault that this evil chance hath come upon thee. I am distressed for thee, my son, I am sorely distressed. How sweet was thy life to me, and how bitter is thy death! Would God I had died for thee, O Joseph, my son, for now I am distressed on thy account. O my son Joseph, where art thou, and where is thy soul? Arise, arise from thy place, and look upon my grief for thee. Come and count the tears that roll down my cheeks, and bring the tale of them before God, that His wrath be turned away from me. O Joseph, my son, how painful and appalling was thy death! None hath died a death like thine since the world doth stand. I know well that it came to pass by reason of my sins. O that thou wouldst return and see the bitter sorrow thy misfortune hath brought upon me! But it is true, it was not I that created thee, and formed thee. I gave thee neither spirit nor soul, but God created thee. He formed thy bones, covered them with flesh, breathed the breath of life into thy nostrils, and then gave thee unto me. And God who gave thee unto me, He hath taken thee from me, and from Him hath this dispensation come upon me. What the Lord doeth is well done"! In these words and many others like them Jacob mourned and bewailed his son, until he fell to the ground prostrate and immovable.

When the sons of Jacob saw the vehemence of their father's grief, they repented of their deed, and wept bitterly. Especially Judah was grief-stricken. He laid his father's head upon his knees, and wiped his tears away as they flowed from his eyes, while he himself broke out in violent weeping. The sons of Jacob and their wives all sought to comfort their father. They arranged a great memorial service, and they wept and mourned over Joseph's death and over their father's sorrow. But Jacob refused to be comforted.

The tidings of his son's death caused the loss of two members of Jacob's family. Bilhah and Dinah could not survive their grief. Bilhah passed away the very day whereon the report reached Jacob, and Dinah died soon after, and so he had three losses to mourn in one month.

He received the tidings of Joseph's death in the seventh month, Tishri, and on the tenth day of the month, and therefore the children of Israel are bidden to weep and afflict their souls on this day. Furthermore, on this day the sin offering of atonement shall be a kid of the goats, because the sons of Jacob transgressed with a kid, in the blood of which they dipped Joseph's coat, and thus they brought sorrow upon Jacob.

When he had recovered somewhat from the stunning blow which the tidings of his favorite son's death had dealt him, Jacob rose up from the ground and addressed his sons, tears streaming down his cheeks all the while. "Up", he said, "take your swords and your bows, go out in the field, and make search, perhaps you will find the body of my son, and you will bring it to me, so that I may bury it. Keep a lookout, too, for beasts of prey, and catch the first you meet. Seize it and bring it to me. It may be that God will have pity upon my sorrow, and put the beast between your hands that hath torn my child in pieces, and I will take my revenge upon it".

The sons of Jacob set out on the morrow to do the bidding of their father, while he remained at home and wept and lamented for Joseph. In the wilderness they found a wolf, which they caught and brought to Jacob alive, saying: "Here is the first wild beast we encountered, and we have brought it to thee. But of thy son's corpse we saw not a trace". Jacob seized the wolf, and, amid loud weeping, he addressed these words to him: "Why didst thou devour my son Joseph, without any fear of the God of the earth, and without taking any thought of the grief thou wouldst bring down upon me? Thou didst devour my son without reason, he was guilty of no manner of transgression, and thou didst roll the responsibility for his death upon me. But God avengeth him that is persecuted".

To grant consolation to Jacob, God opened the mouth of the beast, and he spake: "As the Lord liveth, who hath created me, and as thy soul liveth, my lord, I have not seen thy son, and I did not rend him in pieces. From a land afar off I came to seek mine own son, who suffered a like fate with thine. He hath disappeared, and I know not whether he be dead or alive, and therefore I came hither ten days ago to find him. This day, while I was searching for him, thy sons met me, and they seized me, and, adding more grief to my grief over my lost son, they brought me hither to thee. This is my story, and now, O son of man, I am in thy hands, thou canst dispose of me this day as seemeth well in thy sight, but I swear unto thee by the God that bath created me, I have not seen thy son, nor have I torn him in pieces, never hath the flesh of man come into my mouth". Astonished at the speech of the wolf, Jacob let him go, unhindered, whithersoever he would, but he mourned his son Joseph as before.

It is a law of nature that however much one may grieve over the death of a dear one, at the end of a year consolation finds its way to the heart of the mourner. But the disappearance of a living man can never be wiped out of one's memory. Therefore the fact that he was inconsolable made Jacob suspect that Joseph was alive, and he did not give entire credence to the report of his sons. His vague suspicion was strengthened by something that happened to him. He went up into the mountains, hewed twelve stones out of the quarry, and wrote the names of his sons thereon, their constellations, and the months corresponding to the constellations, a stone for a son, thus, "Reuben, Ram, Nisan", and so for each of his twelve sons. Then he addressed the stones and bade them bow down before the one marked with Reuben's name, constellation, and month, and they did not move. He gave the same order regarding the stone marked for Simon, and again the stones stood still. And so he did respecting all his sons, until he reached the stone for Joseph. When he spoke concerning this one, "I command you to fall down before Joseph", they all prostrated themselves. He tried the same test with other things, with trees and sheaves, and always the result was the same, and Jacob could not but feel that his suspicion was true, Joseph was alive.

There was a reason why God did not reveal the real fate of Joseph to Jacob. When his brethren sold Joseph, their fear that the report of their iniquity might reach the ears of Jacob led them to pronounce the ban upon any that should betray the truth without the consent of all the others. Judah advanced the objection that a ban is invalid unless it is decreed in the presence of ten persons, and there were but nine of them, for Reuben and Benjamin were not there when the sale of Joseph was concluded. To evade the difficulty, the brothers counted God as the tenth person, and therefore God felt bound to refrain from revealing the true state of things to Jacob. He had regard, as it were, for the ban pronounced by the brethren of Joseph. And as God kept the truth a secret from Jacob, Isaac did not feel justified in acquainting him with his grandson's fate, which was well known to him, for he was a prophet. Whenever he was in the company of Jacob, he mourned with him, but as soon as he quitted him, he left off from manifesting grief, because he knew that Joseph lived.

Jacob was thus the only one among Joseph's closest kinsmen that remained in ignorance of his son's real fortunes, and he was the one of them all that had the greatest reason for regretting his death. He spoke: "The covenant that God made with me regarding the twelve tribes is null and void now. I did strive in vain to establish the twelve tribes, seeing that now the death of Joseph hath destroyed the covenant. All the works of God were made to correspond to the number of the tribes--twelve are the signs of the zodiac, twelve the months, twelve hours hath the day, twelve the night, and twelve stones are set in Aaron's breastplate--and now that Joseph hath departed, the covenant of the tribes is set at naught".

He could not replace the lost son by entering into a new marriage, for he had made the promise to his father-in-law to take none beside his daughters to wife, and this promise, as he interpreted it, held good after the death of Laban's daughters as well as while they were alive.

Beside grief over his loss and regret at the breaking of the covenant of the tribes, Jacob had still another reason for mourning the death of Joseph. God had said to Jacob, "If none of thy sons dies during thy lifetime, thou mayest look upon it as a token that thou wilt not be put in Gehenna after thy death". Thinking Joseph to be dead, Jacob had his own fate to bewail, too, for he now believed that he was doomed to Gehenna. His mourning lasted all of twenty-two years, corresponding to the number of the years he had dwelt apart from his parents, and had not fulfilled the duty of a son toward them.

In his mourning Jacob put sackcloth upon his loins, and therein be became a model for the kings and princes in Israel, for David, Ahab, Joram, and Mordecai did likewise when a great misfortune befell the nation.

Judah and His Sons

When the sons of Jacob saw how inconsolable their father was, they went to Judah, and said to him, "This great misfortune is thy fault". Judah replied: "It was I that asked you, What profit is it if we slay our brother and conceal his blood? and now you say the sin lies at my door". The brethren continued to argue: "But it was thou that didst say, Come and let us sell him to the Ishmaelites, and we followed thy advice. Hadst thou said, Let us restore him to his father, we had heeded these words of thine as well".

The brethren hereupon deprived Judah of his dignity, for hitherto he had been their king, and they also excluded him from their fellowship, and he had to seek his fortune alone. Through the mediation of his chief shepherd Hirah, he became acquainted with the Canaanitish king of Adullam, Barsan by name. Though he was well aware of the corruption of the generations of Canaan, he permitted passion to get the better of him, and took a Canaanite to wife. The Adullamite king gave a banquet in his honor, at which his daughter Bath-shua poured the wine, and intoxicated by wine and passion Judah took her and married her. Judah's action may be compared to that of the lion who passes a carrion and eats of it, though a cur preceding him on the way had refused to touch it. Even Esau came in time to acknowledge that the daughters of Canaan were wicked, and the lion Judah must needs take one of them to wife. The holy spirit cried out against Judah when he married the Canaanite woman of Adullam, saying, "The glory of Israel went down in Adullam".

The first-born son of Judah from this marriage was named Er, "the childless", a suitable name for him that died without begetting any issue. At Judah's desire, Er married Tamar, a daughter of Aram, the son of Shem, but because she was not a Canaanitish woman, his mother used artifices against her, and he did not know her, and an angel of the Lord killed him on the third day after his wedding. Then Judah gave Tamar to his second son Onan, the marriage taking place before the week of the wedding festivities for Er had elapsed. A whole year Onan lived with Tamar without knowing her, and when, finally, Judah uttered threats against him on that account, he did, indeed, have intercourse with her, but, giving heed to the injunctions of his mother, he took care not to beget any children with her. He, too, died on account of his iniquity, and his name Onan "mourning", was well chosen, for very soon was his father called upon to mourn for him. Now Judah conceived the plan of marrying Tamar to his youngest son Shelah, but his wife would not permit it. She hated Tamar because she was not of the daughters of Canaan like herself, and while Judah was away from home, Bath-shua chose a wife for her son Shelah from the daughters of Canaan. Judah was very angry at Bath-shua for what she had done, and also God poured out His wrath upon her, for on account of her wickedness she had to die, and her death happened a year after that of her two sons.

Now that Bath-shua was dead, Judah might have carried out his wish and married Tamar to his youngest son. But he waited for Shelah to grow up, because he feared for his life, seeing that Tamar had brought death to two husbands before him. So she remained a widow in her father's house for two years. Endowed with the gift of prophecy, Tamar knew that she was appointed to be the ancestress of David and of the Messiah, and she determined to venture upon an extreme measure in order to make sure of fulfilling her destiny. Accordingly, when the holy spirit revealed to her that Judah was going up to Timnah, she put off from her the garments of her widowhood, and sat in the gate of Abraham's tent, and there she encountered Judah. All the time she lived in the house of her father-in-law, he had never seen her face, for in her virtue and chastity she had always kept it covered, and now when Judah met her, he did not recognize her. It was as a reward for her modesty that God made her to become the mother of the royal line of David, and the ancestress of Isaiah, and his father Amoz as well, both of whom were prophets and of royal blood.

Judah passed Tamar by without paying any attention to her, and she raised her eyes heavenward, and said, "O Lord of the world, shall I go forth empty from the house of this pious man"? Then God sent the angel that is appointed over the passion of love, and he compelled Judah to turn back. With prophetic caution, Tamar demanded that, as a pledge for the reward he promised her, he leave with her his signet, his mantle, and his staff, the symbols of royalty, judgeship, and Messiahship, the three distinctions of the descendants of Tamar from her union with Judah. When Judah sent her the promised reward, a kid of the goats, by the hand of his friend, in order to receive the pledges from her hand, Tamar could not be found, and he feared to make further search for her, lest he be put to shame. But Tamar, who soon discerned that she was with child, felt very happy and proud, for she knew that she would be the mother of kings and redeemers.

When her state became known, she was forcibly dragged before the court, in which Isaac, Jacob, and Judah sat as judges. Judah, being the youngest of the judges and the least considerable in dignity, was the first to give a decision, for thus it is prescribed in criminal cases, that the prominent judges overawe not the lesser and influence their decisions unduly. It was the opinion of Judah that the woman was liable to the penalty of death by burning, for she was the daughter of the high priest Shem, and death by fire is the punishment ordained by the law for a high priest's daughter that leads an unchaste life.

The preparations for her execution were begun. In vain Tamar searched for the three pledges she had received from Judah, she could not find them, and almost she lost hope that she would be able to wring a confession from her father-in-law. She raised her eyes to God, and prayed: "I supplicate Thy grace, O God, Thou who givest ear to the cry of the distressed in the hour of his need, answer me, that I may be spared to bring forth the three holy children, who will be ready to suffer death by fire, for the sake of the glory of Thy Name". And God granted her petition, and sent the angel Michael down to succor her. He put the pledges in a place in which Tamar could not fail to see them, and she took them, and threw them before the feet of the judges, with the words: "By the man whose these are am I with child, but though I perish in the flames, I will not betray him. I hope in the Lord of the world, that He will turn the heart of the man, so that he will make confession thereof". Then Judah rose up, and said: "With your permission, my brethren, and ye men of my father's house, I make it known that with what measure a man metes, it shall be measured unto him, be it for good or for evil, but happy the man that acknowledgeth his sins. Because I took the coat of Joseph, and colored it with the blood of a kid, and then laid it at the feet of my father, saying, Know now whether it be thy son's coat or not, therefore must I now confess, before the court, unto whom belongeth this signet, this mantle, and this staff. But it is better that I be put to shame in this world than I should be put to shame in the other world, before the face of my pious father. It is better that I should perish in a fire that can be extinguished than I should be cast into hell fire, which devoureth other fires. Now, then, I acknowledge that Tamar is innocent. By me is she with child, not because she indulged in illicit passion, but because I held back her marriage with my son Shelah". Then a heavenly voice was heard to say: "Ye are both innocent! It was the will of God that it should happen"!

The open confession of Judah induced his oldest brother Reuben to make public acknowledgment of the sin he had committed against his father, for he had kept it a secret until then.

Tamar gave birth to twin sons, Perez and Zerah, both resembling their father in bravery and piety. She called the first Perez, "mighty", because she said, "Thou didst show thyself of great power, and it is meet and proper that thou shouldst be strong, for thou art destined to possess the kingdom". The second son was called Zerah, because he appeared from out of the womb before his brother, but he was forced back again to make way for Perez. These two, Perez and Zerah. were sent out as spies by Joshua, and the line that Rahab bound in the window of her house as a token to the army of the Israelites, she received from Zerah. It was the scarlet thread that the midwife had bound upon his hand, to mark him as the child that appeared first and withdrew.

The Wives of the Sons of Jacob

Judah was the first of the sons of Jacob to enter wedlock. After the sale of Joseph to the Midianites, his brethren had said to Judah, "If conditions were as before, our father would provide wives for us now. As it is, he is entirely absorbed by his grief for Joseph, and we must look about for wives ourselves. Thou art our chief, and thou shouldst marry first".

Judah's marriage with Alit the daughter of the noble merchant Shua, which was consummated at Adullam, the residence of his friend Hirah, or, as he was called later, Hiram, king of Tyre, was not happy. His two oldest sons died, and shortly thereafter his wife also. It was Judah's punishment for having begun a good deed and left it unfinished, for "he who begins a good deed, and does not execute it to the end, brings down misfortune upon his own head". Judah had rescued Joseph from death, but it was his suggestion to sell him into slavery. Had he urged them to restore the lad to his father, his brethren would have obeyed his words. He was lacking in constancy to persist until he had completed the work of Joseph's deliverance, which he had begun.

In the same year, the year of Joseph's misfortune, all his other brethren married, too. Reuben's wife was named Elyoram, the daughter of the Canaanite Uzzi of Timnah. Simon married his sister Dinah first, and then a second wife. When Simon and Levi massacred the men of Shechem, Dinah refused to leave the city and follow her brethren, saying, "Whither shall I carry my shame"? But Simon swore he would marry her, as he did later, and when she died in Egypt, he took her body to the Holy Land and buried it there. Dinah bore her brother a son, and from her union with Shechem, the son of Hamor, sprang a daughter, Asenath by name, afterward the wife of Joseph. When this daughter was born to Dinah, her brethren, the sons of Jacob, wanted to kill her, that the finger of men might not point at the fruit of sin in their father's house. But Jacob took a piece of tin, inscribed the Holy Name upon it, and bound it about the neck of the girl, and he put her under a thornbush, and abandoned her there. An angel carried the babe down to Egypt, where Potiphar adopted her as his child, for his wife was barren. Years thereafter, when Joseph travelled through the land as viceroy, the maidens threw gifts at him, to make him turn his eyes in their direction and give them the opportunity of gazing upon his beauty. Asenath possessed nothing that would do as a present, therefore she took off the amulet suspended from her neck, and gave it to him. Thus Joseph became acquainted with her lineage, and he married her, seeing that she was not an Egyptian, but one connected with the house of Jacob through her mother.

Beside the son of Dinah, Simon had another son, whose name was Saul, by Bunah, the damsel he had taken captive in the campaign against Shechem.Levi and Issachar married two daughters of Jobab, the grandson of Eber; the wife of the former was named Adinah, the wife of the latter, Aridah. Dan's wife was Elflalet, a daughter of the Moabite Hamudan. For a long time their marriage remained childless, finally they had a son, whom they called Hushim. Gad and Naphtali married women from Haran, two sisters, daughters of Amoram, a grandson of Nahor. Naphtali's wife, Merimit, was the older of the two, and the younger, the wife of Gad, was named Uzit.

Asher's first wife was Adon, the daughter of Ephlal, a grandson of Ishmael. She died childless, and he married a second wife, Hadorah, a daughter of Abimael, the grandson of Shem. She had been married before, her first husband having been Malchiel, also a grandson of Shem, and the issue of this first marriage was a daughter, Serah by name. When Asher brought his wife to Canaan, the three year old orphan Serah came with them. She was raised in the house of Jacob, and she walked in the way of pious children, and God gave her beauty, wisdom, and sagacity.

Zebulon's wife was Maroshah, the daughter of Molad, a grandson of Midian, the son of Abraham by Keturah.

For Benjamin, when he was but ten years old, Jacob took Mahlia to wife, the daughter of Aram, the grandson of Terah, and she bore him five sons. At the age of eighteen he married a second wife, Arbat, the daughter of Zimran, a son of Abraham by Keturah, and by her also he had five sons.

Joseph the Slave of Potiphar

When Joseph was sold as a slave to the Ishmaelites, he kept silent out of respect for his brethren, and did not tell his masters that he was a son of Jacob, a great and powerful man. Even when he came to the Midianites with the Ishmaelites, and the former asked after his parentage, he still said he was a slave, only in order not to put his brethren to shame. But the most distinguished of the Midianites rebuked Joseph, saying, "Thou art no slave, thy appearance betrayeth thee", and he threatened him with death unless he acknowledged the truth. Joseph, however, was steadfast, he would not act treacherously toward his brethren.

Arrived in Egypt, the owners of Joseph could come to no agreement regarding him. Each desired to have sole and exclusive possession of him. They therefore decided to leave him with a shopkeeper until they should come back to Egypt again with their merchandise. And God let Joseph find grace in the sight of the shopkeeper. All that he had, his whole house, he put into Joseph's hand, and therefore the Lord blessed him with much silver and gold, and Joseph remained with him for three months and five days.

At that time there came from Memphis the wife of Potiphar, and she cast her eyes upon Joseph, of whose comeliness of person she had heard from the eunuchs. She told her husband how that a certain shopkeeper had grown rich through a young Hebrew, and she added: "But it is said that the youth was stolen away out of the land of Canaan. Go, therefore, and sit in judgment upon his owner, and take the youth unto thy house, that the God of the Hebrews may bless thee, for the grace of heaven rests upon the youth".

Potiphar summoned the shopkeeper, and when he appeared before him, he spoke harshly to him, saying: "What is this I hear? that thou stealest souls from the land of Canaan, and dost carry on traffic with them"? The shopkeeper protested his innocence, and he could not be made to recede from his assertion, that a company of Ishmaelites had left Joseph in his charge temporarily, until they should return. Potiphar had him stripped naked and beaten, but he continued to reiterate the same statement.

Then Potiphar summoned Joseph. The youth prostrated himself before this chief of the eunuchs, for he was third in rank of the officers of Pharaoh. And he addressed Joseph, and said, "Art thou a slave or a free-born man"? and Joseph replied, "A slave". Potiphar continued to question him, "Whose slave art thou"? Joseph: "I belong to the Ishmaelites". Potiphar: "How wast thou made a slave"? Joseph: "They bought me in the land of Canaan".

But Potiphar refused to give credence to what he said, and he had also him stripped and beaten. The wife of Potiphar, standing by the door, saw how Joseph was abused, and she sent word to her husband, "Thy verdict is unjust, for thou punishest the free-born youth that was stolen away from his place as though he were the one that had committed a crime". As Joseph held firmly to what he had said, Potiphar ordered him to prison, until his masters should return. In her sinful longing for him, his wife wanted to have Joseph in her own house, and she remonstrated with her husband in these words: "Wherefore dost thou keep the captive, nobly-born slave a prisoner? Thou shouldst rather set him at liberty and have him serve thee". He answered, "The law of the Egyptians does not permit us to take what belongs to another before all titles are made clear", and Joseph stayed in prison for twenty-four days, until the return of the Ishmaelites to Egypt.

Meanwhile they had heard somewhere that Joseph was the son of Jacob, and they therefore said to him: "Why didst thou pretend that thou wast a slave? See, we have information that thou art the son of a powerful man in Canaan, and thy father mourns for thee in sackcloth". Joseph was on the point of divulging his secret, but he kept a check upon himself for the sake of his brethren, and he repeated that he was a slave.

Nevertheless the Ishmaelites decided to sell him, that he be not found in their hands, for they feared the revenge of Jacob, who, they knew, was in high favor with the Lord and with men. The shopkeeper begged the Ishmaelites to rescue him from the legal prosecution of Potiphar, and clear him of the suspicion of man theft. The Ishmaelites in turn had a conference with Joseph, and bade him testify before Potiphar that they had bought him for money. He did so, and then the chief of the eunuchs liberated him from prison, and dismissed all parties concerned.

With the permission of her husband, Potiphar's wife sent a eunuch to the Ishmaelites, bidding him to buy Joseph, but he returned and reported that they demanded an exorbitant price for the slave. She dispatched a second eunuch, charging him to conclude the bargain, and though they asked one mina of gold, or even two, he was not to be sparing of money, he was to be sure to buy the slave and bring him to her. The eunuch gave the Ishmaelites eighty pieces of gold for Joseph, telling his mistress, however, that he had paid out a hundred pieces. Joseph noticed the deception, but he kept silent, that the eunuch might not be put to shame.

Thus Joseph became the slave of the idolatrous priest Potiphar, or Potiphera, as he was sometimes called. He had secured possession of the handsome youth for a lewd purpose, but the angel Gabriel mutilated him in such manner that he could not accomplish it. His master soon had occasion to notice that Joseph was as pious as he was beautiful, for whenever he was occupied with his ministrations, he would whisper a prayer: "O Lord of the world, Thou art my trust, Thou art my protection. Let me find grace and favor in Thy sight and in the sight of all that see me, and in the sight of my master Potiphar". When Potiphar noticed the movement of his lips, he said to Joseph, "Dost thou purpose to cast a spell upon me"? "Nay", replied the youth, "I am beseeching God to let me find favor in thine eyes".

His prayer was heard. Potiphar convinced himself that God was with Joseph. Sometimes he would make a test of Joseph's miraculous powers. If he brought him a glass of hippocras, he would say, "I would rather have wine mixed with absinthe", and straightway the spiced wine was changed into bitter wine. Whatever he desired, he could be sure to get from Joseph, and he saw clearly that God fulfilled the wishes of his slave. Therefore he put all the keys of his house into his hand, and he knew not aught that was with him, keeping back nothing from Joseph but his wife. Seeing that the Shekinah rested upon him, Potiphar treated Joseph not as a slave, but as a member of his family, for he said, "This youth is not cut out for a slave's work, he is worthy of a prince's place". Accordingly, he provided instruction for him in the arts, and ordered him to have better fare than the other slaves.

Joseph thanked God for his new and happy state. He prayed, "Blessed art Thou, O Lord, that Thou hast caused me to forget my father's house". What made his present fortunes so agreeable was that he was removed from the envy and jealousy of his brethren. He said: "When I was in my father's house, and he gave me something pretty, my brethren begrudged me the present, and now, O Lord, I thank Thee that I live amid plenty". Free from anxieties, he turned his attention to his external appearance. He painted his eyes, dressed his hair, and aimed to be elegant in his walk. But God spake to him, saying, "Thy father is mourning in sackcloth and ashes, while thou dost eat, drink, and dress thy hair. Therefore I will stir up thy mistress against thee, and thou shalt be embarrassed". Thus Joseph's secret wish was fulfilled, that he might be permitted to prove his piety under temptation, as the piety of his fathers had been tested.

Joseph and Zuleika

"Throw the stick up in the air, it will always return to its original place". Like Rachel his mother, Joseph was of ravishing beauty, and the wife of his master was filled with invincible passion for him". Her feeling was heightened by the astrologic forecast that she was destined to have descendants through Joseph. This was true, but not in the sense in which she understood the prophecy. Joseph married her daughter Asenath later on, and she bore him children, thus fulfilling what had been read in the stars".

In the beginning she did not confess her love to Joseph. She tried first to seduce him by artifice. On the pretext of visiting him, she would go to him at night, and, as she had no sons, she would pretend a desire to adopt him. Joseph then prayed to God in her behalf, and she bore a son. However, she continued to embrace him as though he were her own child, yet he did not notice her evil designs. Finally, when he recognized her wanton trickery, he mourned many days, and endeavored to turn her away from her sinful passion by the word of God. She, on her side, often threatened him with death, and surrendered him to castigations in order to make him amenable to her will, and when these means had no effect upon Joseph, she sought to seduce him with enticements. She would say, "I promise thee, thou shalt rule over me and all I have, if thou wilt but give thyself up to me. and thou shalt be to me the same as my lawful husband". But Joseph was mindful of the words of his fathers, and he went into his chamber, and fasted, and prayed to God, that He would deliver him from the toils of the Egyptian woman.

In spite of the mortifications he practiced, and though he gave the poor and the sick the food apportioned to him, his master thought he lived a luxurious life, for those that fast for the glory of God are made beautiful of countenance.

The wife of Potiphar would frequently speak to her husband in praise of Joseph's chastity in order that he might conceive no suspicion of the state of her feelings. And, again, she would encourage Joseph secretly, telling him not to fear her husband, that he was convinced of his purity of life, and though one should carry tales to him about Joseph and herself, Potiphar would lend them no credence. And when she saw that all this was ineffectual, she approached him with the request that he teach her the word of God, saying, "If it be thy wish that I forsake idol worship, then fulfil my desire, and I will persuade that Egyptian husband of mine to abjure the idols, and we shall walk in the law of thy God". Joseph replied, "The Lord desireth not that those who fear Him shall walk in impurity, nor hath He pleasure in the adulterer".

Another time she came to him, and said, "If thou wilt not do my desire, I will murder the Egyptian and wed with thee according to the law". Whereat Joseph rent his garment, and he said, "O woman, fear the Lord, and do not execute this evil deed, that thou mayest not bring destruction down upon thyself, for I will proclaim thy impious purposes to all in public".

Again, she sent him a dish prepared with magic spells, by means of which she hoped to get him into her power. But when the eunuch set it before him, he saw the image of a man handing him a sword together with the dish, and, warned by the vision, he took good care not to taste of the food. A few days later his mistress came to him, and asked him why he had not eaten of what she had sent him. He reproached her, saying, "How couldst thou tell me, I do not come nigh unto the idols, but only unto the Lord? The God of my fathers hath revealed thy iniquity to me through an angel, but that thou mayest know that the malice of the wicked has no power over those who fear God in purity, I shall eat thy food before thine eyes, and the God of my fathers and the angel of Abraham will be with me". The wife of Potiphar fell upon her face at the feet of Joseph, and amid tears she promised not to commit this sin again.

But her unholy passion for Joseph did not depart from her, and her distress over her unfulfilled wish made her look so ill that her husband said to her, "Why is thy countenance fallen"? And she replied, "I have a pain at my heart, and the groanings of my spirit oppress me".

Once when she was alone with Joseph, she rushed toward him, crying, "I will throttle myself, or I will jump into a well or a pit, if thou wilt not yield thyself to me". Noticing her extreme agitation, Joseph endeavored to calm her with these words, "Remember, if thou makest away with thyself, thy husband's concubine, Asteho, thy rival, will maltreat thy children, and extirpate thy memory from the earth". These words, gently spoken, had the opposite effect from that intended. They only inflamed her passion the more by feeding her hopes. She said: "There, seest thou, thou dost love me now! It sufficeth for me that thou takest thought for me and for the safety of my children. I expect now that my desire will be fulfilled". She did not know that Joseph spoke as he did for the sake of God, and not for her sake.

His mistress, or, as she was called, Zuleika, pursued him day after day with her amorous talk and her flattery, saying: "How fair is thy appearance, how comely thy form! Never have I seen so well-favored a slave as thou art". Joseph would reply: "God, who formed me in my mother's womb, hath created all men".

Zuleika: "How beautiful are thine eyes, with which thou hast charmed all Egyptians, both men and women"!

Joseph: "Beautiful as they may be while I am alive, so ghastly they will be to look upon in the grave".

Zuleika: "How lovely and pleasant are thy words! I pray thee, take thy harp, play and also sing, that I may hear thy words".

Joseph: "Lovely and pleasant are my words when I proclaim the praise of my God".

Zuleika: "How beautiful is thy hair! Take my golden comb, and comb it".

Joseph: "How long wilt thou continue to speak thus to me? Leave off! It were better for thee to care for thy household".

Zuleika: "There is nothing in my house that I care for, save thee alone".

But Joseph's virtue was unshaken. While she spoke thus, he did not so much as raise his eyes to look at his mistress. He remained equally steadfast when she lavished gifts upon him, for she provided him with garments of one kind for the morning, another for noon, and a third kind for the evening. Nor could threats move him. She would say, "I will bring false accusations against thee before thy master", and Joseph would reply, "The Lord executeth judgment for the oppressed". Or, "I will deprive thee of food;" whereupon Joseph, "The Lord giveth food to the hungry". Or, "I will have thee thrown into prison;" whereupon Joseph, "The Lord looseth the prisoners". Or, "I will put heavy labor upon thee that will bend thee double;" whereupon Joseph, "The Lord raiseth up them that are bowed down". Or, "I will blind thine eyes;" whereupon Joseph, "The Lord openeth the eyes of the blind".

When she began to exercise her blandishments upon him, he rejected them with the words, "I fear my master". But Zuleika would say, "I will kill him". Joseph replied with indignation, "Not enough that thou wouldst make an adulterer of me, thou wouldst have me be a murderer, besides"? And he spoke furthermore, saying, "I fear the Lord my God"!

Zuleika: "Nonsense! He is not here to see thee!

Joseph: "Great is the Lord and highly to be praised, and His greatness is unsearchable".

Thereupon she took Joseph into her chamber, where an idol hung above the bed. This she covered, that it might not be a witness of what she was about to do. Joseph said: "Though thou coverest up the eyes of the idol, remember, the eyes of the Lord run to and fro through the whole earth. Yes", continued Joseph, "I have many reasons not to do this thing for the sake of God. Adam was banished from Paradise on account of violating a light command; how much more should I have to fear the punishment of God, were I to commit so grave a sin as adultery! The Lord is in the habit of choosing a favorite member of our family as a sacrifice unto Himself. Perhaps He desireth to make choice of me, but if I do thy will, I make myself unfit to be a sacrifice unto God. Also the Lord is in the habit of appearing suddenly, in visions of the night, unto those that love Him. Thus did He appear unto Abraham, Isaac, and Jacob, and I fear that He may appear unto me at the very moment while I am defiling myself with thee. And as I fear God, so I fear my father, who withdrew the birthright from his first-born son Reuben, on account of an immoral act, and gave it to me. Were I to fulfil thy desire, I would share the fate of my brother Reuben".

With such words, Joseph endeavored to cure the wife of his master of the wanton passion she had conceived for him, while he took heed to keep far from a heinous sin, not from fear of the punishment that would follow, nor out of consideration for the opinion of men, but because he desired to sanctify the Name of God, blessed be He, before the whole world. It was this feeling of his that Zuleika could not comprehend, and when, finally, carried away by passion, she told him in unmistakable language what she desired, and he recoiled from her, she said to Joseph: "Why dost thou refuse to fulfil my wish? Am I not a married woman? None will find out what thou hast done". Joseph replied: "If the unmarried women of the heathen are prohibited unto us, how much more their married women? As the Lord liveth, I will not commit the crime thou biddest me do". In this Joseph followed the example of many pious men, who utter an oath at the moment when they are in danger of succumbing to temptation, and seek thus to gather moral courage to control their evil instincts".

When Zuleika could not prevail upon him, to persuade him, her desire threw her into a grievous sickness, and all the women of Egypt came to visit her, and they said unto her, "Why art thou so languid and wasted, thou that lackest nothing? Is not thy husband a prince great and esteemed in the sight of the king? Is it possible that thou canst want aught of what thy heart desireth"? Zuleika answered them, saying, "This day shall it be made known unto you whence cometh the state wherein you see me".

She commanded her maid-servants to prepare food for all the women, and she spread a banquet before them in her house. She placed knives upon the table to peel the oranges, and then ordered Joseph to appear, arrayed in costly garments, and wait upon her guests. When Joseph came in, the women could not take their eyes off him, and they all cut their hands with the knives, and the oranges in their hands were covered with blood, but they, not knowing what they were doing, continued to look upon the beauty of Joseph without turning their eyes away from him.

Then Zuleika said unto them: "What have ye done? Behold, I set oranges before you to eat, and you have cut your hands". All the women looked at their hands, and, lo, they were full of blood, and it flowed down and stained their garments. They said to Zuleika, "This slave in thy house did enchant us, and we could not turn our eyes away from him on account of his beauty". She then said: "This happened to you that looked upon him but a moment, and you could not refrain yourselves! How, then, can I control myself in whose house he abideth continually, who see him go in and out day after day? How, then, should I not waste away, or keep from languishing on account of him"! And the women spake, saying: "It is true, who can look upon this beauty in the house, and refrain her feelings? But he is thy slave! Why dost thou not disclose to him that which is in thy heart, rather than suffer thy life to perish through this thing"? Zuleika answered them: "Daily do I endeavor to persuade him, but he will not consent to my wishes. I promised him everything that is fair, yet have I met with no return from him, and therefore I am sick, as you may see".

Her sickness increased upon her. Her husband and her household suspected not the cause of her decline, but all the women that were her friends knew that it was on account of the love she bore Joseph, and they advised her all the time to try to entice the youth. On a certain day, while Joseph was doing his master's work in the house, Zuleika came and fell suddenly upon him, but Joseph was stronger than she, and he pressed her down to the ground. Zuleika wept, and in a voice of supplication, and in bitterness of soul, she said to Joseph: "Hast thou ever known, seen, or heard of a woman my peer in beauty, let alone a woman with beauty exceeding mine? Yet I try daily to persuade thee, I fall into decline through love of thee, I confer all this honor upon thee, and thou wilt not hearken unto my voice! Is it by reason of fear of thy master, that he punish thee? As the king liveth, no harm shall come upon thee from thy master on account of this thing. Now, therefore, I pray thee, listen to me, and consent unto my desire for the sake of the honor that I have conferred upon thee, and take this death away from me. For why should I die on account of thee"? Joseph remained as steadfast under these importunities as before. Zuleika, however, was not discouraged; she continued her solicitations unremittingly, day after day, month after month, for a whole year, but always without the least success, for Joseph in his chastity did not permit himself even to look upon her, wherefore she resorted to constraint. She had an iron shackle placed upon his chin, and he was compelled to keep his head up and look her in the face".

Joseph Resists Temptation

Seeing that she could not attain her object by entreaties or tears, Zuleika finally used force, when she judged that the favorable chance had come. She did not have long to wait. When the Nile overflowed its banks, and, according to the annual custom of the Egyptians, all repaired to the river, men and women, people and princes, accompanied by music, Zuleika remained at home under pretense of being sick. This was her long-looked-for opportunity, she thought. She rose up and ascended to the hall of state, and arrayed herself in princely garments. She placed precious stones upon her head, onyx stones set in silver and gold, she beautified her face and her body with all sorts of things for the purifying of women, she perfumed the hall and the whole house with cassia and frankincense, spread myrrh and aloes all over, and afterward sat herself down at the entrance to the hall, in the vestibule leading to the house, through which Joseph had to pass to his work.

And, behold, Joseph came from the field, and he was on the point of entering the house to do his master's work, but when he reached the place where Zuleika sat, and saw all she had done, he turned back. His mistress, perceiving it, called out to him, "What aileth thee, Joseph? Go to thy work, I will make room for thee, that thou mayest pass by to thy seat". Joseph did as she bade him, he entered the house, took his seat, and set about his master's work as usual. Then Zuleika stood before him suddenly in all her beauty of person and magnificence of raiment, and repeated the desire of her heart. It was the first and the last time that Joseph's steadfastness deserted him, but only for an instant. When he was on the point of complying with the wish of his mistress, the image of his mother Rachel appeared before him, and that of his aunt Leah, and the image of his father Jacob. The last addressed him thus: "In time to come the names of thy brethren will be graven upon the breastplate of the high priest. Dost thou desire to have thy name appear with theirs? Or wilt thou forfeit this honor through sinful conduct? For know, he that keepeth company with harlots wasteth his substance". This vision of the dead, and especially the image of his father, brought Joseph to his senses, and his illicit passion departed from him.

Astonished at the swift change in his countenance, Zuleika said, "My friend and true-love, why art thou so affrighted that thou art near to swooning?

Joseph: "I see my father"!

Zuleika: "Where is he? Why, there is none in the house".

Joseph: "Thou belongest to a people that is like unto the ass, it perceiveth nothing. But I belong to those who can see things".

Joseph fled forth, away from the house of his mistress, the same house in which aforetime wonders had been done for Sarah kept a captive there by Pharaoh. But hardly was he outside when the sinful passion again overwhelmed him, and he returned to Zuleika's chamber. Then the Lord appeared unto him, holding the Eben Shetiyah in His hand, and said to him: "If thou touchest her, I will cast away this stone upon which the earth is founded, and the world will fall to ruin". Sobered again, Joseph started to escape from his mistress, but Zuleika caught him by his garment, and she said: "As the king liveth, if thou wilt not fulfil my wish, thou must die", and while she spoke thus, she drew a sword with her free hand from under her dress, and, pressing it against Joseph's throat, she said, "Do as I bid thee, or thou diest". Joseph ran out, leaving a piece of his garment in the hands of Zuleika as he wrenched himself loose from the grasp of the woman with a quick, energetic motion.

Zuleika's passion for Joseph was so violent that, in lieu of its owner, whom she could not succeed in subduing to her will, she kissed and caressed the fragment of cloth left in her hand. At the same time she was not slow to perceive the danger into which she had put herself, for, she feared, Joseph might possibly betray her conduct, and she considered ways and means of obviating the consequences of her folly.

Meanwhile her friends returned from the Nile festival, and they came to visit her and inquire after her health. They found her looking wretchedly ill, on account of the excitement she had passed through and the anxiety she was in. She confessed to the women what had happened with Joseph, and they advised her to accuse him of immorality before her husband, and then he would be thrown into prison. Zuleika accepted their advice, and she begged her visitors to support her charges by also lodging complaints against Joseph, that he had been annoying them with improper proposals.

But Zuleika did not depend entirely upon the assistance of her friends. She planned a ruse, besides, to be sure of convincing her husband of Joseph's guilt. She laid aside her rich robes of state, put on her ordinary clothes, and took to her sick-bed, in which she had been lying when the people left to go to the festival. Also she took Joseph's torn garment, and laid it out next to her. Then she sent a little boy to summon some of the men of her house, and to them she told the tale of Joseph's alleged outrage, saying: "See the Hebrew slave, whom your master hath brought in unto my house, and who attempted to do violence to me to-day! You had scarcely gone away to the festival when be entered the house, and making sure that no one was here he tried to force me to yield to his lustful desire. But I grasped his clothes, tore them, and cried with a loud voice. When he heard that I lifted up my voice and cried, he was seized with fear, and be fled, and got him out, but he left his garment by me". The men of her house spake not a word, but, in a rage against Joseph, they went to their master, and reported to him what had come to pass. In the meantime the husbands of Zuleika's friends had also spoken to Potiphar, at the instigation of their wives, and complained of his slave, that he molested them.

Potiphar hastened home, and he found his wife in low spirits, and though the cause of her dejection was chagrin at not having succeeded in winning Joseph's love, she pretended that it was anger at the immoral conduct of the slave. She accused him in the following words: "O husband, mayest thou not live a day longer, if thou dost not punish the wicked slave that hath desired to defile thy bed, that hath not kept in mind who he was when he came to our house, to demean himself with modesty, nor hath he been mindful of the favors he hath received from thy bounty. He did lay a privy design to abuse thy wife, and this at the time of observing a festival, when thou wouldst be absent". These words she spoke at the moment of conjugal intimacy with Potiphar, when she was certain of exerting an influence upon her husband.

Potiphar gave credence to her words, and he had Joseph flogged unmercifully. While the cruel blows fell upon him, he cried to God, "O Lord, Thou knowest that I am innocent of these things, and why should I die to-day on account of a false accusation by the hands of these uncircumcised, impious men"? God opened the mouth of Zuleika's child, a babe of but eleven months, and he spoke to the men that were beating Joseph, saying: "What is your quarrel with this man? Why do you inflict such evil upon him? Lies my mother doth speak, and deceit is what her mouth uttereth. This is the true tale of that which did happen", and the child proceeded to tell all that had passed--how Zuleika had tried first to persuade Joseph to act wickedly, and then had tried to force him to do her will. The people listened in great amazement. But the report finished, the child spake no word, as before.

Abashed by the speech of his own infant son, Potiphar commanded his bailiffs to leave off from chastising Joseph, and the matter was brought into court, where priests sat as judges. Joseph protested his innocence, and related all that had happened according to the truth, but Potiphar repeated the account his wife had given him. The judges ordered the garment of Joseph to be brought which Zuleika had in her possession, and they examined the tear therein. It turned out to be on the front part of the mantle, and they came to the conclusion that Zuleika had tried to hold him fast, and had been foiled in her attempt by Joseph, against whom she was now lodging a trumped up charge. They decided that Joseph had not incurred the death penalty, but they condemned him to incarceration, because he was the cause of a stain upon Zuleika's fair name".

Potiphar himself was convinced of Joseph's innocence, and when he cast him into prison, he said to him, "I know that thou art not guilty of so vile a crime, but I must put thee in durance, lest a taint cling to my children".

Joseph in Prison

By way of punishment for having traduced his ten brethren before his father, Joseph had to languish for ten years in the prison to which the wiles of traducers had in turn condemned him. But, on the other hand, as he had sanctified the Name of God before the world by his chastity and his steadfastness, he was rewarded. The letter He, which occurs twice in the Name of God, was added to his name. He had been called Joseph, but now he was called also Jehoseph.

Though he was bound in prison, Joseph was not yet safe from the machinations of his mistress, whose passion for him was in no wise lessened. In truth it was she that had induced her husband to change his intention regarding Joseph; she urged him to imprison the slave rather than kill him, for she hoped that as a prisoner he could be made amenable to her wishes more easily. She spake to her husband, saying: "Do not destroy thy property. Cast the slave in prison and keep him there until thou canst sell him, and receive back the money thou didst pay out for him". Thus she had the opportunity of visiting Joseph in his cell and trying to persuade him to do her will. She would say, "This and that outrage have I executed against thee, but, as thou livest, I will put yet other outrages upon thee if thou dost not obey me". But Joseph replied, "The Lord executeth judgment for the oppressed".

Zuleika: "I will push matters so far that all men will hate thee".

Joseph: "The Lord loveth the righteous".

Zuleika: "I will sell thee into a strange land".

Joseph: "The Lord preserveth the strangers".

Then she would resort to enticements in order to obtain her desire. She would promise to release him from prison, if he would but grant her wish. But he would say, "Better it is to remain here than be with thee and commit a trespass against God". These visits to Joseph in prison Zuleika continued for a long time, but when, finally, she saw that all her hopes were vain, she let him alone.

As the mistress persisted in her love for Joseph, so his master, her husband, could not separate himself from his favorite slave. Though a prisoner, Joseph continued to minister to the needs of Potiphar, and he received permission from the keeper of the prison to spend some of his time in his master's house.

In many other ways the jailer showed himself kindly disposed toward Joseph. Seeing the youth's zeal and conscientiousness in executing the tasks laid upon him, and under the spell of his enchanting beauty, he made prison life as easy as possible for his charge. He even ordered better dishes for him than the common prison fare, and he found it superfluous caution to keep watch over Joseph, for he could see no wrong in him, and he observed that God was with him, in good days and in bad. He even appointed him to be the overseer of the prison, and as Joseph commanded, so the other prisoners were obliged to do.

For a long time the people talked of nothing but the accusation raised against Joseph by his mistress. In order to divert the attention of the public from him, God ordained that two high officers, the chief butler and the chief baker, should offend their lord, the king of Egypt, and they were put in ward in the house of the captain of the guard. Now the people ceased their talk about Joseph, and spoke only of the scandal at court. The charges laid at the door of the noble prisoners were that they had attempted to do violence to the daughter of Pharaoh, and they had conspired to poison the king himself.

Besides, they had shown themselves derelict in their service. In the wine the chief butler had handed to the king to drink, a fly had been discovered, and the bread set upon the royal board by the chief baker contained a little pebble". On account of all these transgressions they were condemned to death by Pharaoh, but for the sake of Joseph it was ordained by Divine providence that the king should first detain them in prison before he ordered their execution. The Lord had enkindled the wrath of the king against his servants only that the wish of Joseph for liberty might be fulfilled, for they were the instruments of his deliverance from prison, and though they were doomed to death, yet in consideration of the exalted office they had held at court, the keeper of the prison accorded them privileges, as, for instance, a man was detailed to wait upon them, and the one appointed thereto was Joseph.

The chief butler and the chief baker had been confined in prison ten years, when they dreamed a dream, both of them, but as for the interpretation, each dreamed only that of the other one's dream. In the morning when Joseph brought them the water for washing, he found them sad, depressed in spirits, and, in the manner of the sages, he asked them why they looked different on that day from other days. They said unto him, "We have dreamed a dream this night, and our two dreams resemble each other in certain particulars, and there is none that can interpret them". And Joseph said unto them: "God granteth understanding to man to interpret dreams. Tell them me, I pray you". It was as a reward for ascribing greatness and credit to Him unto whom it belongeth that Joseph later attained to his lofty position.

The chief butler proceeded to tell his dream: "In my dream, behold, a vine was before me; and in the vine were three branches; and it was as though it budded, and its blossoms shot forth, and the clusters thereof brought forth ripe grapes; and Pharaoh's cup was in my hand; and I took the grapes, and pressed them into Pharaoh's cup, and I gave the cup into Pharaoh's hand". The chief butler was not aware that his dream contained a prophecy regarding the future of Israel, but Joseph discerned the recondite meaning, and he interpreted the dream thus: The three branches are the three Fathers, Abraham, Isaac, and Jacob, whose descendants in Egypt will be redeemed by three leaders, Moses, Aaron, and Miriam; and the cup given into the hand of Pharaoh is the cup of wrath that he will have to drain in the end. This interpretation of the dream Joseph kept for himself, and he told the chief butler nothing thereof, but out of gratitude for the glad tidings of the deliverance of Israel from the bondage of Egypt, he gave him a favorable interpretation of his dream, and begged him to have him in his remembrance, when it should be well with him, and liberate him from the dungeon in which he was confined.

When the chief baker heard the interpretation of the butler's dream, he knew that Joseph had divined its meaning correctly, for in his own he had seen the interpretation of his friend's dream, and he proceeded to tell Joseph what he had dreamed in the night: "I also was in my dream, and, behold, three baskets of white bread were on my head; and in the uppermost basket there was of all manner of bake- meats for Pharaoh; and the birds did eat them out of the basket upon my head". Also this dream conveyed a prophecy regarding the future of Israel: The three baskets are the three kingdoms to which Israel will be made subject, Babylon, Media, and Greece; and the uppermost basket indicates the wicked rule of Rome, which will extend over all the nations of the world, until the bird shall come, who is the Messiah, and annihilate Rome. Again Joseph kept the prophecy a secret. To the chief baker he gave only the interpretation that had reference to his person, but it was unfavorable to him, because through his dream Joseph had been made acquainted with the suffering Israel would have to undergo.And all came to pass, as Joseph had said, on the third day. The day whereon he explained the meaning of their dreams to the two distinguished prisoners, a son was born unto Pharaoh and to celebrate the joyous event, the king arranged a feast for his princes and servants that was to last eight days. He invited them and all the people to his table, and he entertained them with royal splendor. The feast had its beginning on the third day after the birth of the child, and on that occasion the chief butler was restored in honor to his butlership, and the chief baker was hanged, for Pharaoh's counsellors had discovered that it was not the butler's fault that the fly had dropped into the king's wine, but the baker had been guilty of carelessness in allowing the pebble to get into the bread. Likewise it appeared that the butler had had no part in the conspiracy to poison the king, while the baker was revealed as one of the plotters, and he had to expiate his crime with his life.

Pharaoh's Dreams

Properly speaking, Joseph should have gone out free from his dungeon on the same day as the butler. He had been there ten years by that time, and had made amends for the slander he had uttered against his ten brethren.

However, he remained in prison two years longer. "Blessed is the man that trusteth in the Lord, and whose hope is the Lord", but Joseph had put his confidence in flesh and blood. He had prayed the chief butler to have him in remembrance when it should be well with him, and make mention of him unto Pharaoh, and the butler forgot his promise, and therefore Joseph had to stay in prison two years more than the years originally allotted to him there. The butler had not forgotten him intentionally, but it was ordained of God that his memory should fail him. When he would say to himself, If thus and so happens, I will remember the case of Joseph, the conditions he had imagined were sure to be reversed, or if he made a knot as a reminder, an angel came and undid the knot, and Joseph did not enter his mind.

But "the Lord setteth an end to darkness", and Joseph's liberation was not delayed by a single moment beyond the time decreed for it. God said, "Thou, O butler, thou didst forget Joseph, but I did not", and He caused Pharaoh to dream a dream that was the occasion for Joseph's release.

In his dream Pharaoh saw seven kine, well-favored and fat-fleshed, come up out of the Nile, and they all together grazed peaceably on the brink of the river, In years when the harvest is abundant, friendship reigns among men, and love and brotherly harmony, and these seven fat kine stood for seven such prosperous years. After the fat kine, seven more came up out of the river, ill-favored and lean- fleshed, and each had her back turned to the others, for when distress prevails, one man turns away from the other. For a brief space Pharaoh awoke, and when he went to sleep again, he dreamed a second dream, about seven rank and good ears of corn, and seven ears that were thin and blasted with the east wind, the withered cars swallowing the full ears. He awoke at once, and it was morning, and dreams dreamed in the morning are the ones that come true.

This was not the first time Pharaoh had had these dreams. They had visited him every night during a period of two years, and he had forgotten them invariably in the morning. This was the first time he remembered them, for the day had arrived for Joseph to come forth from his prison house. Pharaoh's heart beat violently when he called his dreams to mind on awaking. Especially the second one, about the ears of corn, disquieted him. He reflected that whatever has a mouth can eat, and therefore the dream of the seven lean kine that ate up the seven fat kine did not appear strange to him. But the ears of corn that swallowed up other ears of corn troubled his spirit. He therefore called for all the wise men of his land, and they endeavored in vain to find a satisfactory interpretation. They explained that the seven fat kine meant seven daughters to be born unto Pharaoh, and the seven lean kine, that he would bury seven daughters; the rank ears of corn meant that Pharaoh would conquer seven countries, and the blasted ears, that seven provinces would rebel against him. About the ears of corn they did not all agree. Some thought the good ears stood for seven cities to be built by Pharaoh, and the seven withered ears indicated that these same cities would be destroyed at the end of his reign.

Sagacious as he was, Pharaoh knew that none of these explanations hit the nail on the head. He issued a decree summoning all interpreters of dreams to appear before him on pain of death, and he held out great rewards and distinctions to the one who should succeed in finding the true meaning of his dreams. In obedience to his summons, all the wise men appeared, the magicians and the sacred scribes that were in Mizraim, the city of Egypt, as well as those from Goshen, Raamses, Zoan, and the whole country of Egypt, and with them came the princes, officers, and servants of the king from all the cities of the land.

To all these the king narrated his dreams, but none could interpret them to his satisfaction. Some said that the seven fat kine were the seven legitimate kings that would rule over Egypt, and the seven lean kine betokened seven princes that would rise up against these seven kings and exterminate them. The seven good ears of corn were the seven superior princes of Egypt that would engage in a war for their overlord, and would be defeated by as many insignificant princes, who were betokened by the seven blasted ears.

Another interpretation was that the seven fat kine were the seven fortified cities of Egypt, at some future time to fall into the hands of seven Canaanitish nations, who were foreshadowed in the seven lean kine. According to this interpretation, the second dream supplemented the first. It meant that the descendants of Pharaoh would regain sovereign authority over Egypt at a subsequent period, and would subdue the seven Canaanitish nations as well.There was a third interpretation, given by some: The seven fat kine are seven women whom Pharaoh would take to wife, but they would die during his lifetime, their loss being indicated by the seven lean kine. Furthermore, Pharaoh would have fourteen sons, and the seven strong ones would be conquered by the seven weaklings, as the blasted ears of corn in his dream had swallowed up the rank ears of corn.

And a fourth: "Thou wilt have seven sons, O Pharaoh, these are the seven fat kine. These sons of thine will be killed by the seven powerful rebellious princes. But then seven minor princes will come, and they will kill the seven rebels, avenge thy descendants, and restore the dominion to thy family".

The king was as little pleased with these interpretations as with the others, which he had heard before, and in his wrath he ordered the wise men, the magicians and the scribes of Egypt, to be killed, and the hangmen made ready to execute the royal decree.

However, Mirod, Pharaoh's chief butler, took fright, seeing that the king was so vexed at his failure to secure an interpretation of his dreams that he was on the point of giving up the ghost. He was alarmed about the king's death, for it was doubtful whether the successor to the throne would retain him in office. He resolved to do all in his power to keep Pharaoh alive. Therefore he stepped before him, and spake, saying, "I do remember two faults of mine this day, I showed myself ungrateful to Joseph, in that I did not bring his request before thee, and also I saw thee in distress by reason of thy dream, without letting thee know that Joseph can interpret dreams. When it pleased the Lord God to make Pharaoh wroth with his servants, the king put me in ward in the house of the captain of the guard, me and the chief baker. And with us there was a simple young man, one of the despised race of the Hebrews, slave to the captain of the guard, and he interpreted our dreams to us, and it came to pass, as he interpreted to us, so it was. Therefore, O king, stay the hand of the hangmen, let them not execute the Egyptians. The slave I speak of is still in the dungeon, and if the king will consent to summon him hither, he will surely interpret thy dreams".

Joseph Before Pharaoh

"Accursed are the wicked that never do a wholly good deed". The chief butler described Joseph contemptuously as a "slave" in order that it might be impossible for him to occupy a distinguished place at court, for it was a law upon the statute books of Egypt that a slave could never sit upon the throne as king, nor even put his foot in the stirrup of a horse.

Pharaoh revoked the edict of death that he had issued against the wise men of Egypt, and he sent and called Joseph. He impressed care upon his messengers, they were not to excite and confuse Joseph, and render him unfit to interpret the king's dream correctly. They brought him hastily out of the dungeon, but first Joseph, out of respect for the king, shaved himself, and put on fresh raiment, which an angel brought him from Paradise, and then he came in unto Pharaoh.

The king was sitting upon the royal throne, arrayed in princely garments, clad with a golden ephod upon his breast, and the fine gold of the ephod sparkled, and the carbuncle, the ruby, and the emerald flamed like a torch, and all the precious stones set upon the king's head flashed like a blazing fire, and Joseph was greatly amazed at the appearance of the king. The throne upon which he sat was covered with gold and silver and with onyx stones, and it had seventy steps. If a prince or other distinguished person came to have an audience with the king, it was the custom for him to advance and mount to the thirty-first step of the throne, and the king would descend thirty-six steps and speak to him. But if one of the people came to have speech with the king, he ascended only to the third step, and the king would come down four steps from his seat, and address him thence. It was also the custom that one who knew all the seventy languages ascended the seventy steps of the throne to the top, but if a man knew only some of the seventy languages, he was permitted to ascend as many steps as he knew languages, whether they were many or, few. And another custom of the Egyptians was that none could reign over them unless he was master of all the seventy languages.

When Joseph came before the king, he bowed down to the ground, and he ascended to the third step, while the king sat upon the fourth from the top, and spake with Joseph, saying: "O young man, my servant beareth witness concerning thee, that thou art the best and most discerning person I can consult with. I pray thee, vouchsafe unto me the same favors which thou didst bestow on this servant of mine, and tell me what events they are which the visions of my dreams foreshow. I desire thee to suppress naught out of fear, nor shalt thou flatter me with lying words, or with words that please me. Tell me the truth, though it be sad and alarming".

Joseph asked the king first whence he knew that the interpretation given by the wise men of his country was not true, and Pharaoh replied, "I saw the dream and its interpretation together, and therefore they cannot make a fool of me". In his modesty Joseph denied that he was an adept at interpreting dreams. He said, "It is not in me; it is in the hand of God, and if it be the wish of God, He will permit me to announce tidings of peace to Pharaoh". And for such modesty he was rewarded by sovereignty over Egypt, for the Lord doth honor them that honor Him. Thus was also Daniel rewarded for his speech to Nebuchadnezzar:

"There is a God in heaven that revealeth secrets, but as for me, this secret is not revealed to me for any wisdom that I have more than any living, but to the intent that the interpretation may be made known to the king, and that thou mayest know the thoughts of thy heart".

Then Pharaoh began to tell his dream, only he omitted some points and narrated others inaccurately in order that he might test the vaunted powers of Joseph. But the youth corrected him, and pieced the dreams together exactly as they had visited Pharaoh in the night, and the king was greatly amazed. Joseph was able to accomplish this feat, because he had dreamed the same dream as Pharaoh, at the same time as he. Thereupon Pharaoh retold his dreams, with all details and circumstances, and precisely as he had seen them in his sleep, except that he left out the word Nile in the description of the seven lean kine, because this river was worshipped by the Egyptians, and he hesitated to say that aught that is evil had come from his god.

Now Joseph proceeded to give the king the true interpretation of the two dreams. They were both a revelation concerning the seven good years impending and the seven years of famine to follow them. In reality, it had been the purpose of God to bring a famine of forty-two years' duration upon Egypt, but only two years of this distressful period were inflicted upon the land, for the sake of the blessing of Jacob when he came to Egypt in the second year of the famine. The other forty years fell upon the land at the time of the prophet Ezekiel.

Joseph did more than merely interpret the dreams. When the king gave voice to doubts concerning the interpretation, he told him signs and tokens. He said: "Let this be a sign to thee that my words are true, and my advice is excellent: Thy wife, who is sitting upon the birthstool at this moment, will bring forth a son, and thou wilt rejoice over him, but in the midst of thy joy the sad tidings will be told thee of the death of thine older son, who was born unto thee but two years ago, and thou must needs find consolation for the loss of the one in the birth of the other".

Scarcely had Joseph withdrawn from the presence of the king, when the report of the birth of a son was brought to Pharaoh, and soon after also the report of the death of his first-born, who had suddenly dropped to the floor and passed away. Thereupon he sent for all the grandees of his realm, and all his servants, and he spake to them, saying: "Ye have heard the words of the Hebrew, and ye have seen that the signs which he foretold were accomplished, and I also know that he hath interpreted the dream truly. Advise me now how the land may be saved from the ravages of the famine. Look hither and thither whether you can find a man of wisdom and understanding, whom I may set over the land, for I am convinced that the land can be saved only if we heed the counsel of the Hebrew". The grandees and the princes admitted that safety could be secured only by adhering to the advice given by Joseph, and they proposed that the king, in his sagacity, choose a man whom he considered equal to the great task. Thereupon Pharaoh said: "If we traversed and searched the earth from end to end, we could find none such as Joseph, a man in whom is the spirit of God. If ye think well thereof, I will set him over the land which he hath saved by his wisdom".

The astrologers, who were his counsellors, demurred, saying, "A slave, one whom his present owner hath acquired for twenty pieces of silver, thou proposest to set over us as master"? But Pharaoh maintained that Joseph was not only a free-born man beyond the peradventure of a doubt, but also the scion of a noble family. However, the princes of Pharaoh were not silenced, they continued to give utterance to their opposition to Joseph, saying: "Dost thou not remember the immutable law of the Egyptians, that none may serve as king or as viceroy unless he speaks all the languages of men? And this

Hebrew knows none but his own tongue, and how were it possible that a man should rule over us who cannot even speak the language of our land? Send and have him fetched hither, and examine him in respect to all the things a ruler should know and have, and then decide as seemeth wise in thy sight".

Pharaoh yielded, he promised to do as they wished, and he appointed the following day as the time for examining Joseph, who had returned to his prison in the meantime, for, on account of his wife, his master feared to have him stay in his house. During the night Gabriel appeared unto Joseph, and taught him all the seventy languages, and he acquired them quickly after the angel had changed his name from Joseph to Jehoseph. The next morning, when he came into the presence of Pharaoh and the nobles of the kingdom, inasmuch as he knew every one of the seventy languages, he mounted all the steps of the royal throne, until he reached the seventieth, the highest, upon which sat the king, and Pharaoh and his princes rejoiced that Joseph fulfilled all the requirements needed by one that was to rule over Egypt.

The king said to Joseph: "Thou didst give me the counsel to look out a man discreet and wise, and set him over the land of Egypt, that he may in his wisdom save the land from the famine. As God hath showed thee all this, and as thou art master of all the languages of the world, there is none so discreet and wise as thou. Thou shalt therefore be the second in the land after Pharaoh, and according unto thy word shall all my people go in and go out; my princes and my servants shall receive their monthly appanage from thee; before thee the people shall prostrate themselves, only in the throne will I be greater than thou".

The Ruler of Egypt

Now Joseph reaped the harvest of his virtues, and according to the measure of his merits God granted him reward. The mouth that refused the kiss of unlawful passion and sin received the kiss of homage from the people; the neck that did not bow itself unto sin was adorned with the gold chain that Pharaoh put upon it; the hands that did not touch sin wore the signet ring that Pharaoh took from his own hand and put upon Joseph's; the body that did not come in contact with sin was arrayed in vestures of byssus; the feet that made no steps in the direction of sin reposed in the royal chariot, and the thoughts that kept themselves undefiled by sin were proclaimed as wisdom.

Joseph was installed in his high position, and invested with the insignia of his office, with solemn ceremony. The king took off his signet ring from his hand, and put it upon Joseph's hand, and arrayed him in princely apparel, and set a gold crown upon his head, and laid a gold chain about his neck. Then he commanded his servants to make Joseph to ride in his second chariot, which went by the side of the chariot wherein sat the king, and he also made him to ride upon a great and strong horse of the king's horses, and his servants conducted him through the streets of the city of Egypt. Musicians, no less than a thousand striking cymbals and a thousand blowing flutes, and five thousand men with drawn swords gleaming in the air formed the vanguard. Twenty thousand of the king's grandees girt with gold-embroidered leather belts marched at the right of Joseph, and as many at the left of him. The women and the maidens of the nobility looked out of the windows to gaze upon Joseph's beauty, and they poured down chains upon him, and rings and jewels, that he might but direct his eyes toward them. Yet he did not look up, and as a reward God made him proof against the evil eye, nor has it ever had the power of inflicting harm upon any of his descendants. Servants of the king, preceding him and following him, burnt incense upon his path, and cassia, and all manner of sweet spices, and strewed myrrh and aloes wherever he went. Twenty heralds walked before him, and they proclaimed: "This is the man whom the king bath chosen to be the second after him. All the affairs of state will be administered by him, and whoever resisteth his commands, or refuseth to bow down to the ground before him, he will die the death of the rebel against the king and the king's deputy".

Without delay the people prostrated themselves, and they cried, "Long live the king, and long live the deputy of the king"! And Joseph, looking down from his horse upon the people and their exultation, exclaimed, his eyes directed heavenward: "The Lord raiseth up the poor out of the dust, and lifteth up the needy from the dunghill. O Lord of hosts, blessed is the man that trusteth in Thee".

After Joseph, accompanied by Pharaoh's officers and princes, had journeyed through the whole city of Egypt, and viewed all there was therein, he returned to the king on the selfsame day, and the king gave him fields and vineyards as a present, and also three thousand talents of silver, and a thousand talents of gold, and onyx stones and bdellium, and many other costly things. The king commanded, moreover, that every Egyptian give Joseph a gift, else he would be put to death. A platform was erected in the open street, and there all deposited their presents, and among the things were many of gold and silver, as well as precious stones, carried thither by the people and also the grandees, for they saw that Joseph enjoyed the favor of the king. Furthermore, Joseph received one hundred slaves from Pharaoh, and they were to do all his bidding, and he himself acquired many more, for he resided in a spacious palace. Three years it took to build it. Special magnificence was lavished upon the hall of state, which was his audience chamber, and upon the throne fashioned of gold and silver and inlaid with precious stones, whereon there was a representation of the whole land of Egypt and of the river Nile. And as Joseph multiplied in riches, so he increased also in wisdom, for God added to his wisdom that all might love and honor him. Pharaoh called him Zaphenath-paneah, he who can reveal secret things with ease, and rejoiceth the heart of man therewith. Each letter of the name Zaphenath-paneah has a meaning, too. The first, Zadde, stands for Zofeh, seer; Pe for Podeh, redeemer; Nun for Nabi, prophet; Taw for Tomek, supporter; Pe for Poter, interpreter of dreams; Ain for Arum, clever; Nun for Nabon, discreet; and Het for Hakam, wise.

The name of Joseph's wife pointed to her history in the same way. Asenath was the daughter of Dinah and Hamor, but she was abandoned at the borders of Egypt, only, that people might know who she was, Jacob engraved the story of her parentage and her birth upon a gold plate fastened around her neck. The day on which Asenath was exposed, Potiphar went walking with his servants near the city wall, and they heard the voice of a child. At the captain's bidding they brought the baby to him, and when he read her history from the gold plate, he determined to adopt her. He took her home with him, and raised her as his daughter. The Alef in Asenath stands for On, where Potiphar was priest; the Samek for Setirah, Hidden, for she was kept concealed on account of her extraordinary beauty; the Nun for Nohemet, for she wept and entreated that she might be delivered from the house of the heathen Potiphar; and the Taw for Tammah, the perfect one, on account of her pious, perfect deeds.

Asenath had saved Joseph's life while she was still an infant in arms. When Joseph was accused of immoral conduct by Potiphar's wife and the other women, and his master was on the point of having him hanged, Asenath approached her foster-father, and she assured him under oath that the charge against Joseph was false. Then spake God, "As thou livest, because thou didst try to defend Joseph, thou shalt be the woman to bear the tribes that he is appointed to beget.

Asenath bore him two sons, Manasseh and Ephraim, during the seven years of plenty, for in the time of famine Joseph refrained from all indulgence in the pleasures of life. They were bred in chastity and fear of God by their father, and they were wise, and well-instructed in all knowledge and in the affairs of state, so that they became the favorites of the court, and were educated with the royal princes.

Before the famine broke over the land, Joseph found an opportunity of rendering the king a great service. He equipped an army of four thousand six hundred men, providing all the soldiers with shields and spears and bucklers and helmets and slings. With this army, and aided by the servants and officers of the king, and by the people of Egypt, he carried on a war with Tarshish in the first year after his appointment as viceroy. The people of Tarshish had invaded the territory of the Ishmaelites, and the latter, few in number at that time, were sore pressed, and applied to the king of Egypt for help against their enemies. At the head of his host of heroes, Joseph marched to the land of Havilah, where he was joined by the Ishmaelites, and with united forces they fought against the people of Tarshish, routed them utterly, settled their land with the Ishmaelites, while the defeated men took refuge with their brethren in Javan. Joseph and his army returned to Egypt, and not a man had they lost.

In a little while Joseph's prophecy was confirmed: that year and the six following years were years of plenty, as he had foretold. The harvest was so ample that a single ear produced two heaps of grain, and Joseph made circumspect arrangements to provide abundantly for the years of famine. He gathered up all the grain, and in the city situated in the middle of each district he laid up the produce from round about, and had ashes and earth strewn on the garnered food from the very soil on which it had been grown; also he preserved the grain in the ear; all these being precautions taken to guard against rot and mildew. The inhabitants of Egypt also tried, on their own account, to put aside a portion of the superabundant harvest of the seven fruitful years against the need of the future, but when the grievous time of dearth came, and they went to their storehouses to bring forth the treasured grain, behold, it had rotted, and become unfit for food. The famine broke in upon the people with such suddenness that the bread gave out unexpectedly as they sat at their tables, they had not even a bite of bran bread.

Thus they were driven to apply to Joseph and beseech his help, and he admonished them, saying, "Give up your allegiance to your deceitful idols, and say, Blessed is He who giveth bread unto all flesh". But they refused to deny their lying gods, and they betook themselves to Pharaoh, only to be told by him, "Go unto Joseph; what he saith to you, do"! For this Pharaoh was rewarded. God granted him long life and a long reign, until he became arrogant, and well-merited punishment overtook him.

When the Egyptians approached Joseph with the petition for bread, he spoke, saying, "I give no food to the uncircumcised. Go hence, and circumcise yourselves, and then return hither". They entered the presence of Pharaoh, and complained to him regarding Joseph, but he said as before, "Go unto Joseph"! And they replied, "We come from Joseph, and he hath spoken roughly unto us, saying, Go hence and circumcise yourselves! We warned thee in the beginning that he is a Hebrew, and would treat us in such wise". Pharaoh said to them: "O ye fools, did he not prophesy through the holy spirit and proclaim to the whole world, that there would come seven years of plenty to be followed by seven years of dearth? Why did you not save the yield of one or two years against the day of your need"?

Weeping, they made reply: "The grain that we put aside during the good years hath rotted".

Pharaoh: "Have ye nothing over of the flour of yesterday"?

The Egyptians: "The very bread in the basket rotted"!

Pharaoh: "Why"?

The Egyptians: "Because Joseph willed thus"!

Pharaoh: "O ye fools, if his word hath power over the grain, making it to rot when he desireth it to rot, then also must we die, if so be his wish concerning us. Go, therefore, unto him, and do as he bids you".

Joseph's Brethren in Egypt

The famine, which inflicted hardships first upon the wealthy among the Egyptians, gradually extended its ravages as far as Phoenicia, Arabia, and Palestine. Though the sons of Jacob, being young men, frequented the streets and the highways, yet they were ignorant of what their old home-keeping father Jacob knew, that corn could be procured in Egypt. Jacob even suspected that Joseph was in Egypt. His prophetic spirit, which forsook him during the time of his grief for his son, yet manifested itself now and again in dim visions, and he was resolved to send his sons down into Egypt. There was another reason. Though he was not yet in want, he nevertheless had them go thither for food, because he was averse from arousing the envy of the sons of Esau and Ishmael by his comfortable state. For the same reason, to avoid friction with the surrounding peoples, he bade his sons not appear in public with bread in their hands, or in the accoutrements of war. And as he knew that they were likely to attract attention, on account of their heroic stature and handsome appearance, he cautioned them against going to the city all together through the same gate, or, indeed, showing themselves all together anywhere in public, that the evil eye be not cast upon them.

The famine in Canaan inspired Joseph with the hope of seeing his brethren. To make sure of their coming, he issued a decree concerning the purchase of corn in Egypt, as follows: "By order of the king and his deputy, and the princes of the realm, be it enacted that he who desireth to buy grain in Egypt may not send his slave hither to do his bidding, but he must charge his own sons therewith. An Egyptian or a Canaanite that hath bought grain and then selleth it again shall be put to death, for none may buy more than he requireth for the needs of his household. Also, who cometh with two or three beasts of burden, and loads them up with grain, shall be put to death".

At the gates of the city of Egypt, Joseph stationed guards, whose office was to inquire and take down the name of all that should come to buy corn, and also the name of their father and their grandfather, and every evening the list of names thus made was handed to Joseph. These precautions were bound to bring Joseph's brethren down to Egypt, and also acquaint him with their coming as soon as they entered the land.

On their journey his brethren thought more of Joseph than of their errand. They said to one another: "We know that Joseph was carried down into Egypt, and we will make search for him there, and if we should find him, we will ransom him from his master, and if his master should refuse to sell him, we will use force, though we perish ourselves".

At the gates of the city of Egypt, the brethren of Joseph were asked what their names were, and the names of their father and grandfather. The guard on duty happened to be Manasseh, the son of Joseph. The brethren submitted to being questioned, saying "Let us go into the town, and we shall see whether this taking down of our names be a matter of taxes. If it be so, we shall not demur; but if it be something else, we shall see to-morrow what can be done in the case".

On the evening of the day they entered Egypt, Joseph discovered their names in the list, which he was in the habit of examining daily, and he commanded that all stations for the sale of corn be closed, except one only. Furthermore, even at this station no sales were to be negotiated unless the name of the would-be purchaser was first obtained. His brethren, with whose names Joseph furnished the overseer of the place, were to be seized and brought to him as soon as they put in appearance.

But the first thought of the brethren was for Joseph, and their first concern, to seek him. For three days they made search for him everywhere, even in the most disreputable quarters of the city. Meantime Joseph was in communication with the overseer of the station kept open for the sale of corn, and, hearing that his brethren had not appeared there, he dispatched some of his servants to look for them, but they found them neither in Mizraim, the city of Egypt, nor in Goshen, nor in Raamses. Thereupon he sent sixteen servants forth to make a house to house search for them in the city, and they discovered the brethren of Joseph in a place of ill-fame and haled them before their master.

Joseph Meets His Brethren

A large crown of gold on his head, apparelled in byssus and purple, and surrounded by his valiant men, Joseph was seated upon his throne in his palace. His brethren fell down before him in great admiration of his beauty, his stately appearance, and his majesty. They did not know him, for when Joseph was sold into slavery, he was a beardless youth. But he knew his brethren, their appearance had not changed in aught, for they were bearded men when he was separated from them.

He was inclined to make himself known to them as their brother, but an angel appeared unto him, the same that had brought him from Shechem to his brethren at Dothan, and spoke, saying, "These came hither with intent to kill thee". Later, when the brethren returned home, and gave an account of their adventures to Jacob, they told him that a man had accused them falsely before the ruler of Egypt, not knowing that he who incited Joseph against them was an angel. It was in reference to this matter, and meaning their accuser, that Jacob, when he dispatched his sons on their second expedition to Egypt, prayed to God, "God Almighty give you mercy before the man".

Joseph made himself strange unto his brethren, and he took his cup in his hand, knocked against it, and said, "By this magic cup I know that ye are spies". They replied, "Thy servants came from Canaan into Egypt for to buy corn".

Joseph: "If it be true that ye came hither to buy corn, why is it that each one of you entered the city by a separate gate"?

The brethren: "We are ALL the sons of one man in the land of Canaan, and he bade us not enter a city together by the same gate, that we attract not the attention of the people of the place". Unconsciously they had spoken as seers, for the word ALL included Joseph as one of their number.

Joseph: "Verily, ye are spies! All the people that come to buy corn return home without delay, but ye have lingered here three days, without making any purchases, and all the time you have been gadding about in the disreputable parts of the city, and only spies are wont to do thus".

The brethren: "We thy servants are twelve brethren, the sons of Jacob, the son of Isaac, the son of the Hebrew Abraham. The youngest is this day with our father in Canaan, and one hath disappeared. Him did we look for in this land, and we looked for him even in the disreputable houses".

Joseph: "Have ye made search in every other place on earth, and was Egypt the only land left? And if it be true that he is in Egypt, what should a brother of yours be doing in a house of ill-fame, if, indeed, ye are the descendants of Abraham, Isaac, and Jacob"?

The brethren: "We did hear that some Ishmaelites stole our brother, and sold him into slavery in Egypt, and as our brother was exceeding fair in form and face, we thought he might have been sold for illicit uses, and therefore we searched even the disreputable houses to find him".

Joseph: "You speak deceitful words, when you call yourselves sons of Abraham. By the life of Pharaoh, ye are spies, and you did go from one disreputable house to another that none might discover you".

The expression "by the life of Pharaoh" might have betrayed Joseph's real feeling to his brethren, had they but known his habit of taking this oath only when he meant to avoid keeping his word later.

Joseph continued to speak to his brethren: "Let us suppose you should discover your brother serving as a slave, and his master should demand a high sum for his ransom, would you pay it"?

The brethren: "Yes"!

Joseph: "But suppose his master should refuse to surrender him for any price in the world, what would you do"?

The brethren: "If he yields not our brother to us, we will kill the master, and carry off our brother".

Joseph: "Now see how true my words were, that ye are spies. By your own admission ye have come to slay the inhabitants of the land. Report hath told us that two of you did massacre the people of Shechem on account of the wrong done to your sister, and now have ye come down into Egypt to kill the Egyptians for the sake of your brother. I shall be convinced of your innocence only if you consent to send one of your number home and fetch your youngest brother hither".

His brethren refused compliance, and Joseph caused them to be put into prison by seventy of his valiant men, and there they remained for three days. God never allows the pious to languish in distress longer than three days, and so it was a Divine dispensation that the brethren of Joseph were released on the third day, and were permitted by Joseph to return home, on condition, however, that one of them remain behind as hostage.

The difference between Joseph and his brethren can be seen here. Though he retained one of them to be bound in the prison house, he still said, "I fear God", and dismissed the others, but when he was in their power, they gave no thought to God. At this time, to be sure, their conduct was such as is becoming to the pious, who accept their fate with calm resignation, and acknowledge the righteousness of God, for He metes out reward and punishment measure for measure. They recognized that their present punishment was in return for the heartless treatment they had dealt out to

Joseph, paying no heed to his distress, though he fell at the feet of each of them, weeping, and entreating them not to sell him into slavery. Reuben reminded the others that they had two wrongs to expiate, the wrong against their brother and the wrong against their father, who was so grieved that he exclaimed, "I will go down to the grave to my son mourning".

The brethren of Joseph knew not that the viceroy of Egypt understood Hebrew, and could follow their words, for Manasseh stood and was an interpreter between them and him.

Joseph decided to keep Simon as hostage in Egypt, for he had been one of the two--Levi was the other--to advise that Joseph be put to death, and only the intercession of Reuben and Judah had saved him. He did not detain Levi, too, for he feared, if both remained behind together, Egypt might suffer the same fate at their hands as the city of Shechem. Also, he preferred Simon to Levi, because Simon was not a favorite among the sons of Jacob, and they would not resist his detention in Egypt too violently, while they might annihilate Egypt, as aforetime Shechem, if they were deprived of Levi, their wise man and high priest. Besides, it was Simon that had lowered Joseph into the pit, wherefore he had a particular grudge against him.

When the brethren yielded to Joseph's demand, and consented to leave their brother behind as hostage, Simon said to them, "Ye desire to do with me as ye did with Joseph"! But they replied, in despair: "What can we do? Our households will perish of hunger". Simon made answer, "Do as ye will, but as for me, let me see the man that will venture to cast me into prison". Joseph sent word to Pharaoh to let him have seventy of his valiant men, to aid him in arresting robbers. But when the seventy appeared upon the scene, and were about to lay hands on Simon, he uttered a loud cry, and his assailants fell to the floor and knocked out their teeth. Pharaoh's valiant men, as well as all the people that stood about Joseph, fled affrighted, only Joseph and his son Manasseh remained calm and unmoved. Manasseh rose up, dealt Simon a blow on the back of his neck, put manacles upon his hands and fetters upon his feet, and cast him into prison. Joseph's brethren were greatly amazed at the heroic strength of the youth, and Simon said, "This blow was not dealt by an Egyptian, but by one belonging to our house".

He was bound and taken to prison before the eyes of the other brethren of Joseph, but as soon as they were out of sight, Joseph ordered good fare to be set before him, and he treated him with great kindness.

Joseph permitted his nine other brethren to depart, carrying corn with them in abundance, but he impressed upon them that they must surely return and bring their youngest brother with them. On the way, Levi, who felt lonely without his constant companion Simon, opened his sack, and he espied the money he had paid for the corn. They all trembled, and their hearts failed them, and they said, “Where, then, is the lovingkindness of God toward our fathers Abraham, Isaac, and Jacob, seeing that He hath delivered us into the hands of the Egyptian king, that he may raise false accusations against us”? And Judah said, “Verily, we are guilty concerning our brother, we have sinned against God, in that we sold our brother, our own flesh, and why do ye ask, Where, then, is the lovingkindness of God toward our fathers”?

Reuben spoke in the same way: “Spake I not unto you, saying, Do not sin against the child, and ye would not hear? And now the Lord doth demand him of us. How can you say, Where, then, is the lovingkindness of God toward our fathers, though you have sinned against Him”?

They proceeded on their journey home, and their father met them on the way. Jacob was astonished not to see Simon with them, and in reply to his questions, they told him all that had befallen them in Egypt. Then Jacob cried out: “What have ye done? I sent Joseph to you to see whether it be well with you, and ye said, An evil beast hath devoured him. Simon went forth with you for to buy corn, and you say, The king of Egypt hath cast him into prison. And now ye will take Benjamin away and kill him, too. Ye will bring down my gray hairs with sorrow to the grave”.

The words of Jacob, which he uttered, “Me have ye bereaved of my children”, were meant to intimate to his sons that he suspected them of the death of Joseph and of Simon’s disappearance as well, and their reports concerning both he regarded as inventions. What made him inconsolable was that now, having lost two of his sons, he could not hope to see the Divine promise fulfilled, that he should be the ancestor of twelve tribes. He was quite resolved in his mind, therefore, not to let Benjamin go away with his brethren under any condition whatsoever, and he vouchsafed Reuben no reply when he said, “Slay my two sons, if I bring him not to thee”. He considered it beneath his dignity to give an answer to such balderdash. “My first-born son”, he said to himself, “is a fool. What will it profit me, if I slay his two sons? Does he not know that his sons are equally mine”? Judah advised his brethren to desist from urging their father then; he would consent, he thought, to whatever expedients were found necessary, as soon as their bread gave out, and a second journey to Egypt became imperative.

The Second Journey to Egypt

When the supplies bought in Egypt were eaten up, and the family of Jacob began to suffer with hunger, the little children came to him, and they said, “Give us bread, that we die not of hunger before thee”. The words of the little ones brought scorching tears to the eyes of Jacob, and he summoned his sons and bade them go again down into Egypt and buy food. But Judah spake unto him, "The man did solemnly protest unto us, saying that we should not see his face, except our brother Benjamin be with us, and we cannot appear before him with idle pretexts". And Jacob said, "Wherefore dealt ye so ill with me as to tell the man whether ye had yet a brother"? It was the first and only time Jacob indulged in empty talk, and God said, "I made it My business to raise his son to the position of ruler of Egypt, and he complains, and says, Wherefore dealt ye so ill with-me"? And Judah protested against the reproach, that he had initiated the Egyptian viceroy in their family relations, with the words: "Why, he knew the very wood of which our baby coaches are made! Father", he continued, "if Benjamin goes with us, he may, indeed, be taken from us, but also he may not. This is a doubtful matter, but it is certain that if he does not go with us, we shall all die of hunger. It is better not to concern thyself about what is doubtful, and guide thy actions by what is certain. The king of Egypt is a strong and mighty king, and if we go to him without our brother, we shall all be put to death. Dost thou not know, and hast thou not heard, that this king is very powerful and wise, and there is none like unto him in all the earth? We have seen all the kings of the earth, but none like unto the king of Egypt. One would surely say that among all the kings of the earth there is none greater than Abimelech king of the Philistines, yet the king of Egypt is greater and mightier than he, and Abimelech can hardly be compared with one of his officers. Father, thou hast not seen his palace and his throne, and all his servants standing before him. Thou hast not seen that king upon his throne, in all his magnificence and with his royal insignia, arrayed in his royal robes, with a large golden crown upon his head. Thou hast not seen the honor and the glory that God hath given unto him, for there is none like unto him in all the earth. Father, thou hast not seen the wisdom, the understanding, and the knowledge that God has given in his heart. We heard his sweet voice when he spake unto us. We know not, father, who acquainted him with our names, and all that befell us. He asked also concerning thee, saying, Is your father still alive, and is it well with him? Thou hast not seen the affairs of the government of Egypt regulated by him, for none asketh his lord Pharaoh about them. Thou hast not seen the awe and the fear that he imposes upon all the Egyptians. Even we went out from his presence threatening to do unto Egypt as unto the cities of the Amorites, and exceedingly wroth by reason of all his words that he spake concerning us as spies, yet when we came again before him, his terror fell upon us all, and none of us was able to speak a word to him, great or small. Now, therefore, father, send the lad with us, and we will arise and go down into Egypt, and buy food to eat, that we die not of hunger".

Judah offered his portion in the world to come as surety for Benjamin, and thus solemnly he promised to bring him back safe and sound, and Jacob granted his request, and permitted Benjamin to go down into Egypt with his other sons. They also carried with them choice presents from their father for the ruler of Egypt, things that arouse wonder outside of Palestine, such as the murex, which is the snail that produces the Tyrian purple, and various kinds of balm, and almond oil, and pistachio oil, and honey as hard as stone. Furthermore, Jacob put double money in their hand to provide against a rise in prices in the meantime. And after all these matters were attended to, he spake to his sons, saying: "Here is money, and here is a present, and also your brother. Is there aught else that you need"? And they replied, Yes, we need this, besides, that thou shouldst intercede for us with God". Then their father prayed: "O Lord, Thou who at the time of creation didst call Enough! to heaven and earth when they stretched themselves out further and further toward infinity, set a limit to my sufferings, too, say unto them, Enough! God Almighty give you mercy before the ruler of Egypt, that he may release unto you Joseph, Simon, and Benjamin".

This prayer was an intercession, not only for the sons of Jacob, but also for their descendants--that God would deliver the Ten Tribes in time to come, as He delivered the two, Judah and Benjamin, and after He permitted the destruction of two Temples, He would grant endless continuance to the third.Jacob also put a letter addressed to the viceroy of Egypt into the hands of his son. The letter ran thus: "From thy servant Jacob, the son of Isaac, the grandson of Abraham, prince of God, to the mighty and wise king Zaphenathpaneah, the ruler of Egypt, peace! I make known unto my lord the king that the famine is sore with us in the land of Canaan, and I have therefore sent my sons unto thee, to buy us a little food, that we may live, and not die. My children surrounded me, and begged for something to eat, but, alas, I am very old, and I cannot see with mine eyes, for they are heavy with the weight of years, and also on account of my never-ceasing tears for my son Joseph, who hath been taken from me. I charged my sons not to pass through the gate all together at the same time, when they arrived in the city of Egypt, in consideration of the inhabitants of the land, that they might not take undue notice of them. Also I bade them go up and down in the land of Egypt and seek my son Joseph, mayhap they would find him there.

"This did they do, but thou didst therefore account them as spies. We have heard the report of thy wisdom and sagacity. How, then, canst thou look upon their countenances, and yet declare them to be spies? Especially as we have heard thou didst interpret Pharaoh's dream, and didst foretell the coming of the famine, are we amazed that thou, in thy discernment, couldst not distinguish whether they be spies or not.

"And, now, O my lord king, I send unto thee my son Benjamin, as thou didst demand of my other sons. I pray thee, take good care of him until thou sendest him back to me in peace with his brethren. Hast thou not heard, and dost thou not know, what our God did unto Pharaoh when he took our mother Sarah unto himself? Or what happened unto Abimelech on account of her? And what our father Abraham did unto the nine kings of Elam, how he killed them and exterminated their armies, though he had but few men with him? Or hast thou not heard what my two sons Simon and Levi did to the eight cities of the Amorites, which they destroyed on account of their sister Dinah? Benjamin consoled them for the loss of Joseph. What, then, will they do unto him that stretcheth forth the hand of power to snatch him away from them?

"Knowest thou not, O king of Egypt, that the might of our God is with us, and that He always hearkens unto our prayers, and never forsakes us? Had I called upon God to rise up against thee when my sons told me how thou didst act toward them, thou and thy people, ye all would have been annihilated ere Benjamin could come down to thee. But I reflected that Simon my son was abiding in thy house, and perhaps thou wast doing kindnesses unto him, and therefore I invoked not the punishment of God upon thee. Now my son Benjamin goeth down unto thee with my other sons. Take heed unto thyself, keep thy eyes directed upon him, and God will direct His eye upon all thy kingdom.

"I have said all now that is in my heart. My sons take their youngest brother down into Egypt with them, and do thou send them all back to me in peace".This letter Jacob put into the keeping of Judah, charging him to deliver it to the ruler of Egypt. His last words to his sons were an admonition to take good care of Benjamin and not leave him out of their sight, either on the journey or after their arrival in Egypt. He bade farewell to them, and then turned in prayer to God, saying: "O Lord of heaven and earth! Remember Thy covenant with our father Abraham. Remember also my father Isaac, and grant grace unto my sons, and deliver them not into the hands of the king of Egypt. O my God, do it for the sake of Thy mercy, redeem my sons and save them from the hands of the Egyptians, and restore their two brethren unto them".

Also the women and the children in the house of Jacob prayed to God amid tears, and entreated Him to redeem their husbands and their fathers out of the hands of the king of Egypt.

Joseph and Benjamin

Great was the joy of Joseph when his brethren stood before him and Benjamin was with them. In his youngest brother he saw the true counterpart of his father. He ordered his son Manasseh, the steward of his house, to bring the men into the palace, and make ready a meal for them. But he was to take care to prepare the meat dishes in the presence of the guests, so that they might see with their own eyes that the cattle had been slaughtered according to the ritual prescriptions, and the sinew of the hip which is upon the hollow of the thigh had been removed.

The dinner to which Joseph invited his brethren was a Sabbath meal, for he observed the seventh day even before the revelation of the law. The sons of Jacob refused the invitation of the steward, and a scuffle ensued. While he tried to force them into the banqueting hall, they tried to force him out, for they feared it was but a ruse to get possession of them and their asses, on account of the money they had found in their sacks on their return from their first journey to Egypt. In their modesty they put the loss of their beasts upon the same level as the loss of their personal liberty. To the average man property is as precious as life itself.

Standing at the door of Joseph's house, they spake to the steward, and said: "We are in badly reduced circumstances. In our country we supported others, and now we depend upon thee to support us". After these introductory words, they offered him the money they had found in their sacks. The steward reassured them concerning the money, saying, "However it may be, whether for the sake of your own merits, or for the sake of the merits of your fathers, God hath caused you to find a treasure, for the money ye paid for the corn came into my hand". Then he brought Simon out to them. Their brother looked like a leather bottle, so fat and rotund had he grown during his sojourn in Egypt. He told his brethren what kind treatment had been accorded unto him. The very moment they left the city he had been released from prison, and thereafter he had been entertained with splendor in the house of the ruler of Egypt.

When Joseph made his appearance, Judah took Benjamin by the hand, and presented him to the viceroy, and they all bowed down themselves to him to the earth. Joseph asked them concerning the welfare of their father and their grandfather, and they made reply, "Thy servant our father is well; he is yet alive", and Joseph knew from their words that his grandfather Isaac was no more. He had died at the time when Joseph was released from prison, and the joy of God in the liberation of Joseph was overcast by His sorrow for Isaac. Then Judah handed his father's letter to Joseph, who was so moved at seeing the well-known handwriting that he had to retire to his chamber and weep. When he came back, he summoned Benjamin to approach close to him, and he laid his hand upon his youngest brother's head, and blessed him with the words, "God be gracious unto thee, my son". His father had once mentioned "the children which God hath graciously given Thy servant", and as Benjamin was not among the children thus spoken of, for he was born later, Joseph compensated him now by blessing him with the grace of God.

The table was set in three divisions, for Joseph, for his brethren, and for the Egyptians. The sons of Jacob did not venture to eat of the dishes set before them, they were afraid they might not have been prepared according to the ritual prescriptions--a punishment upon Joseph for having slandered his brethren, whom he once charged with not being punctilious in the observance of the dietary laws. The Egyptians, again, could not sit at the same table with the sons of Jacob, because the latter ate the flesh of the animals to which the former paid divine worship.

When all was ready, and the guests were to be seated, Joseph raised his cup, and, pretending to inhale his knowledge from it, he said, "Judah is king, therefore let him sit at the head of the table, and let Reuben the first-born take the second seat", and thus he assigned places to all his brethren corresponding to their dignity and their age. Moreover, he seated the brothers together who were the sons of the same mother, and when he reached Benjamin, he said, "I know that the youngest among you has no brother borne by his own mother, next to whom he might be seated, and also I have none, therefore he may take his place next to me".

The brethren marvelled one with another at all this. During the meal, Joseph took his portion, and gave it to Benjamin, and his wife Asenath followed his example, and also Ephraim and Manasseh, so that Benjamin had four portions in addition to that which he had received like the other sons of Jacob.

Wine was served at the meal, and it was the first time in twenty-two years that Joseph and his brethren tasted of it, for they had led the life of Nazarites, his brethren because they regretted the evil they had done to Joseph, and Joseph because he grieved over the fate of his father.

Joseph entered into conversation with his brother Benjamin. He asked him whether he had a brother borne by his own mother, and Benjamin answered, "I had one, but I do not know what hath become of him". Joseph continued his questions: "Hast thou a wife"?

Benjamin: "Yes, I have a wife and ten sons".

Joseph: "And what are their names"?

Benjamin: "Bela, and Becher, and Ashbel, Gera, and Naaman, Ehi, and Rosh, Muppim, and Huppim, and Ard".

Joseph: "Why didst thou give them such peculiar names"?

Benjamin: "In memory of my brother and his sufferings: Bela, because my brother disappeared among the peoples; Becher, he was the first-born son of my mother; Ashbel, he was taken away from my father; Gera, he dwells a stranger in a strange land; Naaman, he was exceedingly lovely; Ehi, he was my only brother by my father and my mother together; Rosh, he was at the head of his brethren; Muppim, he was beautiful in every respect; Huppim, he was slandered; and Ard, because he was as beautiful as a rose".

Joseph ordered his magic astrolabe to be brought to him, whereby he knew all things that happen, and he said unto Benjamin, "I have heard that the Hebrews are acquainted with all wisdom, but dost thou know aught of this"? Benjamin answered, "Thy servant also is skilled in all wisdom, which my father hath taught me". He then looked upon the astrolabe, and to his great astonishment he discovered by the aid of it that he who was sitting upon the throne before him was his brother Joseph. Noticing Benjamin's amazement, Joseph asked him, "What hast thou seen, and why art thou astonished"? Benjamin said, "I can see by this that Joseph my brother sitteth here before me upon the throne". And Joseph said: "I am Joseph thy brother! Reveal not the thing unto our brethren. I will send thee with them when they go away, and I will command them to be brought back again into the city, and I will take thee away from them. If they risk their lives and fight for thee, then shall I know that they have repented of what they did unto me, and I will make myself known unto them. But if they forsake thee, I will keep thee, that thou shouldst remain with me. They shall go away, and I will not make myself known unto them".

Then Joseph inquired of Benjamin what his brethren had told their father after they had sold him into slavery, and he heard the story of the coat dipped in the blood of a kid of the goats. "Yes, brother", spoke Joseph, "when they had stripped me of my coat, they handed me over to the Ishmaelites, who tied an apron around my waist, scourged me, and bade me run off. But a lion attacked the one that beat me, and killed him, and his companions were alarmed, and they sold me to other people".

Dismissed by Joseph with kind words, his brethren started on their homeward journey as soon as the morning was light, for it is a good rule to "leave a city after sunrise, and enter a city before sundown". Besides, Joseph had a specific reason for not letting his brethren depart from the city during the night. He feared an encounter between them and his servants, and that his men might get the worst of it, for the sons of Jacob were like the wild beasts, which have the upper hand at night.

The Thief Caught

They were not yet far beyond the city gates, when Joseph dispatched Manasseh, the steward of his house, to follow after them, and look for the silver cup that he had concealed in Benjamin's sack. He knew his brethren well, he did not venture to let them get too far from the city before he should attempt to force their return. He hoped that the nearness of the city would intimidate them and make them heed his commands. Manasseh therefore received the order to bring them to a halt, by mild speech if he could, or by rough speech if he must, and carry them back to the city. He acted according to his instructions. When the brethren heard the accusation of theft , they said: "With whomsoever of thy servants the cup be found, let him die, and we also will be my lord's bondmen". And Manasseh said, "As you say, so were it proper to do, for if ten persons are charged with theft, and the stolen object is found with one of them, all are held responsible. But I will not be so hard. He with whom the cup is found shall be the bondman, and the rest shall be blameless".

He searched all the sacks, and in order not to excite the suspicion that he knew where the cup was, he began at Reuben, the eldest, and left off at Benjamin, the youngest, and the cup was found in Benjamin's sack. In a rage, his brethren shouted at Benjamin, "O thou thief and son of a thief! Thy mother brought shame upon our father by her thievery, and now thou bringest shame upon us". But he replied, "Is this matter as evil as the matter of the kid of the goats--as the deed of the brethren that sold their own brother into slavery"?

In their fury and vexation, the brethren rent their clothes. God paid them in their own coin. They had caused Jacob to tear his clothes in his grief over Joseph, and now they were made to do the same on account of their own troubles. And as they rent their clothes for the sake of their brother Benjamin, so Mordecai, the descendant of Benjamin, was destined to rend his on account of his brethren, the people of Israel. But because mortification was inflicted upon the brethren through Manasseh, the steward of Joseph, the allotment of territory given to the tribe of Manasseh was "torn" in two, one-half of the tribe had to live on one side of the Jordan, the other half on the other side. And Joseph, who had not shrunk from vexing his brethren so bitterly that they rent their clothes in their abasement, was punished, in that his descendant Joshua was driven to such despair after the defeat of Ai that he, too, rent his clothes.

Convicted of theft beyond the peradventure of a doubt, the brethren of Joseph had no choice but to comply with the steward's command and return to the city. They accompanied him without delay. Each of them loaded his ass himself, raising the burden with one hand from the ground to the back of the beast, and then they retraced their steps cityward, and as they walked, they rapped Benjamin roughly on the shoulder, saying, "O thou thief and son of a thief, thou hast brought the same shame upon us that thy mother brought upon our father". Benjamin bore the blows and the abusive words in patient silence, and he was rewarded for his humility. For submitting to the blows upon his shoulder, God appointed that His Shekinah should "dwell between his shoulders", and He also called him "the beloved of the Lord".

Joseph's brethren returned to the city without fear. Though it was a great metropolis, in their eyes it appeared but as a hamlet of ten persons, which they could wipe out with a turn of the hand. They were led into the presence of Joseph, who, contrary to his usual habit, was not holding a session of the court in the forum on that day. He remained at home, that his brethren might not be exposed to shame in public. They fell to the earth before him, and thus came true his dream of the eleven stars that made obeisance to him. But even while paying homage to Joseph, Judah was boiling inwardly with suppressed rage, and he said to his brethren, "Verily, this man hath forced me to come back hither only that I should destroy the city on this day".

Guarded by his valiant men on the right and on the left, Joseph addressed his brethren, snarling, "What deed is this that ye have done, to steal away my cup? I know well, ye took it in order to discover with its help the whereabouts of your brother that hath disappeared". Judah was spokesman, and he replied: "What shall we say unto my lord concerning the first money that he found in the mouth of our sacks? What shall we speak concerning the second money that also was in our sacks? And how shall we clear ourselves concerning the cup? We cannot acknowledge ourselves guilty, for we know ourselves to be innocent in all these matters. Yet we cannot avow ourselves innocent, because God hath found out the iniquity of thy servants, like a creditor that goes about and tries to collect a debt owing to him. Two brothers take care not to enter a house of mirth and festivity together, that they be not exposed to the evil eye, but we all were caught together in one place, by reason of the sin which we committed in company".

Joseph: "But if your punishment is for selling Joseph, why should this brother of yours suffer, the youngest, he that had no part in your crime.

Judah: "A thief and his companions are taken together".

Joseph: "If you could prevail upon yourselves to report to your father concerning a brother that had not stolen, and had brought no manner of shame upon you, that a wild beast had torn him, you will easily persuade yourselves to say it concerning a brother that hath stolen, and hath brought shame upon you. Go hence, and tell your father, 'The rope follows after the water bucket'. But", continued Joseph, shaking his purple mantle, "God forbid that I should accuse you all of theft. Only the youth that stole the cup in order to divine his brother's whereabouts shall remain with me as my bondman; but as for you, get you up in peace unto your father".

The holy spirit called out, "Great peace have they which love thy law"!

The brethren all consented to yield Benjamin to the ruler of Egypt, only Judah demurred, and he cried out, "Now it is all over with peace"! and he prepared to use force, if need be, to rescue Benjamin from slavery.

Judah Pleads and Threatens

Joseph dismissed his brethren, and carried Benjamin off by main force, and locked him up in a chamber. But Judah broke the door open and stood before Joseph with his brethren. He determined to use in turn the three means of liberating Benjamin at his disposal. He was prepared to convince Joseph by argument, or move him by entreaties, or resort to force, in order to accomplish his end.

He spake: "Thou doest a wrong unto us. Thou who didst say, 'I fear God', thou showest thyself to be like unto Pharaoh, who hath no fear of God. The judgments which thou dost pronounce are not in accordance with our laws, nor are they in accordance with the laws of the nations. According to our law, a thief must pay double the value of what he hath stolen. Only, if he hath no money, he is sold into slavery, but if he hath the money, he maketh double restitution. And according to the law of the nations, the thief is deprived of all he owns. Do so, but let him go free. If a man buys a slave, and then discovers him to be a thief, the transaction is void. Yet thou desirest to make one a slave whom thou chargest with being a thief. I suspect thee of wanting to keep him in thy power for illicit purposes, and in this lustfulness thou resemblest Pharaoh. Also thou art like Pharaoh in that thou makest a promise and keepest it not. Thou saidst unto thy servants, Bring thy youngest brother down unto me, that I may set mine eyes upon him. Dost thou call this setting thine eyes upon him? If thou didst desire nothing beside a slave, then wouldst thou surely accept our offer to serve thee as bondmen instead of Benjamin. Reuben is older than he, and I exceed him in strength. It cannot but be as I say, thou hast a lustful purpose in mind with our brother.

"Therefore let these words of mine which I am about to speak find entrance into thy heart: For the sake of the grandmother of this lad were Pharaoh and his house stricken with sore plagues, because he detained her in his palace a single night against her will. His mother died a premature death, by reason of a curse which his father uttered in inconsiderate haste. Take heed, then, that this man's curse strike thee not and slay thee. Two of us destroyed the whole of a city on account of one woman, how much more would we do it for the sake of a man, and that man the beloved of the Lord, in whose allotment it is appointed that God shall dwell!

"If I but utter a sound, death-dealing pestilence will stalk through the land as far as No. In this land Pharaoh is the first, and thou art the second after him, but in our land my father is the first, and I am the second. If thou wilt not comply with our demand, I will draw my sword, and hew thee down first, and then Pharaoh".

When Judah gave utterance to this threat, Joseph made a sign, and Manasseh stamped his foot on the ground so that the whole palace shook. Judah said, "Only one belonging to our family can stamp thus"! and intimidated by this display of great strength, he moderated his tone and manner. "From the very beginning", he continued to speak, "thou didst resort to all sorts of pretexts in order to embarrass us. The inhabitants of many countries came down into Egypt to buy corn, but none of them didst thou ask questions about their family relations. In sooth, we did not come hither to seek thy daughter in marriage, or peradventure thou desirest an alliance with our sister? Nevertheless we gave thee an answer unto all thy questions".

Joseph replied: "Verily, thou canst talk glibly! Is there another babbler like thee among thy brethren? Why dost thou speak so much, while thy brethren that are older than thou, Reuben, Simon, and Levi, stand by silent"?

Judah: "None of my brethren has so much at stake as I have, if Benjamin returns not to his father. I was a surety to my father for him, saying, If I bring him not unto thee, and set him before thee, then let me bear the blame forever, in this world and in the world to come.

The other brethren withheld themselves intentionally from taking part in the dispute between Judah and Joseph, saying, "Kings are carrying on a dispute, and it is not seemly for us to interfere between them". Even the angels descended from heaven to earth to be spectators of the combat between Joseph the bull and Judah the lion, and they said, "It lies in the natural course of things that the bull should fear the lion, but here the two are engaged in equal, furious combat".

In reply to Judah, when he explained that his great interest in Benjamin's safety was due to the pledge he had given to his father, Joseph spoke: "Why wast thou not a surety for thy other brother, when ye sold him for twenty pieces of silver? Then thou didst not regard the sorrow thou wast inflicting upon thy father, but thou didst say, A wild beast hath devoured Joseph. And yet Joseph had done no evil, while this Benjamin has committed theft. Therefore, go up and say unto thy father, The rope hath followed after the water bucket".

These words had such an effect upon Judah that he broke out in sobs, and cried aloud, "How shall I go up to my father, and the lad be not with me"?

His outcry reached to a distance of four hundred parasangs, and when Hushim the son of Dan heard it in Canaan, he jumped into Egypt with a single leap and joined his voice with Judah's, and the whole land was on the point of collapsing from the great noise they produced. Joseph's valiant men lost their teeth, and the cities of Pithom and Raamses were destroyed, and they remained in ruins until the Israelites built them up again under taskmasters. Also Judah's brethren, who had kept quiet up to that moment, fell into a rage, and stamped on the ground with their feet until it looked as though deep furrows had been torn in it by a ploughshare. And Judah addressed his brethren, "Be brave, demean yourselves as men, and let each one of you show his heroism, for the circumstances demand that we do our best".

Then they resolved to destroy Mizraim, the city of Egypt, and Judah said, "I will raise my voice, and with it destroy Egypt".

Reuben: "I will raise my arm, and crush it out of existence".

Simon: "I will raise my hand, and lay waste its palaces".

Levi: "I will draw my sword, and slay the inhabitants of Egypt".

Issachar: "I will make the land like unto Sodom".

Zebulon: "Like unto Gomorrah will I render it".

Dan: "I will reduce it to a desert".

Then Judah's towering rage began to show signs of breaking out: his right eye shed tears of blood; the hair above his heart grew so stiff that it pierced and rent the five garments in which he was clothed; and he took brass rods, bit them with his teeth, and spat them out as fine powder. When Joseph observed these signs, fear befell him, and in order to show that he, too, was a man of extraordinary strength, he pushed with his foot against the marble pedestal upon which he sat, and it broke into splinters. Judah exclaimed, "This one is a hero equal to myself"! Then he tried to draw his sword from its scabbard in order to slay Joseph, but the weapon could not be made to budge, and Judah was convinced thereby that his adversary was a God-fearing man, and he addressed himself to the task of begging him to let Benjamin go free, but he remained inexorable.

Judah then said: "What shall we say unto our father, when he seeth that our brother is not with us, and he will grieve over him"?

Joseph: "Say that the rope hath followed after the water bucket".

Judah: "Thou art a king, why dost thou speak in this wise, counselling a falsehood? Woe unto the king that is like thee"!

Joseph: "Is there a greater falsehood than that ye spake concerning your brother Joseph, whom you sold to the Midianites for twenty pieces of silver, telling your father, An evil beast bath devoured him"?

Judah: "The fire of Shechem burneth in my heart, now will I burn all thy land with fire".

Joseph: "Surely, the fire kindled to burn Tamar, thy daughter-in-law, who did kill thy sons, will extinguish the fire of Shechem".

Judah: "If I pluck out a single hair from my body, I will fill the whole of Egypt with its blood".

Joseph: "Such is it your custom to do; thus ye did unto your brother whom you sold, and then you dipped his coat in blood, brought it to your father, and said, An evil beast hath devoured him, and here is his blood".

When Judah heard this, he was exceedingly wroth, and he took a stone weighing four hundred shekels that was before him, cast it toward heaven with one hand, caught it with his left hand, then sat upon it, and the stone turned into dust. At the command of Joseph, Manasseh did likewise with another stone, and Joseph said to Judah: "Strength hath not been given to you alone, we also are powerful men. Why, then, will ye all boast before us"? Then Judah sent Naphtali forth, saying, "Go and count all the streets of the city of Egypt and come and tell me the number", but Simon interposed, saying, "Let not this thing trouble you, I will go to the mount, and take up one huge stone from the mount, throw it over the whole of Mizraim, the city of Egypt, and kill all therein".

Hearing all these words, which they spake aloud, because they did not know that he understood Hebrew, Joseph bade his son Manasseh make haste and gather together all the inhabitants of Egypt, and all the valiant men, and let them come to him on horseback and afoot. Meantime Naphtali had gone quickly to execute Judah's bidding, for he was as swift as the nimble hart, he could run across a field of corn without breaking an ear. And he returned and reported that the city of Egypt was divided into twelve quarters. Judah bade his brethren destroy the city; he himself undertook to raze three quarters, and he assigned the nine remaining quarters to the others, one quarter to each.

In the meantime Manasseh had assembled a great army, five hundred mounted men and ten thousand on foot, among them four hundred valiant heroes, who could fight without spear or sword, using only their strong, unarmed hands. To inspire his brethren with more terror, Joseph ordered them to make a loud noise with all sorts of instruments, and their appearance and the hubbub they produced did, indeed, cause fear to fall upon some of the brethren of Joseph. Judah, however, called to them, "Why are you terrified, seeing that God grants us His mercy"? He drew his sword, and uttered a wild cry, which threw all the people into consternation, and in their disordered flight many fell over each other and perished, and Judah and his brethren followed after the fleeing people as far as the house of Pharaoh. Returning to Joseph, Judah again broke out in loud roars, and the reverberations caused by his cries were so mighty that all the city walls in Egypt and in Goshen fell in ruins, the pregnant women brought forth untimely births, and Pharaoh was flung from his throne. Judah's cries were heard at a great distance, as far off as Succoth.

When Pharaoh learnt the reason of the mighty uproar, he sent word to Joseph that he would have to concede the demands of the Hebrews, else the land would suffer destruction. "Thou canst take thy choice", were the words of Pharaoh, "between me and the Hebrews, between Egypt and the land of the Hebrews. If thou wilt not heed my command, then leave me and go with them into their land".

Joseph Makes Himself Knows

Seeing that his brethren were, indeed, on the point of destroying Egypt, Joseph resolved to make himself known to them, and he cast around for a proper opening, which would lead naturally to his announcement. At his behest, Manasseh laid his hand upon Judah's shoulder, and his touch allayed Judah's fury, for he noticed that he was in contact with a kinsman of his, because such strength existed in no other family. Then Joseph addressed Judah gently, saying: "I should like to know who advised him to steal the cup. Could it have been one of you"? Benjamin replied: "Neither did they counsel theft, nor did I touch the cup". "Take an oath upon it", demanded Joseph, and Benjamin complied with his brother's request: "I swear that I did not touch the cup! As true as my brother Joseph is separated from me; as true as I had nothing to do with the darts that my brethren threw at him; as true as I was not one of those to take off his coat; as true as I had no part in the transaction by which he was given over to the Ishmaelites; as true as I did not help the others dip his coat in blood; so true is my oath, that they did not counsel theft, and that I did not commit theft".

Joseph: "How can I know that this oath of thine taken upon thy brother's fate is true"?

Benjamin: "From the names of my ten sons, which I gave them in memory of my brother's life and trials, thou canst see how dearly I loved him. I pray thee, therefore, do not bring down my father with sorrow to the grave".

Hearing these words of abiding love, Joseph could refrain himself no longer. He could not but make himself known unto his brethren. He spake these words to them: "Ye said the brother of this lad was dead. Did you yourselves see him dead before you"? They answered, "Yes"!

Joseph: "Did you stand beside his grave"?

The brethren: "Yes"!

Joseph: "Did you throw clods of earth upon his corpse"?

The brethren: "No".

Then Joseph reflected, saying to himself: "My brethren are as pious as aforetime, and they speak no lies. They said I was dead, because when they abandoned me, I was poor, and 'a poor man is like unto a dead man;' they stood beside my grave, that is the pit into which they cast me; but they did not say that they had shovelled earth upon me, for that would have been a falsehood".

Turning to his brethren, he said: "Ye lie when ye say that your brother is dead. He is not dead. You sold him, and I did buy him. I shall call him, and set him before your eyes", and he began to call, "Joseph, son of Jacob, come hither! Joseph, son of Jacob, come hither! Speak to thy brethren who did sell thee". The others turned their eyes hither and thither, to the four corners of the house, until Joseph called to them: "Why look ye here and there? Behold, I am Joseph your brother! "Their souls fled away from them, and they could make no answer, but God permitted a miracle to happen, and their souls came back to them.

Joseph continued, "Ye see it with your own eyes, and also my brother Benjamin seeth it with his eyes, that I speak with you in Hebrew, and I am truly your brother". But they would not believe him. Not only had he been transformed from a smooth-faced youth into a bearded man since they had abandoned him, but also the forsaken youth now stood before them the ruler of Egypt. Therefore Joseph bared his body and showed them that he belonged to the descendants of Abraham.

Abashed they stood there, and in their rage they desired to slay Joseph as the author of their shame and their suffering. But an angel appeared and flung them to the four corners of the house. Judah raised so loud an outcry that the walls of the city of Egypt tumbled down, the women brought forth untimely births, Joseph and Pharaoh both rolled down off their thrones, and Joseph's three hundred heroes lost their teeth, and their heads remained forever immobile, facing backward, as they had turned them to discover the cause of the tumult. Yet the brethren did not venture to approach close to Joseph, they were too greatly ashamed of their behavior toward their brother.

He sought to calm them, saying, "Now be not grieved, nor angry with yourselves, that ye sold me hither, for God did send me before you to preserve life".

Even such kind words of exhortation did not banish their fear, and Joseph continued to speak, "As little as I harbor vengeful thoughts in my heart against Benjamin, so little do I harbor them against you".And still his brethren were ill at case, and Joseph went on, "Think you that it is possible for me to inflict harm upon you? If the smoke of ten candles could not extinguish one, how can one extinguish ten"?

At last the brethren were soothed, and they went up to Joseph, who knew each by name, and, weeping, he embraced and kissed them all in turn. The reason why he wept was that his prophetic spirit showed him the descendants of his brethren enslaved by the nations. Especially did he weep upon Benjamin's neck, because he foresaw the destruction decreed for the two Temples to be situated in the allotment of Benjamin. And Benjamin also wept upon Joseph's neck, for the sanctuary at Shiloh, in the territory of Joseph which was likewise doomed to destruction.

Pharaoh was well pleased with the report of the reconciliation between Joseph and the Hebrews, for he had feared that their dissensions might cause the ruin of Egypt, and he sent his servants to Joseph, that they take part in his joy. Also he sent word to Joseph that it would please him well if his brethren took up their abode in Egypt, and he promised to assign the best parts of the land to them for their dwelling-place.

Not all the servants of Pharaoh were in agreement with their master concerning this invitation to the Hebrews. Many among them were disquieted, saying, "If one of the sons of Jacob came hither, and he was advanced to a high position over our heads, what evil will happen to us when ten more come hither"?

Joseph gave all his brethren two changes of raiment, one for use on the ordinary days of the week and one for use on the Sabbath, for, when the cup was found with Benjamin, they had rent their clothes, and Joseph would not have his brethren go about in torn garments. But to Benjamin he gave five changes of raiment, though not in order to distinguish him above his brethren. Joseph remembered only too well what mischief his father had caused by giving him the coat of many colors, thereby arousing the envy of his brethren. He desired only to intimate that Mordecai, a descendant of Benjamin, would once be arrayed in five royal garments.

Joseph presented his brethren, apparelled in their gold and silver embroidered clothes, before Pharaoh, who was well pleased to become acquainted with them when he saw that they were men of heroic stature and handsome appearance. He gave them wagons, to bring their families down into Egypt, but as they were ornamented with images of idols, Judah burnt them, and Joseph replaced them with eleven other wagons, among them the one he had ridden in at his accession to office, to view the land of Egypt. This was to be used by his father on his journey to Egypt. For each of his brothers' children, he sent raiments, and also one hundred pieces of silver for each, but for each of the children of Benjamin he sent ten changes of raiment. And for the wives of his brethren he gave them rich garments of state, such as were worn by the wives of the Pharaohs, and also ointments and aromatic spices. To his sister Dinah he sent silver and gold embroidered clothes, and myrrh, aloes, and other perfumes, and such presents he gave also to the wife and the daughters-in-law of Benjamin. For themselves and for their wives the brethren received all sorts of precious stones and jewelled ornaments, like those that are worn by the Egyptian nobility.

Joseph accompanied his eleven brethren to the frontier, and there he took leave of them with the wish that they and all their families come down to Egypt, and he enjoined upon them, besides, three maxims to be observed by travellers: Do not take too large steps; do not discuss Halakic subjects, that you lose not your way; and enter the city at the latest with the going down of the sun.

Jacob Receives the Glad Tidings

In blithe spirits the sons of Jacob journeyed up to the land of Canaan, but when they reached the boundary line, they said to one another, "How shall we do? If we appear before our father and tell him that Joseph is alive, he will be greatly frightened, and he will not be inclined to believe us". Besides, Joseph's last injunction to them had been to take heed and not startle their father with the tidings of joy.

On coming close to their habitation, they caught sight of Serah, the daughter of Asher, a very beautiful maiden, and very wise, who was skilled in playing upon the harp. They summoned her unto them and gave her a harp, and bade her play before Jacob and sing that which they should tell her. She sat down before Jacob, and, with an agreeable melody, she sang the following words, accompanying herself upon the harp: "Joseph, my uncle, liveth, he ruleth over the whole of Egypt, he is not dead"! She repeated these words several times, and Jacob grew more and more pleasurably excited. His joy awakened the holy spirit in him, and he knew that she spoke the truth. The spirit of prophecy never visits a seer when he is in a state of lassitude or in a state of grief; it comes only together with joy. All the years of Joseph's separation from him Jacob had had no prophetic visions, because he was always sad, and only when Serah's words reawakened the feeling of happiness in his heart, the prophetic spirit again took possession of him. Jacob rewarded her therefor with the words, "My daughter, may death never have power over thee, for thou didst revive my spirit". And so it was. Serah did not die, she entered Paradise alive. At his bidding, she repeated the words she had sung again and again, and they gave Jacob great joy and delight, so that the holy spirit waxed stronger and stronger within him.

While he was sitting thus in converse with Serah, his sons appeared arrayed in all their magnificence, and with all the presents that Joseph had given them, and they spake to Jacob, saying: "Glad tidings! Joseph our brother liveth! He is ruler over the whole land of Egypt, and he sends thee a message of joy". At first Jacob would not believe them, but when they opened their packs, and showed him the presents Joseph had sent to all, he could not doubt the truth of their words any longer.

Joseph had had a premonition that his father would refuse to give his brethren credence, because they had tried to deceive him before, and "it is the punishment of the liar that his words are not believed even when he speaks the truth". He had therefore said to them, "If my father will not believe your words, tell him that when I took leave of him, to see whether it was well with you, he had been teaching me the law of the heifer whose neck is broken in the valley". When they repeated this, every last vestige of Jacob's doubt disappeared, and he said: "Great is the steadfastness of my son Joseph. In spite of all his sufferings he has remained constant in his piety. Yea, great are the benefits that the Lord hath conferred upon me. He saved me from the hands of Esau, and from the hands of Laban, and from the Canaanites who pursued after me. I have tasted many joys, and I hope to see more, but never did I hope to set eyes upon Joseph again, and now I shall go down to him and behold him before my death".

Then Jacob and the members of his family put on the clothes Joseph had sent, among them a turban for Jacob, and they made all preparations to journey down into Egypt and dwell there with Joseph and his family. Hearing of his good fortune, the kings and the grandees of Canaan came to wait upon Jacob and express sympathy with him in his joy, and he prepared a three days' banquet for them.

Jacob, however, would not go down into Egypt without first inquiring whether it was the will of God that he should leave the Holy Land. He said, "How can I leave the land of my fathers, the land of my birth, the land in which the Shekinah dwells, and go into an unclean land, inhabited by slaves of the sons of Ham, a land wherein there is no fear of God"? Then he brought sacrifices in honor of God, in the expectation that a Divine vision would descend upon him and instruct him whether to go down into Egypt or have Joseph come up to Canaan. He feared the sojourn in Egypt, for he remembered the vision he had had at Beth-el on leaving his father's house, and he said to God: "I resemble my father. As he was greedy in filling his maw, so am I, and therefore I would go down into Egypt in consequence of the famine. As my father preferred one son to the other, so had I a favorite son, and therefore I would go down into Egypt to see Joseph. But in this I do not resemble my father, he had only himself to provide for, and my house consists of seventy souls, and therefore am I compelled to go down into Egypt. The blessing which my father gave me was not fulfilled in me, but in my son Joseph, whom peoples serve, and before whom nations bow down".

Then the Shekinah addressed Jacob, calling his name twice in token of love, and bidding him not to fear the Egyptian slavery foretold for the descendants of Abraham, for God would have pity upon the suffering of his children and deliver them from bondage. God furthermore said, "I will go down into Egypt with thee", and the Shekinah accompanied Jacob thither, bringing the number of the company with which he entered Egypt up to seventy. But as Jacob entertained fears that his descendants would stay there forever, God gave him the assurance that He would lead him forth together with all the pious that were like unto him. And God also told Jacob that Joseph had remained steadfast in his piety even in Egypt, and he might dismiss all doubts from his mind on this score, for it was his anxiety on this account that had induced Jacob to consider going down into Egypt; he wanted only to make sure of Joseph's faithfulness, and then return home, but God commanded him to go thither and remain there.

Before Jacob left Canaan, he went to Beer-sheba, to hew down the cedars that Abraham had planted there, and take them with him to Egypt. For centuries these cedar trees remained in the possession of his descendants; they carried them with them when they left Egypt, and they used them in building the Tabernacle.

Although Joseph had put wagons at the disposal of his brethren for the removal of his family from Canaan to Egypt, they yet carried Jacob upon their arms, for which purpose they divided themselves into three divisions, one division after the other assuming the burden. As a reward for their filial devotion, God redeemed their descendants from Egypt.

Judah was sent on ahead by his father, to erect a dwelling in Goshen, and also a Bet ha-Midrash, that Jacob might set about instructing his sons at once after his arrival. He charged Judah with this honorable task in order to compensate him for a wrong he had done him. All the years of Joseph's absence he bad suspected Judah of having made away with Rachel's son. How little the suspicion was justified he realized now when Judah in particular had been assiduous in securing the safety of Benjamin, the other son of Rachel. Jacob therefore said to Judah: "Thou hast done a pious, God-bidden deed, and hast shown thyself to be a man capable of carrying on negotiations with Joseph. Complete the work thou hast begun! Go to Goshen, and together with Joseph prepare all things for our coming. Indeed", continued Jacob, "thou wast the cause of our going down into Egypt, for it was at thy suggestion that Joseph was sold as a slave, and, also, through thy descendants Israel will be led forth out of Egypt".

When Joseph was informed of the approach of his father, he rejoiced exceedingly, chiefly because his coming would stop the talk of the Egyptians, who were constantly referring to him as the slave that had dominion over them. "Now", thought Joseph, "they will see my father and my brethren, and they will be convinced that I am a free-born man, of noble stock".

In his joy in anticipation of seeing his father, Joseph made ready his chariot with his own hands, without waiting for his servants to minister to him, and this loving action redounded later to the benefit of the Israelites, for it rendered of none effect Pharaoh's zeal in making ready his chariot himself, with his own hands, to pursue after the Israelites.

Jacob Arrives in Egypt

When the Egyptian nobles observed their viceroy completing his preparations to meet his father, they did the same. Indeed, Joseph had issued a proclamation throughout the land, threatening with death all that did not go forth to meet Jacob. The procession that accompanied him was composed of countless men, arrayed in byssus and purple, and marching to the sound of all sorts of musical instruments. Even the women of Egypt had a part in the reception ceremonies. They ascended to the roofs of the houses and the walls of the cities, ready to greet Jacob with the music of cymbals and timbrels.

Joseph wore the royal crown upon his head, Pharaoh had yielded it to him for the occasion. He descended from his chariot when he was at a distance of about fifty ells from his father, and walked the rest of the way on foot, and his example was followed by the princes and nobles of Egypt. When Jacob caught sight of the approaching procession, he was rejoiced, and even before he recognized Joseph, he bowed down before him, but for permitting his father to show him this mark of honor, punishment was visited upon Joseph. He died an untimely death, before the years of life assigned to him had elapsed.

That no harm befall Jacob from a too sudden meeting with him, Joseph sent his oldest son ahead with five horses, the second son following close after him in the same way. As each son approached, Jacob thought he beheld Joseph, and so he was prepared gradually to see him face to face.

Meantime Jacob had espied, from where he was seated, a man in royal robes among the Egyptians, a crown upon his head, and a purple mantle over his shoulders, and he asked Judah who it might be. When he was told that it was Joseph, his joy was great over the high dignity attained by his son.By this time Joseph had come close to his father, and he bowed himself before him down to the earth, and all the people with him likewise prostrated themselves. Then Joseph fell upon his father's neck, and he wept bitterly. He was particularly grieved that he had permitted his father to bow down before him but a little while before without hindering it. At the very moment when Joseph embraced his father, Jacob was reciting the Shema', and he did not allow himself to be interrupted in his prayer, but then he said, "When they brought me the report of the death of Joseph, I thought I was doomed to double death--that I should lose this world and the world to come as well. The Lord had promised to make me the ancestor of twelve tribes, and as the death of my son rendered it impossible that this promise should be realized, I feared I had incurred the doom by my own sins, and as a sinner I could not but expect to forfeit the future world, too. But now that I have beheld thee alive, I know that my death will be only for the world here below".

Such was the manner of Jacob's arrival in Egypt. He came with his whole family, sixty-nine persons they were in all, but the number was raised to seventy by the birth of Jochebed, afterward the mother of Moses, which took place when the cavalcade had advanced to the space between the one and the other city wall. All the males in his family were married men; even Pallu and Hezron, the latter of whom was but one year old at the time of their migration, and the former but two years, had the wives with them that had been chosen for them by their parents. In general, all the sons and grandsons of Jacob had married young, some of them had been fathers at the age of seven.

Joseph took some from among his brethren, and presented them to Pharaoh. He chose the weakest of them, that the king might not be tempted to retain them in his service as warriors. And as he did not desire his family to live at close quarters with the Egyptians and perhaps amalgamate with them, he introduced them as shepherds. The Egyptians worshipped the constellation of the rain, and paid divine honors to animals, and they kept aloof from shepherds. Pharaoh therefore was inclined to grant Joseph's wish, to give them the pasture land of Goshen for their sojourning place, the land that was theirs by right, for the Pharaoh that took Sarah away from Abraham by force had given it to her as her irrevocable possession.

In their conversation with Pharaoh the brethren of Joseph made it plain to the Egyptian king that it was not their intention to remain in Egypt forever, it was to be only a temporary dwelling-place.

Then Joseph set Jacob his father before Pharaoh, and when the king saw him, he said to Og, who happened to be with him at that moment, "Seest thou! Thou wast wont to call Abraham a sterile mule, and here is his grandson with a family of seventy persons"! Og would not believe his own eyes, he thought Abraham was standing before him, so close was the resemblance between Jacob and his progenitor. Then Pharaoh asked about Jacob's age, to find out whether he actually was Jacob, and not Abraham. And Jacob said unto Pharaoh, "The days of the years of my pilgrimage are an hundred and thirty years", using the word pilgrimage in reference to life on earth, which the pious regard as a temporary sojourn in alien lands. "Few and evil", he continued, "have been the days of the years of my life. In my youth I had to flee to a strange land on account of my brother Esau, and now, in my old age, I must again go to a strange land, and my days have not attained unto the days of the years of the life of my fathers in the days of their pilgrimage". These words sufficed to convince Pharaoh and Og that the man standing before them was not Abraham, but his grandson.

When Jacob uttered the words, "The days of the years of my pilgrimage have been few and evil", God said to him: "Jacob, I saved thee out of the hands of Esau and Laban, I restored Joseph unto thee, and made him to be a king and a ruler, and yet thou speakest of few and evil days. Because of thy ingratitude, thou wilt not attain unto the days of the years of the life of thy fathers", and Jacob died at an age thirty-three years less than his father Isaac's.

On going out from the presence of Pharaoh, Jacob blessed the king with the words, "May the years still in store for me be given unto thee, and may the Nile overflow its banks henceforth again and water the land". His words were fulfilled. In order to show that the pious are a blessing for the world, God caused the Nile to rise above its bed and fructify the land of Egypt.

Joseph's Kindness and Generosity

Jacob and his family now settled in the land of Goshen, and Joseph provided them with all things needful, not only with food and drink, but also with clothing, and in his love and kindness he entertained his father and his brethren daily at his own table. He banished the wrong done to him by his brethren from his mind, and he besought his father to pray to God for them, that He should forgive their great transgression. Touched by this noble sign of love, Jacob cried out, "O Joseph, my child, thou hast conquered the heart of thy father Jacob".

Joseph had other virtues, besides. The title "the God- fearing one", borne only by him, Abraham, Job, and Obadiah, he gained by reason of his kindness of heart and his generosity. Whatever he gave his brethren, he gave with a "good eye", a liberal spirit. If it was bread for food, it was sure to be abundant enough, not only to satisfy the hunger of all, but also for the children to crumble, as is their habit.

But Joseph was more than a helper to his family. As a shepherd pastures his flock, so he provided for the whole world during the years of famine. The people cursed Pharaoh, who kept the stores of corn in his treasure chambers for his own use, and they blessed Joseph, who took thought for the famishing, and sold grain to all that came. The wealth which he acquired by these sales was lawful gain, for the prices were raised, not by him, but by the Egyptians themselves. One part of his possessions, consisting of gold and silver and precious stones, Joseph buried in four different places, in the desert near the Red Sea, on the banks of the Euphrates, and in two spots in the desert in the vicinity of Persia and Media. Korah discovered one of the hiding- places, and the Roman emperor Antoninus, the son of Severus, another. The other two will never be found, because God has reserved the riches they hold for the pious, to be enjoyed by them in the latter days, the days of the Messiah. The remainder of Joseph's possessions he gave away, partly to his brethren and their families, and partly to Pharaoh, who put them into his treasury.

The wealth of the whole world flowed into Egypt at that time, and it remained there until the exodus of the Israelites. They took it along, leaving Egypt like a net without fish. The Israelites kept the treasure until the time of Rehoboam, who was deprived of it by the Egyptian king Shishak, and he in turn had to yield it to Zerah, the king of Ethiopia. Once more it came into possession of the Jews when King Asa conquered Zerah, but this time they held it for only a short while, for Asa surrendered it to the Aramean king Ben-hadad, to induce him to break his league with Baasha, the king of the Ten Tribes. The Ammonites, in turn, captured it from Ben-hadad, only to lose it in their war with the Jews under Jehoshaphat. Again it remained with the Jews, until the time of King Ahaz, who sent it to Sennacherib as tribute money. Hezekiah won it back, but Zedekiah, the last king of the Jews, lost it to the Chaldeans, from whom it came to Persia, thence to the Greeks, and finally to the Romans, and with the last it remained for all time.

The people were soon left without means to purchase the corn they needed. In a short time they had to part with their cattle, and when the money thus secured was spent, they sold their land to Joseph, and even their persons.

Many of them would cover themselves with clay and appear before Joseph, and say to him, "O lord king, see me and see my possessions"! And so Joseph bought all the land of Egypt, and the inhabitants became his tenants, and they gave a fifth of their ingatherings unto joseph.

The only class of the people permitted to remain in possession of their land were the priests. Joseph owed them gratitude, for they had made it possible for him to become the ruler over Egypt. The Egyptians had hesitated to make him their viceroy, because they shrank from choosing a man accused of adultery for so high an office. It was the priests that made the suggestion to examine Joseph's torn garment, which his mistress had submitted as evidence of his guilt, and see whether the rent was in front or in back. If it was in back, it would show his innocence--he had turned to flee, and his temptress had clutched him so that the garment tore. But if the tear was in front, then it would be a proof of his guilt--he had used violence with the woman, and she had torn the mantle in her efforts to defend her honor. The angel Gabriel came and transferred the rent from the fore part to the back, and the Egyptians were convinced of Joseph's innocence, and their scruples about raising him to the kingship were removed.

As soon as the Egyptians learnt of the advantageous position of the priests, they all tried to prove themselves members of the caste. But Joseph investigated the lists in the archives, and determined the estate of every citizen.

The priests were favored in another way. Beside remaining in possession of their land, they received daily portions from Pharaoh, wherefore God said, "The priests that serve idols receive all they need every day, how much more do the sons of Abraham, Isaac, and Jacob, who are My priests, deserve that I should give them what they need every day".

The rest of the inhabitants of Egypt, who had to part with their land, were not permitted to remain in their native provinces. Joseph removed them from their own cities, and settled them in others. His purpose herein was to prevent the Egyptians from speaking of his brethren derogatorily as "exiles the sons of exiles"; he made them all equally aliens. For the same reason, God later, at the time of the going forth of the Israelites from Egypt, caused all nations to change their dwelling-places about, so that the Israelites could not be reproached with having had to leave their home. And, finally, when Sermacherib carried the Jews away from their land into exile, it also happened that this king first mixed up the inhabitants of all the countries of the world.

Jacob's Last Wish

In return for the seventeen years that Jacob had devoted to the bringing up of Joseph, he was granted seventeen years of sojourn with his favorite son in peace and happiness. The wicked experience sorrow after joy; the pious must suffer first, and then they are happy, for all's well that ends well, and God permits the pious to spend the last years of their lives in felicity.

When Jacob felt his end approach, he summoned Joseph to his bedside, and he told him all there was in his heart. He called for Joseph rather than one of his other sons, because he was the only one in a position to execute his wishes.

Jacob said to Joseph: "If I have found grace in thy sight, bury me not, I pray thee, in Egypt. Only for thy sake did I come down into Egypt, and for thy sake I spoke, Now I can die. Do this for me as a true service of love, and not because thou art afraid, or because decency demands it. And when I sleep with my fathers, thou shalt bury me in their burying-place. Carry me out of the land of idolatry, and bury me in the land where God hath caused His Name to dwell, and put me to rest in the place in which four husbands and wives are to be buried, I the last of them".

Jacob desired not to be buried in Egypt for several reasons. He knew that the soil of Egypt would once swarm with vermin, and it revolted him to think of his corpse exposed to such uncleanness. He feared, moreover, that his descendants might say, "Were Egypt not a holy land, our father Jacob had never permitted himself to be buried there", and they might encourage themselves with this argument to make choice of Egypt as a permanent dwelling- place. Also, if his grave were there, the Egyptians might resort to it when the ten plagues came upon them, and if he were induced to pray for them to God, he would be advocating the cause of the Lord's enemies. If, on the other hand, he did not intercede for them, the Name of God would be profaned among the heathen, who would say, "Jacob is a useless saint"! Besides, it was possible that God might consider him, the "scattered sheep" of Israel, as a sacrifice for the Egyptians, and remit their punishment. From his knowledge of the people, another fear was justified, that his grave would become an object of idolatrous veneration, and the same punishment is appointed by God for the idols worshipped as for the idolaters that worship them.

If Jacob had good reasons for not wanting his body to rest in the soil of Egypt, he had equally good reasons for wanting it to rest in the Holy Land. In the Messianic time, when the dead will rise, those buried in Palestine will awaken to new life without delay, while those buried elsewhere will first have to roll from land to land through the earth, hollowed out for the purpose, until they reach the Holy Land, and only then will their resurrection take place. But over and beyond this, Jacob had an especial reason for desiring to have his body interred in Palestine. God had said to him at Beth-el, "The land whereon thou liest, to thee will I give it, and to thy seed", and hence he made every endeavor to "lie" in the Holy Land, to make sure it would belong to him and his descendants. Nevertheless he bade Joseph strew some Egyptian earth over his dead body.

Jacob expressed these his last wishes three times. Such is the requirement of good breeding in preferring a request.

In the last period of Jacob's life, one can see how true it is that "even a king depends upon favors in a strange land". Jacob, the man for the sake of whose merits the whole world was created, for the sake of whom Abraham was delivered from the fiery furnace, had to ask services of others while he was among strangers, and when Joseph promised to do his bidding, he bowed himself before his own son, for it is a true saying, "Bow before the fox in his day", the day of his power.

He was not satisfied with a simple promise from Joseph, that he would do his wish; he insisted upon his taking an oath by the sign of the covenant of Abraham, putting a hand under his thigh in accordance with the ceremony customary among the Patriarchs! But Joseph said: "Thou treatest me like a slave. With me thou hast no need to require an oath. Thy command sufficeth". Jacob, however, urged him, saying: "I fear Pharaoh may command thee to bury me in the sepulchre with the kings of Egypt. I insist that thou takest an oath, and then I will be at peace". Joseph gave in, though he would not submit to the ceremony that Eliezer had used to confirm the oath he took at the request of his master Abraham. The slave acted in accordance with the rules of slavery, the free man acted in accordance with the dictates of freedom. And in a son that thing would have been unseemly which was becoming in a slave.

When Joseph swore to bury his father in Palestine, he added the words, "As thou commandest me to do, so also will I beg my brethren, on my death-bed, to fulfil my last wish and carry my body from Egypt to Palestine".

Jacob, noticing the Shekinah over the bed's head, where she always rests in a sick room, bowed himself upon the bed's head, saying, "I thank thee, O Lord my God, that none who is unfit came forth from my bed, but my bed was perfect". He was particularly grateful for the revelation God had vouchsafed him concerning his first-born son Reuben, that he had repented of his trespass against his father, and atoned for it by penance. He was thus assured that all his sons were men worthy of being the progenitors of the twelve tribes, and he was blessed with happiness such as neither Abraham nor Isaac had known, for both of them had had unworthy as well as worthy sons.

Until the time of Jacob death had always come upon men suddenly, and snatched them away before they were warned of the imminent end by sickness. Once Jacob spoke to God, saying, "O Lord of the world, a man dies suddenly, and he is not laid low first by sickness, and he cannot acquaint his children with his wishes regarding all he leaves behind. But if a man first fell sick, and felt that his end were drawing nigh, he would have time to set his house in order". And God said, "Verily, thy request is sensible, and thou shalt be the first to profit by the new dispensation", and so it happened that Jacob fell sick a little while before his death.

His sickness troubled him grievously, for he had undergone much during his life. He had worked day and night while he was with Laban, and his conflicts with the angel and with Esau, though he came off victor from both, had weakened him, and he was not in a condition to endure the hardships of disease.

The Blessing of Ephraim and Manasseh

All the years of Jacob's sojourn in Egypt, Asenath, the wife of Joseph, was his constant nurse. When she saw his end drawing nigh, she spoke to Joseph: "I have heard that one who is blessed by a righteous man is as though he had been blessed by the Shekinah. Therefore, bring thy sons hither, that Jacob give them his blessing".

Though Joseph was a devoted and loving son to his father, he was not in constant attendance upon him, because he wanted to avoid giving him the opportunity of inquiring into the circumstances of his coming to Egypt. He was apprehensive that Jacob might curse his sons and bring death upon them, if he discovered the facts connected with their treacherous dealings with Joseph. He took good care therefore never to be alone with his father. But as he desired to be kept informed of his welfare, he arranged a courier service between himself and Jacob.

Now when Joseph received the news of his father's having fallen sick, through his messenger, as well as through Ephraim, whom Jacob was instructing in the Torah, he hastened to the land of Goshen, taking his two sons with him. He desired to have certainty upon five points: Would his father bless his two sons, who were born in Egypt, and, if so, would he appoint them to be heads of tribes? Would he assign the rights of the first-born unto himself, and, if so, would he divest Reuben of such rights altogether? And why had his father buried his mother Rachel by the wayside, and not carried her body to the family tomb at Machpelah?

Jacob had also entertained doubts on five points, when he was about to emigrate from Canaan to Egypt: He did not know whether his descendants would lose themselves among the people of Egypt; whether he would die there and be buried there; and whether he would be permitted to see Joseph and see the sons of Joseph. God gave him the assurance, saying, "I will go down with thee into Egypt, and I will surely bring thee up again after thy death, and thy descendants also, and Joseph shall put his hand upon thine eyes". When the time approached for the fulfilment of the Divine promise, God appeared unto Jacob, and He said, "I promised to fulfil thy wish, and the time of fulfilment hath come".

The holy spirit made known to Jacob that Joseph was coming to him, and he strengthened himself, and sat upon the bed in order to pay due respect to the representative of the government. Though Joseph was his son, he was also viceroy, and entitled to special marks of honor. Besides, Jacob desired to make the impression of being a man in good health. He wanted to avoid the possibility of having his blessing of Joseph and Joseph's sons questioned as the act of an irresponsible person.

He strengthened himself spiritually as well as physically, by prayer to God, in which he besought Him to let the holy spirit descend upon him at the time of his giving the blessing to the sons of Joseph.

When Joseph appeared in the company of his two sons, his father said to him: "In all the seventeen years thou hast been visiting me, thou didst never bring thy sons with thee, but now they have come, and I know the reason. If I bless them, I shall act in opposition to the word of God, who promised to make me the progenitor of twelve tribes, for if I adopt them as my sons, there will be fourteen tribes. But if I do not bless them, it will plunge thee in sorrow. So be it, I will bless them. But think not I do it because thou didst support me all these years. There is quite another reason. When I left my father's house to go to Haran, I offered up a prayer at Beth-el, and I promised to give unto God the tenth of all I owned. So far as my material possessions are concerned, I kept my vow, but I could not give the tithe of my sons, because according to the law I had to withdraw from the reckoning the four sons, Reuben, Joseph, Dan, and Gad, that are the first-born children of their mothers. When I returned, God again appeared unto me in Beth-el, and He said, Be fruitful and multiply. But after this blessing no son was born unto me except Benjamin alone, and it cannot be but that God meant Manasseh and Ephraim when He spoke of 'a nation and a company of nations'. If now I have found favor in thy sight, thy two sons Ephraim and Manasseh, even as Reuben and Simon, shall be mine, and then I shall be able to give a tenth part of my ten sons unto the Lord, and I shall leave this world free from the sin of not keeping my vow to the Lord concerning the tithe-giving".

Joseph consented to do his father's will, and Jacob tithed his sons, consecrating Levi to the Holy One, and appointing him to be the chief of his brethren. He enjoined his sons to have a care that there should never fail them a son of Levi in the priestly succession. And it happened that. of all the tribes Levi was the only one that never proved faithless to the covenant of the fathers.

Thus Jacob adopted Manasseh and Ephraim to be his own sons, even as Reuben and Simon were his sons. They were entitled like the others to a portion in the Holy Land, and like the others they were to bear standards on their journey through the desert.

Satisfied as to Jacob's intentions concerning his sons, Joseph asked his father about his mother's burial-place, and Jacob spoke, saying: "As thou livest, thy wish to see thy mother lying by my side in the grave doth not exceed mine own. I had joy in life only as long as she was alive, and her death was the heaviest blow that ever fell upon me". Joseph questioned him: "Perhaps thou didst have to bury her in the way, because she died during the rainy season, and thou couldst not carry her body through the rain to our family sepulchre"? "No", replied Jacob, "she died in the spring time, when the highways are clean and firm". Joseph: "Grant me permission to take up her body now and place it in our family burial-place". Jacob: "No, my son, that thou mayest not do. I was unwilling to bury her in the way, but the Lord commanded it". The reason of the command was that God knew that the Temple would be destroyed, and Israel would be carried away into banishment, and the exiles would ask the Patriarchs to intercede for them with God, but God would not hearken unto them. On their way to the land of the stranger they would pass the grave of Rachel, and they would throw themselves upon it, and beseech their mother to make intercession for them with God. And Rachel would pray to God in their behalf: "O Lord of the world, look upon my tears, and have compassion upon my children. But if Thou wilt not take pity on them, then indemnify me for the wrong done to me". Unto her prayer God will hearken, and He will have mercy upon Israel. Therefore was Rachel buried in the way.

Now Jacob desired to bless the sons of Joseph, but the holy spirit made him to see Jeroboam, the descendant of Ephraim, and Jehu, the descendant of Manasseh, how they would seduce Israel to idolatry, and the Shekinah forsook him as he was about to lay his hands upon the heads of his grandsons. He said to Joseph, "Is it possible that thou didst not marry the mother of thy children according to the law"? Joseph thereupon brought his wife Asenath to his father, and pointing to her marriage contract, he said,

"This one is my wife, whom I married as is proper, with a marriage contract and due ceremony. I pray thee, my father, bless my sons if only for the sake of this pious woman".

Jacob bade his grandsons approach close to him, and he kissed and embraced them, in the hope that his joy in them would lure back the holy spirit, but his hope was vain. Joseph concluded that the time was not favorable for blessing, and he decided to go away until a more propitious opportunity presented itself, first, however, proving to his father that his sons had been initiated in the covenant of Abraham.

Outside of his father's chamber, alone with his sons, he threw himself down before God and besought Him to show him mercy, and he bade his sons do likewise, saying, "Be not content with your high station, for worldly honors are but for a time. Entreat God to be merciful and let the Shekinah descend upon my father, that he bless you both". Then spake God to the holy spirit: "How long yet shall Joseph suffer? Reveal thyself quickly, and enter into Jacob, that he may be able to bestow blessings".

In the words of Jacob, "Ephraim and Manasseh, even as Reuben and Simon, shall be mine", Joseph had noticed his father's preference for his younger son Ephraim. It made him very anxious about his older son's birthright, and he was careful to put the two lads before his father in such wise that Manasseh should stand opposite Jacob's right hand, and Ephraim opposite his left hand. But Ephraim, on account of his modesty, was destined for greater things than his older brother Manasseh, and God bade the holy spirit prompt Jacob to give the birthright to Ephraim. Now when Joseph observed his father put his right hand upon Ephraim's head, he made an attempt to remove it unto Manasseh's head. But Jacob warded him off, saying: "What, thou wouldst displace my hand against my will, the hand that overcame the prince of the angel hosts, who is as large as one-third of the world! I know things not known to thee--I know what Reuben did to Bilhah, and what Judah did to Tamar. How much more do I know things known to thee! Thinkest thou I know not what thy brethren did to thee, because thou wouldst betray nothing whenever I asked thee? I know it, Manasseh also shall become great, the judge Gideon shall descend from him, but his younger brother will be the ancestor of Joshua, who will bring the sun and the moon to a standstill, though they have dominion over the whole earth from end to end". Thus did Jacob set Ephraim the younger above Manasseh the older, and thus did it remain unto all times. In the list of the generations, Manasseh comes after Ephraim, and so it was in the allotment of the portions in the Holy Land, and so it was in the placing of the camps and the standards of the tribes, and in the dedication of the Tabernacle--everywhere Ephraim preceded Manasseh.

The blessing bestowed upon his grandchildren by Jacob was as follows: "O that it be the will of God that ye walk in the ways of the Lord like unto my fathers Abraham and Isaac, and may the angel that hath redeemed me from all evil give his aid unto Joshua and Gideon, and reveal himself unto them. May your names be named on Israel, and like unto fishes may you grow into a multitude in the midst of the earth, and as fishes are protected by the water, so may you be protected by the merits of Joseph".

The words "like unto fishes" were used by Jacob for the purpose of intimating the manner of death awaiting the Ephraimites, the descendants of Joseph. As fish are caught by their mouth, so the Ephraimites were in later days to invite their doom by their peculiar lisp. At the same time, Jacob's words contained the prophecy that Joshua the son of the man Nun, the "fish", would lead Israel into the Holy Land. And in his words lay still another prophecy, with reference to the sixty thousand men children begot in the same night as Moses, all cast into the river with him, and saved for the sake of his merits. The number of boys thrown to the fishes in the river that night was equal to the number of men in Israel upon the earth.

Ephraim received a special and separate blessing from his grandfather. Jacob said to him, "Ephraim, my son, thou art the head of the Academy, and in the days to come my most excellent and celebrated descendants will be called Ephrati after thee".

Joseph received two gifts from his father. The first was Shechem, the city that Jacob had defended, with sword and bow, against the depredations of the Amorite kings when they tried to take revenge upon his sons for the outrage committed there. And the second gift was the garments made by God for Adam and passed from hand to hand, until they came into the possession of Jacob. Shechem was his reward, because, with his chastity, he stemmed the tide of immorality that burst loose in Shechem first of all. Besides, he had a prior claim upon the city. Shechem, son of Hamor, the master of the city, had given it to Dinah as a present, and the wife of Joseph, Asenath, being the daughter of Dinah, the city belonged to him by right.

Adam's clothes Jacob had received from Esau. He had not taken them from his brother by force, but God had caused them to be given to him as a reward for his good deeds. They had belonged to Nimrod. Once when the mighty hunter caught Esau in his preserves, and forbade him to go on the chase, they agreed to determine by combat what their privileges were. Esau had taken counsel with Jacob, and he had advised him never to fight with Nimrod while he was clothed in Adam's garments. The two now wrestled with each other, and at the time Nimrod was not dressed in Adam's clothes. The end was that he was slain by Esau. Thus the garments worn by Adam fell into the hands of Esau, from him they passed into Jacob's, and he bequeathed them to Joseph.

Jacob also taught Joseph three signs whereby to distinguish the true redeemer, who should deliver Israel from the bondage of Egypt. He would proclaim the Ineffable Name, appoint elders, and use the word Pakod in addressing the people.

The Blessing of the Twelve Tribes

When Joseph and his two sons left Jacob, his brethren, envious of the bountiful blessings bestowed upon the three, said, "The whole world loveth a favorite of fortune, and our father hath blessed Joseph thus because he is a ruler of men". Then spoke Jacob: "They that seek the Lord shall not want any good thing. I have blessings enough for all".

Jacob summoned his sons from the land of Egypt, and bade them come to him at Raamses, first, however, commanding them to make themselves clean, that the blessing he was about to bestow might attach itself to them. Another one of his commands was that they were to establish an Academy, by the members of which they were to be governed.

When his sons were brought into his presence by the angels, Jacob spoke, saying, "Take heed that no dissensions spring up among you, for union is the first condition of Israel's redemption", and he was on the point of revealing the great secret to them concerning the end of time, but while they were standing around the golden bed whereon their father lay, the Shekinah visited him for a moment and departed as quickly, and with her departed also all trace of the knowledge of the great mystery from the mind of Jacob. He had the same experience as his own father Isaac, who also had loss of memory inflicted upon him by God, to prevent him from revealing the secret at the end of time to Esau, when he summoned him to receive his blessing.

The accident made Jacob apprehensive that his sons were not pious enough to be considered worthy of the revelation concerning the Messianic era, and he said to them, "Ishmael and the sons of Keturah were the blemished among the issue of my grandfather Abraham; my father Isaac begot a blemished issue in Esau, and I fear now that among you, too, there is one that harbors the intention to serve idols". The twelve men spake, and said: "Hear, O Israel, our father, the Eternal our God is the One Only God. As thy heart is one and united in avouching the Holy One, blessed be He, to be thy God, so also are our hearts one and united in avouching Him". Whereto Jacob responded, "Praised be the Name of the glory of His majesty forever and ever"! And although the whole mystery of the Messianic time was not communicated to the sons of Jacob, yet the blessing of each contained some reference to the events of the future.

These were the words addressed by Jacob to his oldest son: "Reuben, thou art my first-born, my might, and the beginning of my strength! Thy portion should have been three crowns. Thou shouldst have had the double heritage of thy primogeniture, and the priestly dignity, and the royal power. But by reason of thy sin, the birthright is conferred upon Joseph, kingship upon Judah, and the priesthood upon Levi. My son, I know no healing remedy for thee, but the man Moses, who will ascend to God, he will make thee whole, and God will forgive thy sin. I bless thee--may thy descendants be heroes in the Torah and heroes in war. Though thou must lose thy birthright, yet wilt thou be the first to enter into possession of thy allotment in the Holy Land, and in thy territory shall be the first of the cities of refuge, and always shall thy name stand first in the list of the families of the tribes. Yea, thou shalt also be the first whose heritage will be seized by the enemy, and the first to be carried away into the lands of exile".

After Reuben had had his "ears pulled" thus, he retired, and Jacob called his sons Simon and Levi to his side, and he addressed them in these words: "Brethren ye were of Dinah, but not of Joseph, whom you sold into slavery. The weapons of violence wherewith ye smote Shechem were stolen weapons, for it was not seemly for you to draw the sword. That was Esau's portion. To him was it said, By thy sword shalt thou live. Into the council of the tribe of Simon my soul will not come when they foregather at Shittim to do vicious deeds, and my glory will not be united unto the assembly of Korah, the descendants of Levi. In their anger Simon and Levi slew the prince of Shechem, and in their self-will they sold Joseph the bull into slavery. Accursed was the city of Shechem when they entered to destroy it. If they remain united, no ruler will be able to stand up before them, no war will prosper against them. Therefore will I divide and scatter their possession among the possessions of the other tribes. The descendants of Simon will many of them be poor men, who will wander from tribe to tribe and beg for bread, and also Levi's tribe will gather its tithes and gifts from all the others".

The words of Jacob, "I will divide them in Jacob", spoken of Simon and Levi, were fulfilled on Simon in particular. When twenty-four thousand of Simon fell at Shittim, the widows they left behind married husbands of all the other tribes. Nevertheless Jacob did not dismiss Simon and Levi without blessing them; the tribe of Simon was to bring forth the teachers and the beadles needed by all Israel, and Levi, the scholars that would expound the Torah and render decisions according to its teachings.

When the remaining sons of Jacob heard the rebukes dealt out by their father to these three, they feared to hear like reproaches, and they tried to slip away from his presence. Especially Judah was alarmed, that his father might taunt him with his trespass touching Tamar. But Jacob spoke thus to him: "Judah, thou dost deserve thy name. Thy mother called thee Jehudah, because she gave praise to God at thy birth, and so shall thy brethren praise thee, and they all will call themselves by thy name. And as thou didst confess thy sin openly, so also thy descendants, Achan, David, and Manasseh, will make public avowal of their sins, and the Lord will hear their prayer. Thy hands will send darts after the fleeing foe, and thy father's sons shall pay thee respect. Thou hast the impudence of a dog and the bravery of a lion. Thou didst save Joseph from death, and Tamar and her two sons from the flames. No people and no kingdom will be able to stand up against thee. Rulers shall not cease from the house of Judah, nor teachers of the law from his posterity, until his descendant Messiah come, and the obedience of all peoples be unto him. How glorious is Messiah of the House of Judah! His loins girded, he will go out to do battle with his enemies. No king and no ruler will prevail against him. The mountains will be dyed red with their blood, and the garments of Messiah will be like the garments of him that presseth wine. The eyes of Messiah will be clearer than pure wine, for they will never behold unchastity and bloodshed; and his teeth will be whiter than milk, for never will they bite aught that is taken by violence".

Though Issachar was the older, Zebulon came next to be blessed, as a reward for the sacrifice he had made for his brother's sake, for when Issachar chose the study of the Torah as his vocation, Zebulon decided to devote himself to business and support his brother with the profits of his trade, that he might give himself up to the law undisturbed. His blessing was that he would conquer the seacoast as far as Zidon.

"Issachar", said Jacob, "will take upon himself the burden of the study of the Torah, and all the other tribes will come to him and ask him to decide their doubts on legal questions, and his descendants will be the members of the Sanhedrin and the scholars that will occupy themselves with fixing the calendar". Jacob blessed Issachar also with the blessing, that the fruits of his land should be exceedingly large, and this brought a heavenly as well as an earthly profit in its train, for when the heathen to whom the fruits were sold marvelled thereat, the Jewish merchants explained that their extraordinary size was due to the merits of the tribe of Issachar, whom God rewarded for their devotion to the Torah, and thus many of the heathen were induced to convert to Judaism.

In blessing Dan, Jacob's thoughts were occupied chiefly with his descendant Samson, who, like unto God, without any manner of assistance, conferred victory upon his people. Jacob even believed the strong, heroic man to be the Messiah, but when Samson's death was revealed to him, he exclaimed, "I wait for Thy salvation, O Lord, for Thy help is unto all eternity, while

Samson's help is only for a time. The redemption" continued Jacob, "will not be accomplished by Samson the Danite, but by Elijah the Gadite, who will appear at the end of time".

Asher's blessing was the beauty of his women, who would be sought in marriage by kings and high priests.

In Naphtali's land all fruits would ripen quickly, and they would be brought as presents to kings, and gain royal favor for the givers. This blessing was fulfilled in the plain of Gennesaret. At the same time Naphtali's blessing was a prophecy concerning his descendant Deborah, who was like a hind let loose against Sisera to conquer him, and she gave goodly words in her song of Israel's victory. Naphtali himself deserved the description applied to Deborah, for he was swift as a hart to do the will of God, and he was a fleet messenger unto his father and the tribes. They sent him whithersoever they would, and he executed their errands with dispatch. He served the brethren of Joseph as herald, to announce unto Jacob the glad tidings, "Joseph is yet alive", and when the stricken father saw him approach, he said, "Lo, here cometh Naphtali the lovable, who proclaimeth peace".

Joseph's blessing exceeded the blessing of all his brethren. Jacob spoke: "O son whom I bred up, Joseph, whom I raised, and who wast strong to resist the enticements of sin, thou didst conquer all the magicians and the wise men of Egypt by thy wisdom and thy pious deeds. The daughters of princes cast their jewels before thee, to draw thine eyes upon them when thou didst pass through the land of Egypt, but thou didst not look their way, and therefore wast thou made the father of two tribes. The magicians and the wise men of Egypt sought to defame thee before Pharaoh and slander thee, but thou didst set thy hope in the Almighty. Therefore may He who appeared unto me as El Shaddai bless thee and grant thee fertile soil and much cattle. May the blessing thy father giveth thee now, and the blessing that his fathers Abraham and Isaac gave him, and that called forth the envy of the great of the world, Ishmael, Esau, and the sons of Keturah--may all these blessings be a crown upon the head of Joseph, and a chain upon the neck of him that was the ruler of Egypt, and yet diminished not the honor due to his brethren".

The slander of which Jacob spoke referred to what Potiphar had said of Joseph before Pharaoh. He had complained, saying, "Why didst thou appoint my slave, whom I did buy for twenty pieces of silver, to be ruler over the Egyptians"? Joseph had then taken up his own defense, saying: "When thou didst buy me as a slave, thou didst commit a capital crime. Only a descendant of Canaan may be sold as a slave, and I am a descendant of Shem, and a prince besides. If thou wilt convince thyself of the truth of my words, do but compare me with the likeness of my mother Sarah that Pharaoh had made of her"! They brought Sarah's likeness, and, verily, it appeared that Joseph resembled his ancestress, and all were convinced of his noble lineage.

The blessing that Jacob bestowed upon Benjamin contains the prophecy that his tribe would provide Israel with his first ruler and his last ruler, and so it was, for Saul and Esther both belonged to the tribe of Benjamin. Likewise Benjamin's heritage in the Holy Land harbors two extremes: Jericho ripens its fruits earlier than any other region in Palestine, while Beth-el ripens them latest. In Benjamin's blessing, Jacob referred also to the service in the Temple, because the Holy Place was situated in the territory of Benjamin. And when Jacob called his youngest son a wolf that ravineth, he was thinking of the judge Ehud, the great scholar, a Benjamite, who conquered Eglon king of Moab, and also he had in mind the Benjamites that captured their wives by cunning and force.

Again, if he called Benjamin a wolf, Judah a lion, and Joseph a bull, he wanted to point to the three kingdoms known as wolf, lion, and bull, the doom of which was and will be sealed by the descendants of his three sons: Babylon, the kingdom of the lion, fell through the hands of Daniel of the tribe of Judah; Media, the wolf, found its master in the Benjamite Mordecai; and the bull Joseph will subdue the horned beast, the kingdom of wickedness, before the Messianic time.

The Death of Jacob

After Jacob had blessed each of his sons separately, he addressed himself to all of them together, saying: "According to my power did I bless you, but in future days a prophet will arise, and this man Moses will bless you, too, and he will continue my blessings where I left off". He added, besides, that the blessing of each tribe should redound to the good of all the other tribes: the tribe of Judah should have a share in the fine wheat of the tribe of Benjamin, and Benjamin should enjoy the goodly barley of Judah. The tribes should be mutually helpful, one to another.

Moreover, he charged them not to be guilty of idolatry in any form or shape and not to let blasphemous speech pass their lips, and he taught them the order of transporting his bier, thus: "Joseph, being king, shall not help to bear it, nor shall Levi, who is destined to carry the Ark of the Shekinah. Judah, Issachar, and Zebulon shall grasp its front end, Reuben, Simon, and Gad its right side, Ephraim, Manasseh, and Benjamin the hindmost end, and Dan, Asher, and Naphtali its left side". And this was the order in which the tribes, bearing each its standard, were to march through the desert, the Shekinah dwelling in the midst of them.

Jacob then spake to Joseph, saying: "And thou, my son Joseph, forgive thy brethren for their trespass against thee, forsake them not, and grieve them not, for the Lord hath put them into thine hands, that thou shouldst protect them all thy days against the Egyptians".

Also he admonished his sons, saying that the Lord would be with them if they walked in His ways, and He would redeem them from the hands of the Egyptians. "I know", he continued, "great suffering will befall your sons and your grandsons in this land, but if you will obey God, and teach your sons to know Him, then He will send you a redeemer, who will bring you forth out of Egypt and lead you into the land of your fathers".

In resignation to the will of God, Jacob awaited his end, and death enveloped him gently. Not the Angel of Death ended his life, but the Shekinah took his soul with a kiss. Beside the three Patriarchs, Abraham, Isaac, and Jacob, only Moses, Aaron, and Miriam breathed their last in this manner, through the kiss of the Shekinah. And these six, together with Benjamin, are the only ones whose corpses are not exposed to the ravages of the worms, and they neither corrupt nor decay.

Thus Jacob departed this world, and entered the world to come, a foretaste of which he had enjoyed here below, like the other two Patriarchs, and none beside among men. In another respect their life in this world resembled their life in the world to come, the evil inclination had no power over them, either here or there, wherein David resembled them.

Joseph ordered his father's body to be placed upon a couch of ivory, covered with gold, studded with gems, and hung with drapery of byssus and purple. Fragrant wine was poured out at its side, and aromatic spices burnt next to it. Heroes of the house of Esau, princes of the family of Ishmael, and the lion Judah, the bravest of his sons, surrounded the sumptuous bier of Jacob. "Come", said Judah to his brethren, "let us plant a high cedar tree at the head of our father's grave, its top shall reach up to the skies, its branches shall shade all the inhabitants of the earth, and its roots shall grow down deep into the earth, unto the abyss. For from him are sprung twelve tribes, and from him will arise kings and rulers, chapters of priests prepared to perform the service of the sacrifices, and companies of Levites ready to sing psalms and play upon sweet instruments".

The sons of Jacob tore their garments and girded their loins with sackcloth, threw themselves upon the ground, and strewed earth upon their heads until the dust rose in a high cloud. And when Asenath, the wife of Joseph, heard the tidings of Jacob's death, she came, and with her came the women of Egypt, to weep and mourn over him. And the men of Egypt that had known Jacob repaired thither, and they mourned day after day, and also many journeyed down into Egypt from Canaan, to take part in the seventy days' mourning made for him.

The Egyptians spake to one another, saying, "Let us lament for the pious man Jacob, because the affliction of the famine was averted from our land on account of his merits", for instead of ravaging the land for forty-two years according to the decree of God, the famine had lasted but two years, and that was due to the virtues of Jacob.

Joseph ordered the physicians to embalm the corpse. This he should have refrained from doing, for it was displeasing to God, who spoke, saying: "Have I not the power to preserve the corpse of this pious man from corruption? Was it not I that spoke the reassuring words, Fear not the worm, O Jacob, thou dead Israel"? Joseph's punishment for this useless precaution was that he was the first of the sons of Jacob to suffer death. The Egyptians, on the other hand, who devoted forty days to embalming the corpse and preparing it for burial, were rewarded for the veneration they showed. Before He destroyed their city, God gave the Ninevites a forty days' respite on account of their king, who was the Pharaoh of Egypt. And for the three score and ten days of mourning that the heathen made for Jacob, they were recompensed at the time of Ahasuerus. During seventy days, from the thirteenth of Nisan, the date of Haman's edict ordering the extermination of the Jews, until the twenty-third of Siwan, when Mordecai recalled it, they were permitted to enjoy absolute power over the Jews.

When all preparations for the burial of Jacob had been completed, Joseph asked permission of Pharaoh to carry the body up into Canaan. But he did not himself go to put his petition before Pharaoh, for he could not well appear before the king in the garb of a mourner, nor was he willing to interrupt his lamentation over his father for even a brief space and stand before Pharaoh and prefer his petition. He requested the family of Pharaoh to intercede for him with the king for the additional reason that he was desirous of enlisting the favor of the king's relations, lest they advise Pharaoh not to fulfil his wish. He acted according to the maxim, "Seek to win over the accuser, that he cause thee no annoyance".

Joseph applied first to the queen's hairdresser, and she influenced the queen to favor him, and then the queen put in a good word for him with the king. At first Pharaoh refused the permission craved by Joseph, who, however, urged him to consider the solemn oath he had given his dying father, to bury him in Canaan. Pharaoh desired him to seek absolution from the oath. But Joseph rejoined, "Then will I apply also for absolution from the oath I gave thee", referring to an incident in his earlier history. The grandees of Egypt had advised Pharaoh against appointing Joseph as viceroy, and they did not recede from this counsel until Joseph, in his conversation with the Egyptian king, proved himself to be master of the seventy languages of the world, the necessary condition to be fulfilled before one could become ruler over Egypt. But the conversation proved something else, that Pharaoh himself was not entitled to Egyptian kingship, because he lacked knowledge of Hebrew. He feared, if the truth became known, Joseph would be raised to his own place, for he knew Hebrew beside all the other tongues. In his anxiety and distress, Pharaoh made Joseph swear an oath never to betray the king's ignorance of Hebrew. Now when Joseph threatened to have himself absolved from this oath as well as the one to his dying father, great terror overwhelmed him, and he speedily granted Joseph permission to go up to Canaan and bury his father there.

Moreover, Pharaoh issued a decree in all parts of the land menacing those with death who would not accompany Joseph and his brethren upon their journey to Canaan with their father's remains, and accordingly the procession that followed the bier of Jacob was made up of the princes and nobles of Egypt as well as the common people. The bier was borne by the sons of Jacob. In obedience to his wish not even their children were allowed to touch it. It was fashioned of pure gold, the border thereof inlaid with onyx stones and bdellium, and the cover was gold woven work joined to the bier with threads that were held together with hooks of onyx stones and bdellium. Joseph placed a large golden crown upon the head of his father, and a golden sceptre he put in his hand, arraying him like a living king.

The funeral cortege was arranged in this order: First came the valiant men of Pharaoh and the valiant men of Joseph, and then the rest of the inhabitants of Egypt. All were girt with swords and clothed in coats of mail, and the trappings of war were upon them. The weepers and mourners walked, crying and lamenting, at some distance from the bier, and the rest of the people went behind it, while Joseph and his household followed together after it, with bare feet and in tears, and Joseph's servants were close to him, each man with his accoutrements and weapons of war. Fifty of Jacob's servants preceded the bier, strewing myrrh upon the road in passing, and all manner of perfumes, so that the sons of Jacob trod upon the aromatic spices as they carried the body forward.

Thus the procession moved on until it reached Canaan. It halted at the threshing-floor of Atad, and there they lamented with a very great and sore lamentation. But the greatest honor conferred upon Jacob was the presence of the Shekinah, who accompanied the cortege.

The Canaanites had no intention at first to take part in the mourning made for Jacob, but when they saw the honors shown him, they joined the procession of the Egyptians, loosing the girdles of their garments as a sign of grief. Also the sons of Esau, Ishmael, and Keturah appeared, though their design in coming was to seize the opportunity and make war upon the sons of Jacob, but when they saw Joseph's crown suspended from the bier, the Edomite and Ishmaelite kings and princes followed his example, and attached theirs to it, too, and it was ornamented with thirty-six crowns.

Nevertheless the conflict was not averted; it broke out in the end between the sons of Jacob and Esau and his followers. When the former were about to lower the body of their father into the Cave of Machpelah, Esau attempted to prevent it, saying that Jacob had used his allotted portion of the tomb for Leah, and the only space left for a grave belonged to himself. For, continued Esau, "though I sold my birthright unto Jacob, I yet have a portion in the tomb as a son of Isaac". The sons of Jacob, however, were well aware of the fact that their father had acquired Esau's share in the Cave, and they even knew that a bill of sale existed, but Esau, assuming properly that the document was left behind in Egypt, denied that any such had ever been made out, and the sons of Jacob sent Naphtali, the fleet runner, back to Egypt to fetch the bill. Meantime, while this altercation was going on between Esau and the others, Hushim the son of Dan arose and inquired in astonishment why they did not proceed with the burial of Jacob, for he was deaf and had not understood the words that had passed between the disputants. When he heard what it was all about, and that the ceremonies were interrupted until Naphtali should return from Egypt with the bill of sale, he exclaimed, with indignation, "My grandfather shall lie here unburied until Naphtali comes back"! and he seized a club and dealt Esau a vigorous blow, so that he died, and his eyes fell out of their sockets and dropped upon Jacob's knees, and Jacob opened his own eyes and smiled. Esau being dead, his brother's burial could proceed without hindrance, and Joseph interred him in the Cave of Machpelah in accordance with his wish.

His other children had left all arrangements connected with the burial of their father's body to their brother Joseph, for they reflected that it was a greater honor for Jacob if a king concerned himself about his remains rather than simple private individuals.

The head of Esau, as he lay slain by the side of Jacob's grave, rolled down into the Cave, and fell into the lap of Isaac, who prayed to God to have mercy upon his son, but his supplications were in vain. God spoke, saying, "As I live, he shall not behold the majesty of the Lord".

The Sons of Jacob at War with the Sons of Esau

Jacob having been interred with royal pomp, and the seven days' period of mourning over, the conflict between the sons of Jacob and the sons of Esau broke out anew. In the skirmish that had ensued when Esau advanced a claim upon a place in the Cave of Machpelah, while his brother's remains still lay unburied, he lost forty of his men, and after his death fortune favored his sons as little. Eighty of their followers were slain, while of the sons of Jacob not one was lost. Joseph succeeded in capturing Zepho the son of Eliphaz and fifty of his men, and he clapped them in chains and carried them off to Egypt. Thereupon the rest of the attacking army led by Eliphaz fled to Mount Seir, taking with them the headless corpse of Esau, to bury it in his own territory. The sons of Jacob pursued after them, but they slew none, out of respect for the remains of Esau.

On the third day a great army gathered together, consisting of the inhabitants of Seir and the children of the East, and they marched down into Egypt with the purpose of making war upon Joseph and his brethren. In the battle that came off, this army was almost totally destroyed, not less than six hundred thousand men were mowed down by Joseph and his warriors, and the small remnant fled precipitately. Returned to their own country after this fatal campaign, the sons of Esau and the sons of Seir fell to quarrelling among themselves, and the sons of Seir demanded that their former allies leave the place, because it was they that had brought misfortune upon the country.

The sons of Esau thereupon dispatched a messenger in secret to their friend Agnias, king of Africa, begging his aid against the sons of Seir. He granted their request, and sent them troops consisting of foot-soldiers and mounted men. The sons of Seir, on their part, also sought allies, and they secured the help of the children of the East, and of the Midianites, who put warriors at their disposal. In the encounters that ensued between the hostile forces, the sons of Esau were defeated again and again, partly on account of treachery in their own ranks, for their men sometimes deserted to the enemy while the combat was on. At last, however, in the battle that took place in the desert of Paran, the sons of Esau gained a decisive victory. They massacred all the warriors of the sons of Seir, and the Midianites and the children of the East were put to flight.

Thereafter the sons of Esau returned to Seir, and they slew all the inhabitants of the place, men, women, and children, sparing only fifty lads and maidens. The former they used as slaves, and the latter they took to wife. They also enriched themselves with the spoils, seizing all the possessions of the sons of Seir, and the whole land was divided among the five sons of Esau. Now these descendants of Esau determined to put a king over themselves, but in consequence of the treachery committed during the war there prevailed such hatred and bitterness among them that they decided never to appoint a ruler from their own people. Their choice fell upon Bela, the son of Beor, one of the warriors sent to them by King Agnias. His peer could not be found among the allied troops for bravery, wisdom, and handsome appearance. They set the royal crown upon his head, built a palace for him, and gave him gifts of silver, gold, and gems, until he lived in great opulence. He reigned happily for thirty years, and met his death then in a war against Joseph and his brethren.

This war came about because the sons of Esau could not banish from their memory the disgrace of the defeat inflicted upon them by Joseph and his people. Having enlisted the aid of Agnias, and of the Ishmaelites and other nations of the East, they set forth on a second campaign against Egypt, in the hope of delivering Zepho and his followers from the hands of Joseph. In spite of their enormous host--they had no less than eight hundred thousand men of infantry and cavalry--they were defeated at Raamses by Joseph and his brethren and their little company of six hundred men. Beside their king Bela, they left one-fourth of their army upon the field. The loss of their king discouraged them grievously, and they took to flight, hard pressed by Joseph, who cut down many of the fugitives.

When he returned from the battle, Joseph ordered manacles and fetters to be put upon Zepho and his followers, and their captivity was made more bitter unto them than it had been before.

The sons of Esau appointed Jobab of Bozrah to succeed their dead king Bela. His reign lasted ten years, but they desisted from all further attempts at waging war with the sons of Jacob. Their last experience with them had been too painful, but the enmity they cherished against them was all the fiercer, and their hatred never abated.

Their third king was Husham, and he ruled over them for twenty years. During his reign Zepho succeeded in making good his escape from Egypt. He was received kindly by Agnias, king of Africa, and appointed commander-in-chief of his troops. He used every means of persuasion to induce his sovereign lord to enter into a war with Egypt, but in vain, for Agnias was only too well acquainted with the strength and heroism of the sons of Jacob. For many years he resisted Zepho's arguments and blandishments. Indeed, as it was, Agnias had his hands full with other warlike enterprises. It had happened about this time that a man of the land of Kittim, 'Uzi by name, whom his countrymen venerated as a god, died in the city of Pozimana, and he left behind a fair and clever daughter. Agnias heard of Yaniah's beauty and wisdom, and he sued for her hand, and his request was granted him by the people of Kittim.

The messengers of Agnias were hastening away from Kittim, bearing to their master the promise of the inhabitants that Yaniah should become his wife, when Turnus, king of Benevento, arrived on the same errand. His suit was rejected, for the people of Kittim were afraid-to break the promise given to

Agnias. In his anger, Turnus went to Sardinia to make war upon King Lucus, a brother of Agnias, intending to deal with the latter as soon as the other was rendered harmless. Hearing of the design hatched by Turnus, Agnias hastened to Sardinia to the assistance of his brother, and a battle took place in the Valley of Campania. Against Turnus were arrayed Agnias, his brother Lucus, and the son of the latter, Niblos, whom his father had appointed commander-in-chief of the Sardinian troops. In the first encounter, Turnus was the victor, and the Sardinians lost their general Niblos. But in the second engagement the army of Turnus was routed completely, and he himself was left dead on the field. His army fled, pursued closely by Agnias as far as the cross-road between Rome and Albano. Niblos' body was put inside of a golden statue, and his father erected a high tower over his grave, and another over the grave of Turnus, and these two buildings, connected by a marble pavement, stand opposite to each other, on the cross-road at which Agnias left off from following after the fugitive army.

The king of Africa went on to the city of Benevento, but he took no harsh measures against it and its inhabitants, because it belonged to the land of Kittim at that time. Thenceforth, however, bands of soldiers from Africa made incursions, now and again, into the land of Kittim, under the lead of Zepho, the captain of the African army. Agnias meantime went to Pozimana, to solemnize his marriage with Yaniah, and he returned with her to his capital in Africa.

Zepho King of Kittim

All this time Zepho did not leave off urging Agnias to invade Egypt, and he succeeded finally in persuading the king to consider his wish, and a great army was equipped against Egypt and the sons of Jacob. Among the shield-bearers was Balaam, the fifteen year old son of Beor, a wise youth and an adept in magic, and the king bade him acquaint him with the issue of the war upon which they were entering. Balaam took wax and moulded the figures of men, to represent the army of Agnias and the army of the Egyptians, and he plunged them into magic water and let them swim, and it appeared that the African army was subdued by the Egyptians. Agnias accordingly gave up the campaign, and Zepho, seeing that his sovereign could not be persuaded into war with the sons of Jacob, fled the country and betook himself to Kittim.

The people of Kittim received him with great honors, and they offered him much money to stay with them and conduct their wars. It happened once while Zepho was in the mountains of Koptiziah, where the inhabitants of Kittim had taken refuge before the troops of the African king, that he had to go on a search for an ox that had strayed away, and he discovered a cave the opening of which was barred by a great stone. He shivered the stone in pieces, and entering the cave he saw an animal formed like a man above and a he-goat below, and he killed the strange beast, which was in the very act of devouring his lost ox. There was great rejoicing among the people of Kittim, for the monster had long been doing havoc among their cattle, and in gratitude they set aside one day of the year, which they called by Zepho's name, in honor of their liberator, and all the people brought him presents and offered sacrifices to him.

At this time it came to pass that Yaniah, the wife of King Agnias, fell into a grievous sickness, and the physicians ascribed her illness to the climate, and to the water of Africa, to which she, a native of the land of Kittim, could not get accustomed, because she had been in the habit of using the water of the river Forma, which her forefathers had drawn to her house through a conduit. Agnias sent to the land of Kittim and had some of the water of the Forma brought to Africa. Finding it much lighter than the water of his own country, he built a huge canal from the land of Kittim. to Africa, and the queen henceforth had all the Forma water she needed. Besides, he took earth and stone from Kittim, and built a palace for Yaniah, and she recovered from her illness.

Meantime Zepho had won a decisive victory over the African troops that had made an incursion into the land of Kittim, and the people chose him as king. His first undertaking was a campaign against the sons of Tubal and the Islands of the Sea, and again he was successful, he subdued them completely. On his return, the people built a great palace for Zepho, and they renewed his kingship, and he continued until his death to reign as king of Kittim and of Italy.

During the first thirteen years of his reign, the Africans made no attempt to disturb the peace of Kittim, but then they invaded the land, only to be severely repulsed by Zepho, who pursued the troops up to the very borders of Africa, and Agnias the king was in such consternation that he did not venture to make reprisals for some time. When he finally made a second attempt, his troops were annihilated by Zepho down to the very last man. Now Agnias, in despair, assembled all the inhabitants of Africa, as numerous as the sand on the sea-shore, and he united his great host with the army of his brother Lucus, and thus he made his third attempt upon Zepho and the people of the land of Kittim.

Alarmed, Zepho wrote to his brethren in Seir, and entreated their king Hadad to send him aid. But the people of Seir had concluded an alliance with Agnias as far back as under their first king Bela, and they refused Zepho's request, and the king of Kittim had to face the host of eight hundred thousand men mustered by Agnias with his little band of three thousand.

Then the people of Kittim spake to their king Zepho, saying: "Pray for us unto the God of thy ancestors. Peradventure He may deliver us from the hand of Agnias and his army, for we have heard that He is a great God, and He delivers all that trust in Him". Zepho prayed unto the Lord, saying: "O Lord, God of Abraham and Isaac, my fathers, this day may it be made known that Thou art a true God, and all the gods of the nations are vain and useless. Remember now this day unto me Thy covenant with Abraham our father, which our ancestors related unto us, and do graciously with me this day for the sake of Abraham and Isaac, our fathers, and save me and the sons of Kittim from the hand of the king of Africa, who hath come against us for battle".

God gave ear unto Zepho's prayer, and in the first day's battle one-half of the African army fell. Agnias forthwith dispatched a decree to his country, ordering, on penalty of death and confiscation of property, that all the males of the land, including boys that bad passed their tenth year, were to join the army and fight against the people of Kittim. In spite of these new accessions, three hundred thousand strong, Agnias was beaten again by Zepho in the second battle. The African general Sosipater having fallen slain, the troops broke into flight, at their head Agnias with Lucus the brother and Asdrubal the son of Agnias. After this dire defeat the Africans made no further attempt to disturb the peace of Kittim, and their incursions ceased forever.

In spite of the great victory that Zepho had won with the help of God, the king of Kittim walked in the idolatrous ways of the people whom he ruled, and in the ways of the sons of Esau, for, as saith the proverb of the ancients, "Out of the wicked cometh forth wickedness", and Zepho was not other than the rest of the sons of Esau.

The severe defeat inflicted upon Agnias drove Balaam from Africa to Kittim, and he was received with great honors by Zepho, who welcomed him on account of his deep wisdom.

Now Zepho thought the time had arrived for him to carry out his plan of vengeance against the posterity of Jacob, all the more as in the meantime Joseph had died, and also his brethren and the valiant men of Pharaoh had passed away. He was joined in the enterprise by Hadad, the king of Edom, and by the nations of the East and the Ishmaelites. The allied army was so vast that the space it covered as it stood in rank and file was equal to a three days' journey. It formed in battle array in the Valley of Pathros, and it was met by three hundred thousand Egyptians and one hundred and fifty Israelites from Goshen. But the Egyptians did not trust the Israelites, they feared their defection to the sons of Esau and Ishmael. They therefore made an agreement with them that the Israelites were not to come to the help of the Egyptians until it appeared that the enemy were getting the upper hand.

Zepho, who had a high opinion of Balaam's ability, desired him to use his magic arts and find out what would be the outcome of the war, but Balaam's knowledge failed him, he could not satisfy the king's wish. The Egyptians got the worst of the first encounter between the two hostile armies, but the aspect of things changed as soon as they summoned the Israelites to aid them. The Israelites prayed to God to support them with His help, and the Lord heard their prayer. Then they threw themselves upon Zepho and his allies, and after they had cut down several thousand men, such dismay and confusion took hold of the enemy that they fled hastily, pursued by the Israelites as far as the boundary of the country. The Egyptians, instead of coming to the assistance of the Israelites, had taken to flight, leaving the small band of their allies to dispose of the huge host of their adversaries. Embittered by such treatment, the Israelites slew as many as two hundred Egyptians, under the pretext that they thought they belonged to the enemy.

The Nations at War

Hadad, the king of Edom, who had failed to gain fame and honor in the Egyptian campaign, was favored by fortune in another war, a war against Moab. The Moabites shrank from meeting Hadad alone, and they made an alliance with the Midianites. In the thick of the fight the Moabites fled from the field of battle, leaving the Midianites to their fate, and these deserted allies of theirs were cut down to a man by Hadad and his Edomites. The Moabites saved their skins, and suffered only the inconvenience of having to pay tribute. To avenge the faithlessness practiced against them, the Midianites, supported by their kinsmen, the sons of Keturah, gathered a mighty army, and attacked the Moabites the following year. But Hadad came to their assistance, and again he inflicted a severe defeat upon the Midianites, who had to give up their plan of revenge against Moab. This is the beginning of the inveterate enmity between the Moabites and the Midianites. If a single Moabite is caught in the land of Midian, he is killed without mercy, and a Midianite in Moab fares no better.

After the death of Hadad, the Edomites installed Samlah of Masrekah as their king, and he reigned eighteen years. It was his desire to take up the cause of Agnias, the old ally of the Edomites, and chastise Zepho for having gone to war with him, but his people, the Edomites, would not permit him to undertake aught that was inimical to their kinsman, and Samlah had to abandon the plan. In the fourteenth year of Samlah's reign, Zepho died, having been king of Kittim for fifty years. His successor was Janus, one of the people of Kittim, who enjoyed an equally long reign.

Balaam had made his escape to Egypt after the death of Zepho, and he was received there with great demonstrations of honor by the king and all the nobles, and Pharaoh appointed him to be royal counsellor, for he had heard much about his exceeding great wisdom.

In the Edomite kingdom, Samlah was succeeded by Saul of Pethor, a youth of surpassing beauty, whose reign lasted forty years. His successor upon the throne was Baal Hamon, king for thirty-eight years, during which period the Moabites rose up against the Edomites, to whom they had been paying tribute since the time of Hadad, and they succeeded in throwing off the yoke of the stranger.

The times were troubled everywhere. Agnias, the king of Africa, died, and also the death of Janus occurred, the king of Kittim. The successors to these two rulers, Asdrubal, the son of Agnias, and Latinus, the king of Kittim, then entered upon a long drawn out war of many years. At first the fortune of war favored Latinus. He sailed to Africa in ships, and inflicted one defeat after another upon Asdrubal, and finally this king of Africa lost his life upon the battlefield. After destroying the canal from Kittim to Africa built many years before by Agnias, Latinus returned to his own country, taking with him as his wife Ushpiziwnah, the daughter of Asdrubal, who was so wondrously beautiful that her countrymen wore her likeness upon their garments.

Latinus did not enjoy the fruits of his victory long. Anibal, the younger brother of Asdrubal and his successor in the royal power, went to Kittim in ships and carried on a series of wars lasting eighteen years, in the course of which he killed off eighty thousand of the people of Kittim, not sparing the princes and the nobles. At the end of this protracted period he went back to Africa, and reigned over his people in quiet and peace.

The Edomites, during the forty-eight years of the reign of Hadad, the successor of Baal Hamon, fared no better than the people of Kittim. Hadad's first undertaking was to reduce the Moabites again under the sovereignty of Edom, but he had to desist, because he could not offer successful resistance to a newly chosen king of theirs, one of their own people, who enlisted the aid of their kinsmen the Ammonites. The allies commanded a great host, and Hadad was overwhelmed. These wars were followed by others between Hadad of Edom. and Abimenos of Kittim. The latter was the attacking party, and he invaded Seir with a mighty army. The sons of Seir were defeated abjectly, their king Hadad was taken captive, and then executed by Abimenos, and Seir was made a province subject to Kittim and ruled by a governor.

Thus ended the independence of the sons of Esau. Henceforth they had to pay tribute to Kittim, over which Abimenos ruled until his death, in the thirty-eighth year of his reign.

Joseph's Magnanimity

As Joseph was returning from the burial of his father in the Cave of Machpelah, he passed the pit into which his brethren had once cast him, and he looked into it, and said, "Blessed be God who permitted a miracle to come to pass for me here"! The brethren inferred from these words of gratitude, which Joseph but uttered in compliance with the injunctions of the law, that he cherished the recollection of the evil they had done him, and they feared, that now their father was dead, their brother would requite them in accordance with their deeds. They observed, moreover, that since their father was no more, Joseph had given up the habit of entertaining them at his table, and they interpreted this as a sign of his hatred of them. In reality, it was due to Joseph's respect and esteem for his brethren. "So long as my father was alive", Joseph said to himself, "he bade me sit at the head of the table, though Judah is king, and Reuben is the first-born. It was my father's wish, and I complied with it. But now it is not seemly that I should have the first seat in their presence, and yet, being ruler of Egypt, I cannot yield my place to any other". He thought it best therefore not to have the company of his brethren at his meals.

But they, not fathoming his motives, sent Bilhah to him with the dying message of their father, that he was to forgive the transgression and the sin of his brethren. For the sake of the ways of peace they had invented the message; Jacob had said nothing like it. Joseph, on his part, realized that his brethren spoke thus only because they feared he might do harm unto them, and he wept that they should put so little trust in his affection. When they appeared, and fell down before his face, and said, "Thou didst desire to make one of us a slave unto thyself. Behold, we all are ready to be thy servants", he spoke to them gently, and tried to convince them that he harbored no evil design against them. He said: "Be not afraid, I will do you no harm, for I fear God, and if ye think I failed to have you sit at my table because of enmity toward you, God knows the intentions of my heart, He knows that I acted thus out of consideration for the respect I owe to you".

Furthermore he said: "Ye are like unto the dust of the earth, the sand on the sea-shore, and the stars in the heavens. Can I do aught to put these out of the world? Ten stars could effect nothing against one star, how much less can one star effect anything against ten? Do you believe that I have the power of acting contrary to the laws of nature? Twelve hours hath the day, twelve hours the night, twelve months the year, twelve constellations are in the heavens, and also there are twelve tribes! You are the trunk and I am the head--of what use the head without the trunk? It is to my own good that I should treat you with fraternal affection. Before your advent, I was looked upon as a slave in this country--you proved me a man of noble birth. Now, if I should kill you, my claims upon an aristocratic lineage would be shown to be a lie. The Egyptians would say, He was not their brother, they were strangers to him, he but called them his brethren to serve his purpose, and now he hath found a pretext to put them out of the way. Or they would hold me to be a man of no probity. Who plays false with his own kith and kin, how can he keep faith with others? And, in sooth, how can I venture to lay hand upon those whom God and my father both have blessed"?

As Joseph's dealings were kind and gentle with his brethren, so he was the helper and counsellor of the Egyptians, and when Pharaoh departed this life, Joseph being then a man of seventy-one years of age, the king's last wish was that he might be a father unto his son and successor Magron, and administer the affairs of state for him. Some of the Egyptians desired to make Joseph king after the death of Pharaoh, but this plan met with opposition on the part of others. They objected to an alien on the throne, and so the royal title was left to Magron, called Pharaoh, according to the established custom the name given to all the Egyptian kings. But Joseph was made the actual ruler of the land, and though he was only viceroy in Egypt, he reigned as king over the lands outside of Egypt as far as the Euphrates, parts of which Joseph had acquired by conquest. The inhabitants of these countries brought their yearly tribute to him and other presents besides, and thus did Joseph rule for forty years, beloved of all, and respected by the Egyptians and the other nations, and during all that time his brethren dwelt in Goshen, happy and blithe in the service of God. And in his own family circle Joseph was happy also; he lived to act as godfather at the circumcision of the sons of his grandson Machir.

His end was premature as compared with that of his brethren; at his death he was younger than any of them at their death. It is true, "Dominion buries him that exercises it". He died ten years before his allotted time, because, without taking umbrage, he had permitted his brethren to call his father his "servant" in his presence.

Asenath

God gives every man the wife he deserves, and so Asenath was worthy of being the helpmeet of Joseph the pious. Her father was Potiphar, one of Pharaoh's magnates, ranking among the most distinguished of them by reason of wisdom, wealth, and station. His daughter was slender like unto Sarah, beautiful like Rebekah, and radiant in appearance like Rachel. Noblemen and princes sued for her hand when she was eighteen years of age. Even Pharaoh's appointed successor, his first-born son, demanded her in marriage, but his father refused to comply with his wish, because he did not consider her a proper wife for one destined to sit upon the throne. The daughter of the Moabite king, he insisted, was a more suitable match for him. But Asenath rejected every proposal of marriage, and avoided all intercourse with men. With seven maidens born the same day as herself, she lived in retirement in a magnificent palace adjoining that of her parents.

It happened in the first of the seven years of plenty that Joseph planned to visit the place in which Potiphar resided, and he sent word to him that he would put up with him, at his house. Potiphar was enchanted with the honor in prospect for him, and also with the opportunity it would afford him of bringing about a marriage between Asenath and Joseph. But when he disclosed his plan to his daughter, she rejected it with indignation. "Why shouldst thou desire to see me united with a vagabond, a slave", she cried out, "one that does not even belong to our nation, but is the son of a Canaanitish herdsman, a fellow that attempted to violate the honor of his mistress, and in punishment for this misdemeanor was thrown into prison, to be liberated thence by Pharaoh for interpreting his dream? Nay, father, never will I become his wife. I am willing to marry the son of Pharaoh, the future ruler and king of Egypt".

Potiphar promised his daughter not to speak of the plan again. At that moment Joseph's arrival was announced, and Asenath left the presence of her parents and withdrew to her own apartments. Standing by the window, she saw Joseph pass, and she was so transported with his divine beauty and his indescribably noble carriage that she burst into tears, and said: "Poor, foolish me, what shall I do? I permitted myself to be misled by friends, who told me that Joseph was the son of a Canaanitish shepherd. Now I behold the splendor that emanates from him like unto the splendor of the sun, illuminating our house with his rays. In my audacity and folly I had looked down upon him, and had spoken absurd nonsense against him. I knew not that he was a son of God, as he must be, for among men such beauty as his does not exist. I pray Thee, O God of Joseph, grant me pardon! It was my ignorance that made me speak like a fool. If my father will give me in marriage to Joseph, I will be his forever".

Meantime Joseph had taken his seat at Potiphar's table, and he observed a maiden looking at him from one of the palace windows. He commanded that she be ordered away, for he never permitted women to gaze at him or come near to him. His supernatural beauty always fascinated the noble Egyptian ladies, and they were untiring in the efforts they made to approach him. But their attempts were vain. He cherished the words of his father Jacob, who had admonished his son to keep aloof from the women of the Gentiles.

Potiphar explained to Joseph that the maiden at the window was his virgin daughter, who never permitted men to abide near her; he was the first man she had ever looked upon. The father continued and made the request of Joseph, to allow his daughter to pay him her respects. Joseph granted the favor he desired, and Asenath appeared and greeted him with the words, "Peace be with thee, thou blessed of God Most High", whereunto Joseph returned the salutation, "Be thou blessed of the Lord, from whom flow all blessings".

Asenath desired also to kiss Joseph, but he warded off the intimate greeting with the words: "It is not meet that a God-fearing man, who blesses the living God, and eats the blessed bread of life, who drinks of the blessed cup of immortality and incorruptibility, and anoints himself with the fragrant oil of holiness, should kiss a woman of a strange people, who blesses dead and unprofitable idols, and eats the putrid bread of idolatry, which chokes the soul of man, who drinks the libations of deceit, and anoints herself with the oil of destruction".

These words uttered by Joseph touched Asenath unto tears. Out of compassion with her, he bestowed his blessing upon her, calling upon God to pour out His spirit over her and make her to become a member of His people and His inheritance, and grant her a portion in the life eternal.

The Marriage of Joseph

The appearance and the speech of Joseph made so deep an impression upon Asenath that no sooner had she reached her apartment than she divested herself of her robes of state and took off her jewels, and put on sackcloth instead, strewed ashes upon her head, and supplicated God amid tears to grant her pardon for her sins. In this manner she spent seven days and seven nights in her chamber. Not even her seven attendants were permitted to enter her presence during the time of her penance. The morning of the eighth day an angel appeared unto her, and bade her put away her sackcloth and ashes and array herself in state, for this day she had been born anew, he said, to eat the blessed bread of life, to drink of the cup of life immortal, and anoint herself with the oil of life eternal. Asenath was about to set food and drink before her guest, when she perceived a honeycomb of wondrous form and fragrance. The angel explained to her that it had been produced by the bees of Paradise, to serve as food for the angels and the elect of God. He took a small portion of it for himself, and the rest he put into Asenath's mouth, saying: "From this day forth thy body shall bloom like the eternal flowers in Paradise, thy bones shall wax fat like the cedars thereof, strength inexhaustible shall be thine, thy youth shall never fade, and thy beauty never perish, and thou shalt be like unto a metropolis surrounded by a wall". At the request of Asenath, the angel blessed also her seven attendants, with the words, "May the Lord bless you and make you to be seven pillars in the City of Refuge".

Thereupon the angel left her, and she saw him ascend heavenward in a chariot of fire drawn by four steeds of fire. Now she knew that she had not been entertaining a human being, but an angel.

The celestial messenger had scarcely departed, when a visit from Joseph was announced, and she hastened to array and adorn herself for his reception. When she washed her face, she caught sight of it in the water, and saw it to be of such beauty as never before, so great had been the transformation wrought by the angel. When Joseph came, he did not recognize her. He asked her who she was, whereto she replied, "I am thy maid-servant Asenath! I have cast away my idols, and this day a visitant came to me from heaven. He gave me to eat of the bread of life and to drink of the blessed cup, and he spake these words unto me, 'I give thee unto Joseph as his affianced wife, that he may be thy affianced husband forever'. And furthermore he said, 'Thy name shall not any more be called Asenath, but thy name shall be City of Refuge, whither the nations shall flee for safety'. And he added, 'I go to Joseph, to tell him all these things that have reference to thee'. Now, my lord, thou knowest whether the man was with thee and spoke to thee in my behalf".

Joseph confirmed all she had said, and they embraced and kissed each other in token of their betrothal, which they celebrated by a banquet with Potiphar and his wife. The wedding took place later in the presence of Pharaoh, who set a golden crown upon the head of the bridegroom and the bride, gave them his blessing, and made a seven days' feast in their honor, to which he invited the magnates and princes of Egypt and of other countries. And during the seven days of the wedding festivities the people were prohibited, under penalty of death, from doing any manner of work; they all were to join in the celebration of Joseph's marriage.

Kind and Unkind Brethren

On the twenty-first day of the second month in the second of the seven years of famine, Jacob came down to Egypt, and his daughter-in-law Asenath visited him. She marvelled not a little at his beauty and strength. His shoulders and his arms were like an angel's, and his loins like a giant's. Jacob gave her his blessing, and with her husband she returned home, accompanied by the sons of Leah, while the sons of the handmaids, remembering the evil they had once done unto Joseph, kept aloof. Levi in particular had conceived a fondness for Asenath. He was especially close to the Living God, for he was a prophet and a sage, his eyes were open, and he knew how to read the celestial books written by the finger of God. He revealed to Asenath that he had seen her future resting-place in heaven, and it was built upon a rock and encompassed by a diamond wall.

On their journey they met the son of Pharaoh, his successor to the throne, and he was so transported with Asenath's beauty, that he made the plan of murdering Joseph in order to secure possession of his wife. He summoned Simon and Levi, and by blandishments and promises sought to induce them to put Joseph out of the way. Simon was so enraged that he would have felled him at once, had not his brother Levi, who was endowed with the gift of prophecy, divined his purpose, and frustrated it by stepping upon his foot, while whispering: "Why art thou so angry, and so wroth with the man? We that fear God may not repay evil with evil". Turning to the son of Pharaoh, he told him that nothing would induce them to execute the wickedness he had proposed; rather he advised him not to undertake aught against Joseph, else he would kill him with the sword that had served him in his slaughter of the inhabitants of Shechem. The culprit was seized with frantic alarm, and fell down before Simon and Levi to entreat their mercy. Levi raised him tip, saying, "Fear not, but abandon thy wicked plan, and harbor no evil design against Joseph".

Nevertheless the son of Pharaoh did not give up his criminal purpose. He approached the sons of Bilhah and Zilpah, and sought to accomplish through them what had failed with Simon and Levi. He called them into his presence, and told them of a conversation between Joseph and Pharaoh that he had overheard. The former had said that he waited but to learn of the death of his father Jacob in order to do away with the sons of the handmaids, because they had been the ones to sell him into slavery. Their wrath excited against Joseph by these words, the sons of Bilhah and Zilpah assented to the proposition of the son of Pharaoh. It was arranged that the latter should kill Pharaoh, the friend of Joseph, while they would fall upon their brother, and put him out of the way. They were furnished with six hundred able warriors and fifty spearmen for the purpose. The first part of the plan, the murder of Pharaoh, failed. The palace guard would not allow even the successor to the throne to enter his father's bedchamber, and he had to depart without having effected his object.

Now Dan and Gad gave him the advice to take up his station with fifty archers in a secret place that Asenath had to pass on her homeward journey. Thence he could make a successful attack upon her suite, and gain possession of her. Naphtali and Asher did not care to have anything to do with this hostile enterprise against Joseph, but Dan and Gad forced them into it, insisting that all the sons of the handmaids must stand together as men and repel the danger that threatened them.

Treachery Punished

From their ambush the forces of the son of Pharaoh fell upon Asenath and her six hundred attendants. They succeeded in hewing down the vanguard, and Asenath had to take to flight. To her alarm she encountered the son of Pharaoh with fifty mounted men. Benjamin, seated in the same chariot with her, came to her rescue, for in spite of his youth he was exceedingly courageous. He descended from the chariot, gathered pebbles, and, throwing them at the son of Pharaoh, struck him on his forehead and inflicted a severe wound. The charioteer aided him by keeping him supplied with pebbles, which he cast at the fifty riders with such expert skill that he slew forty-eight of them with as many missiles. Meantime the sons of Leah arrived on the spot and came to Asenath's aid, for Levi, with his prophetic spirit, had seen what was happening, and summoning his five brothers he had hastened thither.

These six attacked the troops in ambush and cut them down. But the danger to Asenath was by no means removed. At this moment the sons of the handmaids threw themselves upon her and Benjamin with drawn swords. It was their intention to kill them both, and flee to cover in the depths of the woods. But as soon as Asenath supplicated God for aid, the swords dropped from the hands of her assailants, and they saw that the Lord was on the side of Asenath. They fell at her feet and entreated her grace. She allayed their anxiety with the words: "Be courageous and have no fear of your brethren, the sons of Leah. They are God-fearing men. Do but keep yourselves in hiding until their wrath is appeased".

When the sons of Leah appeared, Asenath fell down before them, and amid tears she adjured them to spare the sons of the handmaids and not repay with evil the evil they had meditated. Simon would not hear of making concessions. He insisted that the measure of their sins was full, and they must pay for them with their lives, for they had been the ones that had sold Joseph into slavery, and brought down untold misfortune upon Jacob and his sons. But Asenath did not leave off, and her urgent petitions won the day. She succeeded in calming the anger of Simon, and in Levi she had a secret ally, for this prophet knew the hiding-place of the sons of the handmaids, and he did not betray it to Simon, lest his wrath be increased at the sight of them. It was also Levi that restrained Benjamin from giving the death blow to the heavily wounded son of Pharaoh. So far from permitting harm to be done to him, he washed his wounds, put him into a chariot, and took him to Pharaoh, who thanked Levi from his heart for his services of loving- kindness.

Levi's efforts were vain, three days later the son of Pharaoh died of the wounds inflicted by Benjamin, and from grief over the loss of his first-born Pharaoh followed him soon after, departing this life at the age of one hundred and seventy-seven years. His crown he left to Joseph, who ruled over Egypt for forty-eight years thereafter. He in turn handed the crown on to the grandchild of Pharaoh, an infant in arms at the time of his grandfather's death, toward whom Joseph had acted in a father's stead all his life.

The Death and Burial of Joseph

On his death-bed Joseph took an oath of his brethren, and he bade them on their death-bed likewise take an oath of their sons, to carry his bones to Palestine, when God should visit them and bring them up out of the land of Egypt. He said: "I that am a ruler could take my father's body up to the Holy Land while it was still intact. Of you I do but make the request that ye carry my bones from hence, and you may inter them in any spot in Palestine, for I know that the burial-place of the fathers was appointed to be the tomb only of the three Patriarchs and their three wives".

Joseph took the oath, to carry his remains along with them when they left Egypt, from his brethren, and not from his sons, to bury him at once in Palestine, for he feared the Egyptians would not give the latter permission to transport his bones even if they recalled what Joseph had been allowed to do with his father's body. They would object that Joseph had been the viceroy, and a wish preferred by one of so high an estate could not be denied. Furthermore, he adjured his brethren not to leave Egypt until a redeemer should appear and announce his message with the words, "Pakod-- I have surely visited you"--a tradition which Joseph had received from his father, who bad it from Isaac, and Isaac in turn had beard it from Abraham. And he told them that God would redeem Israel through Moses as through the Messiah, in this world as in the world to come, and the Egyptian redemption would begin in Tishri, when Israel would be freed from slave labor, and would be completed in the following Nisan, when they would leave Egypt.

Joseph also admonished his brethren to walk in the ways of the Lord, so that they might become worthy of His grace and help. Especially he impressed upon his brethren and his sons the virtue of chastity and a steadfast moral life. He told them all that had happened to him, the hatred of his brethren, the persecutions of the wife of Potiphar, the slander, envy, and malice of the Egyptians, to show how that those who fear the Lord are not forsaken by Him in darkness, or bondage, or tribulation, or distress. "I was sold into slavery", he said, "but the Lord delivered me; I was thrown into prison, but His strong hand helped me. I was tortured by hunger, but the

Lord Himself gave me sustenance. I was alone, and God comforted me. And as for you, if ye will walk in the ways of chastity and purity in patience and humility of heart, the Lord will dwell among you, for He loveth a chaste life, and if you, my children, will observe the commandments of the Lord, He will raise you up here, in this world, and bless you there, in the world to come. If men seek to do evil unto you, pray for them, and you will be delivered from all evil by the Lord. On account of my forbearing patience I received the daughter of my master to wife, and her dowry was a hundred talents of gold, and God gave me also beauty like the beauty of a flower, more than all the children of Jacob, and He preserved me unto mine old age in vigor and beauty, for in all things did I resemble Jacob".

Joseph continued and told them the visions he had had, in which the future of Israel was revealed to him, and then he closed with the words: "I know that the Egyptians will oppress you after my death, but God will execute vengeance for your sakes, and He will lead you to the land of promise of your fathers. But ye shall surely carry my bones with you from hence, for if my remains are taken to Canaan, the Lord will be with you in the light, and Behar will be with the Egyptians in the darkness. Also take with you the bones of your mother Zilpah, and bury them near the sepulchre of Bilhah and Rachel".

These words ended, he stretched out his feet, and slept his last eternal sleep, and the whole of Israel mourned him, and the whole of Egypt was in great grief, for he had been a compassionate friend to the Egyptians, too, and he had done good unto them, and given them wise counsel and assistance in all their undertakings.

Joseph's wish, that his bones should rest in the Holy Land, was fulfilled when the Israelites went forth from Egypt, and no less a personage than Moses applied himself to its execution. Such was Joseph's reward for the devotion he had displayed in the interment of his father's body, for he had done all things needful himself, leaving naught to others. Therefore so great a man as Moses busied himself with the realization of Joseph's wish.

For three days and three nights preceding the exodus Moses hunted up and down through the land of Egypt for Joseph's coffin, because he knew that Israel could not leave Egypt without heeding the oath given to Joseph. But his trouble was in vain; the coffin was nowhere to be found. Serah, the daughter of Asher, met Moses, tired and exhausted, and in answer to her question about the cause of his weariness, he told her of his fruitless search. Serah took him to the Nile river, and told him that the leaden coffin made for Joseph by the Egyptians had been sunk there after having been scaled up on all sides. The Egyptians had done this at the instigation and with the help of the magicians, who, knowing that Israel could not leave the country without the coffin, had used their arts to put it in a place whence it could not be removed.

Moses now took Joseph's cup, and he cut four flat pieces from it, and engraved a lion on one of them, an eagle on the second, a bull on the third, and a human figure on the fourth. He threw the first, with the lion, into the river, saying at the same time, "Joseph, Joseph, the hour for the redemption of Israel hath arrived, the Shekinah lingers here only for thy sake, the clouds of glory await thy coming. If thou wilt show thyself, well and good; if not, then we are clear from our oath". But the coffin did not appear.

Then Moses threw the second plate into the water, that with the figure of the eagle, repeating the same words, but again the coffin did not rise from the bed of the Nile, and there it remained, too, when he threw in the third plate bearing the figure of the bull, and called upon Joseph a third time to come forth. But the fourth plate with the human figure and the fourth invocation to Joseph brought the coffin to the surface of the water. Moses seized it, and in joy he bore it off. While Israel had been busy gathering gold and silver from the Egyptians, Moses had been thinking of nothing but Joseph's coffin, and his happiness was great that he had been permitted to fulfil the wish of Joseph.

During the forty years of wandering through the desert, the coffin was in the midst of Israel, as a reward for Joseph's promise to his brethren, "I will nourish you and take care of you". God had said, "As thou livest, for forty years they will take care of thy bones".

All this time in the desert Israel carried two shrines with them, the one the coffin containing the bones of the dead man Joseph, the other the Ark containing the covenant of the Living God. The wayfarers who saw the two receptacles wondered, and they would ask, "How doth the ark of the dead come next to the ark of the Ever-living"? The answer was, "The dead man enshrined in the one fulfilled the commandments enshrined in the other. In the latter it is written, I am the Lord thy God, and he said, Am I in the place of God? Here it is written, Thou shalt have no other gods before My face, and he said, I fear God. Here it is written, Thou shalt not take the name of the Lord thy God in vain, and therefore he did not swear by God, but said, By the life of Pharaoh. Here it is written, Remember the Sabbath day, and he said to the overseer of his palace on Friday, Slay and make ready, meaning for the Sabbath. Here it is written, Honor thy father and thy mother, and he said, when his father desired to send him to his brethren, Here am I, although he knew it was perilous for him to go. Here it is written, Thou shalt not kill, and he refrained from murdering Potiphar when Potiphar's wife urged him to do it. Here it is written, Thou shalt not commit adultery, and he scorned the adulterous proposals of Potiphar's wife. Here it is written, Thou shalt not steal, and he stole nothing from Pharaoh, but gathered up all the money and brought it unto Pharaoh's house. Here it is written, Thou shalt not bear false witness against thy neighbor, and he told his father nothing of what his brethren had done to him, though what he might have told was the truth. Here it is written, Thou shalt not covet, and he did not covet Potiphar's wife".On their arrival in the Holy Land, the Israelites buried the bones of Joseph in Shechem, for God spake to the tribes, saying, "From Shechem did ye steal him, and unto Shechem, shall ye return him".

God, who is so solicitous about the dead bodies of the pious, is even more solicitous about their souls, which stand before Him like angels, and do their service ministering unto Him.

II. The Sons of Jacob

Significant Names

Jacob raised all his sons in the fear of God, and taught them the ways of a pious life, using severity when there was need to make his lessons impressive. He reaped the fruits of his labor, for all his sons were godly men of stainless character. The ancestors of the twelve tribes resembled their fathers in piety, and their acts were no less significant than those of Abraham, Isaac, and Jacob. Like these three, they deserve to be called the Fathers of Israel. God made a covenant with them as He had made with the three Patriarchs, and to this covenant their descendants owe their preservation.

The very names of the tribes point to the redemption of Israel. Reuben is so called, because God "sees" the affliction of His people; Simon, because He "hears" its groaning; Levi, He "joins" Himself unto His people when Israel suffers; Judah, Israel will "thank" God for its deliverance; Issachar, it will be "rewarded" for its suffering with a recompense; Zebulon, God will have a "dwelling-place" in Israel; Benjamin, He swore by His "right hand" to succor His people; Dan, He will "judge" the nation that subjugates Israel; Naphtali, He bestowed the Torah upon Israel, and she drops sweetness like the "honeycomb"; Gad, the Lord gave manna unto Israel, and it was like "coriander" seed; Asher, all nations will call Israel "happy"; and Joseph, because God will "add" a second redemption of Israel to the first--redemption from the wicked kingdom at the end as from Egypt in former times.

Not only the names of Jacob's sons are significant, but the names of their sons as well. Thus the names of the sons of Issachar express the activities of the tribe known for its learning above all the others. The oldest was called Tola, "worm"; as the silk worm is distinguished for its mouth, with which it spins, so also the men of the tribe of Issachar for the wise words of their mouth. The second is Puah, "madder plant"; as this plant colors all things, so the tribe of Issachar colors the whole world with its teachings. The third is Jashub, "the returning one", for through the teachings of Issachar Israel will be turned back to its Heavenly Father; and Shimron, the fourth, is "the observing one", to indicate that the tribe of Issachar observes the Torah.

The names of the sons of Gad likewise interpret the history of the tribe. During Israel's sojourn in Egypt, it had strayed from the right path, but when Aaron appeared as prophet and monitor, and called unto the Israelites to cast away the abominations of their eyes and forsake the idols of Egypt, they hearkened unto his words. Hence the double name Ozni and Ezbon borne by one of the sons of Gad, for this tribe "hearkened" to the word of God, and fulfilled His "will".

The grandsons of Asher bear the names Heber and Malchiel, because they were the "associates" of kings, and their inheritance yielded "royal dainties".Partly the history of the tribe of Benjamin can be read in the names of its chiefs. It consisted originally of ten divisions, descended from Benjamin's ten sons, but five of them perished in Egypt on account of their ungodly ways, from which no admonition availed to turn them aside. Of the five families remaining, two, the descendants of Bela and those of Ashbel, had always been God-fearing; the others, the Ahiramites, the Shephuphamites, and the Huphamites, repented of their sins, and in accordance with the change in their conduct had been the change in their names. Ehi had become Ahiram, because the breach with the "Exalted" One was healed; Muppira was called Shephupham, because they "afflicted" themselves in their penance; and Huppim was turned into Hupham, to indicate that they had "cleansed" themselves from sin. As a reward for their piety, the family springing from Bela was permitted to have two subdivisions, the Ardites and the Naamites. Their names point them out as men that know well how the fear of God is to be manifested, whose deeds are exceedingly lovely.

Naphtali was another tribe of steadfast piety, and the names of his sons testify thereto: Jahzeel, because the tribesmen raised a "partition wall" between God and the idols, inasmuch as they trusted in God and contemned the idols; Guni, because God was their "protection"; and Jezer and Shillem designate the Naphtalites as men devoted to God with all their hearts.

Reuben's Testament

Two years after the death of Joseph, Reuben fell sick. Feeling that his end was nigh, he called together his sons, his grandsons, and his brethren, to give them his last admonitions from out of the fulness of his experience. He spake: "Hear, my brethren, and do ye, my children, give ear unto Reuben your father in the commands that I enjoin upon you. And, behold, I adjure you this day by the God of heaven that ye walk not in the follies of youth and the fornications to which I was addicted, and wherewith I defiled the bed of my father Jacob. For I tell you now that for seven months the Lord afflicted my loins with a terrible plague, and if my father Jacob had not interceded for me, the Lord had swept me away. I was twenty years of age when I did what was evil before the Lord, and for seven months I was sick unto death. Then I did penance for seven years in the innermost depths of my soul. Wine and strong drink I drank not, the flesh of animals passed not my lips, dainties I tasted not, because I mourned over my sins, for they were great".

He admonished those gathered around him to beware of the seven tempter spirits, which are the spirit of fornication, gluttony, strife, love of admiration, arrogance, falsehood, and injustice. He cautioned them especially against unchastity, saying: "Pay no heed to the glances of a woman, and remain not alone with a married woman, and do not occupy yourselves with the affairs of women. Had I not seen Bilhah bathe in a secluded spot, I had not fallen into the great sin I committed, for after my thoughts had once grasped the nakedness of woman, I could not sleep until I had accomplished the abominable deed. For when our father Jacob went to his father Isaac, while we sojourned in Eder, not far from Ephrath, which is Beth-lehem, Bilhah was drunken with wine, and she lay asleep, uncovered, in her bedchamber, and I entered in and saw her nakedness and committed the sin, and I went out again, leaving her asleep. But an angel of God revealed my impious act to my father Jacob at once. He came back and mourned over me, and never again did he approach Bilhah. Unto the very last day of his life, I had not the assurance to look my father in the face or to speak to my brethren regarding my disgrace, and even now my conscience tortures me on account of my sin. Nevertheless my father spake words of comfort to me, and prayed to God in my behalf, that the wrath of the Lord might depart from me, as He showed me".

Reuben admonished his children impressively to join themselves to Levi, "because he will know the law of the Lord", he said, "and he will give ordinances for judgment, and bring sacrifices for all Israel, until the consummation of the times, as the anointed high priest of whom the Lord spake".

After announcing his last will to his sons, Reuben departed this life at the age of one hundred and twenty-five years. His body was laid in a coffin until his sons bore it away from Egypt, and carried it up to Hebron, where they buried it in the Double Cave.

Simon's Admonition Against Envy

As Reuben confessed his sin upon his death-bed, and warned his children and his family to be on their guard against unchastity, the vice that had brought about his fall, so Simon, when he was about to die, assembled his sons around him, and confessed the sin he had committed. He had been guilty of boundless envy of Joseph, and he spoke: "I was the second son begotten by my father Jacob, and my mother Leah called me Simon, because the Lord had heard her prayer. I waxed strong, and shrank from no manner of deed, and I was afraid of naught, for my heart was hard, and my liver unyielding, and my bowels without mercy. And in the days of my youth I was jealous of Joseph, for our father loved him more than all the rest of us, and I resolved to kill him. For the prince of temptation sent the spirit of jealousy to take possession of me, and it blinded me so that I did not consider Joseph to be my brother, and I spared not even my father Jacob. But his God and the God of his fathers sent His angel and saved him out of my hands.

When I went to Shechem to fetch ointment for the herds, and Reuben was in Dothan, where all our supplies and stores were kept, our brother Judah sold Joseph to the Ishmaelites. On his return, when he heard what had happened, Reuben was very sad, for he had been desirous of saving Joseph and bringing him back to our father. But as for me, my wrath was enkindled against Judah, that he had let him escape alive. My anger abode with me all of five months. But the Lord restrained me from using the power of my hands, for my right hand withered for the length of seven days. Then I knew that what had happened was for the sake of Joseph. I repented and prayed to God to restore my hand and withhold me henceforth from all sorts of defilement, envy, and folly. For two years I gave myself up to fasting and the fear of God, for I perceived that redemption from jealousy could come only through the fear of God.

My father, seeing me downcast, asked to know the cause of my sadness, and I replied that I was suffering with my liver, but in truth I was mourning more than all my brethren, seeing that I had been the cause of Joseph's sale. And when we went down into Egypt, and Joseph bound me as a spy, I was not grieved, for I knew in my heart that my suffering was just retribution. But Joseph was good, the spirit of God dwelt within him. Compassionate and merciful as he was, he bore me no resentment for my evil deeds toward him, but he loved me with the same love he showed the others. He paid due honor to us all, and gave us gold, and cattle, and produce. And now, my dear children, do ye love one another, each one his brother, with a clean heart, and remove the spirit of jealousy from the midst of you".

Like Reuben, so also Simon adjured his sons to beware of unchastity, for this vice is the mother of all evil. It separates man from God, and abandons him to Behar. These were the closing words of his exhortation: "In the writings of Enoch I saw that your sons would be corrupted through unchastity, and they would maltreat the sons of Levi with the sword. But they will not be able to do aught against Levi, for the war he will wage is the war of the Lord, and he will vanquish all your armies. As a small remnant you will be scattered among Levi and Judah, and none among you will rise to be a judge or a king of our people, as, my father Jacob prophesied in his blessing".

Having completed his admonitions to his sons, Simon passed away and was gathered to his fathers, at the age of one hundred and twenty years. His sons placed him in a coffin made of imperishable wood, so that they might carry his bones to Hebron, as they did, in secret, during the war between the Egyptians and the Canaanites. Thus did all the tribes during the war; they took the remains each of its founder from Egypt to Hebron. Only the bones of Joseph remained in Egypt until the Israelites went out of the land, for the Egyptians guarded them in their royal treasure chambers. Their magicians had warned them that whenever Joseph's bones should be removed from Egypt, a great darkness would envelop the whole land, and it would be a dire misfortune for the Egyptians, for none would be able to recognize his neighbor even with the light of a lamp.

The Ascension of Levi

When it was disclosed to Levi that he was about to die, he gathered all his children around him, to tell them the story of his life, and he also prophesied unto them what they would do, and what would happen to them until the judgment day. He spoke: "When we were pasturing the flocks in Abel-Meholah, the spirit of understanding of the Lord came upon me, and I saw all mankind, how they corrupt their ways, and that injustice builds up walls for herself, and impiety sits enthroned upon the towers. And I fell to grieving over the generations of men, and I prayed to the Lord to save me. Sleep enshrouded me, and I beheld a tall mountain, and lo! the heavens opened, and an angel of God addressed me, and said: 'Levi, enter'!

"I entered the first heaven, and I saw a great sea hanging there, and farther on I saw a second heaven, brighter and more resplendent than the first. I said to the angel, 'Why is this so'? And the angel said to me, 'Marvel not at this, for thou shalt see another heaven, brilliant beyond compare, and when thou hast ascended thither, thou shalt stand near the Lord, and thou shalt be His minister, and declare His mysteries to men; and of the Lord's portion shall be thy life, and He shall be thy field and vineyard and fruits and gold and silver'."

"Then the angel explained the uses of the different heavens to me, and all that happens in each, and he proclaimed the judgment day. He opened the gates of the third heaven, where I beheld the holy Temple, and God seated upon the Throne of Glory. The Lord spake to me: 'Levi, upon thee have I bestowed the blessing of the priesthood, until I come and dwell in the midst of Israel'. Then the angel carried me back to earth, and gave me a shield and a sword, saying, 'Execute vengeance upon Shechem for Dinah, and I will be with thee, for the Lord hath sent me'. I asked the angel what his name was, and he replied: 'I am the angel that intercedes for the people of Israel, that it may not be destroyed utterly, for every evil spirit attacks it'."

"When I awoke, I betook myself to my father, and on the way, near Gebal, I found a brass shield, such as I had seen in my dream. Then I advised my father and my brother Reuben to bid the sons of Hamor circumcise themselves, for I was quivering with rage on account of the abominable deed they had done. I slew Shechem first of all, and then Simon slew Hamor, and all my other brothers came out and destroyed the whole city. Our father took this in ill part, and in his blessing he remembered our conduct. Although we did a wrong thing in acting thus against his wishes, yet I recognized it to be the judgment of God upon the people of Shechem on account of their sins, and I said to my father: 'Be not wroth, my lord, for God will exterminate the Canaanites through this, and he will give the land to thee and to thy seed after thee. Henceforth Shechem will be called the city of imbeciles, for as a fool is mocked at, so have we made a mockery of them'."

"When we journeyed to Beth-lehem, and had been abiding there for seventy days, another vision was vouchsafed me, like unto the former. I saw seven men clad in white, and they spake to me, saying: 'Rise up, and array thyself in the priestly garments, set the crown of righteousness upon thy head, and put on the ephod of understanding, and the robe of truth, and the mitre-plate of faith, and the mitre of dignity, and the shoulderpieces of prophecy'. And each of the men brought a garment unto me and invested me therewith, and spake: 'Henceforth be the priest of the Lord, thou and thy seed unto eternity. And ye shall eat all that is lovely to look upon, and the table of the Lord thy descendants will appropriate for themselves, and from them will come high priests, judges, and scholars, for all that is holy will be guarded by their mouth'."

"Two days after I was visited by this dream, Judah and I repaired to our grandfather Isaac, who blessed me in accordance with the words I had heard. Jacob also had a vision, and he saw, too, that I was appointed to be the priest of God, and through me he set apart a tenth of his possessions unto the Lord. And when we established ourselves in Hebron, the residence of Isaac, our grandfather taught me the law of the priesthood, and admonished me to hold myself aloof from unchastity.

At the age of twenty-eight years I took Milcah to wife, and she bore me a son, and I named him Gershom, because we were strangers in the land. But I perceived he would not be in the first ranks of men. My second son was born unto me in my thirty-fifth year, and he saw the light of the world at sunrise, and I beheld him in a vision standing among the proud of the assembly, and therefore I gave him the name Kohath. The third son my wife bore me in the fortieth year of my life, and I called his name Merari, because bitter had been her travail in bearing him. My daughter Jochebed was born in Egypt, when I was sixty-three years old, and I called her thus because I was known honorably among my brethren in those days. And in my ninety- fourth year, Amram took Jochebed to wife, he that was born on the same day with her".

Thereupon Levi admonished his children to walk in the ways of the Lord, and fear Him with all their heart, and he told them what he had learnt from the writings of Enoch, that his descendants would sin against the Lord in times to come, and they would suffer the Divine punishment for their transgression, and then God would raise up a new priest, unto whom all the words of the Lord would be revealed. His last words were: "And now, my children, ye have heard all I have to say. Choose, now, light or darkness, the law of the Lord or the works of Beliar". And his sons made answer, "Before the Lord we will walk according to His law". Then Levi spake, "The Lord is witness and the angels are witnesses, I am witness and ye are witnesses, concerning the word of your mouth". And his sons replied, "We are witnesses".

Thus Levi ceased to admonish his sons. He stretched out his feet, and was gathered unto his fathers, at the age of one hundred and thirty-seven years, a greater age than any of his brethren attained.

Judah Warns Against Greed and Unchastity

The last words addressed by Judah to his sons were the following: "I was the fourth son begotten by my father, and my mother called me Judah, saying, 'I thank the Lord that He hath given me a fourth son'. I was zealous in my youth and obedient to my father in all things. When I grew up to manhood, he blessed me, saying, 'Thou wilt be king, and wilt prosper in all thy ways'. The Lord granted me His grace in whatever I undertook, in the field and in the house. I could speed as swiftly as the hind, and overtake it, and prepare a dish of it for my father. A deer I could catch on the run, and all the animals of the valley. A wild mare I could outstrip, hold it, and bridle it. A lion I slew, and snatched a kid from its jaws. A bear I caught by the paw, and flung it adown the cliff, and it lay beneath crushed. I could keep pace with the wild boar, and overtake it, and as I ran I seized it, and tore it to pieces. A leopard sprang at my dog in Hebron, and I grasped its tail, and hurled it away from me, and its body burst on the coast at Gaza. A wild steer I found grazing in the field. I took it by its horns, swung it round and round until it was stunned, and then I cast it to the ground and killed it".

Judah continued and told his children of his heroism in the wars that the sons of Jacob had waged with the kings of Canaan and with Esau and his family. In all these conflicts he bore a distinguished part, beyond the achievements of the others. His father Jacob was free from all anxiety when Judah was with his brethren in their combats, because he had had a vision showing him an angel of strength standing at the side of Judah on all his ways.

Judah did not conceal his shortcomings, either. He confessed how drunkenness and passion had betrayed him first into marriage with a Canaanitish woman, and then into improper relations with his daughter-in-law Tamar. He said to his children:

"Do not walk after the desire of your hearts, and vaunt not the valiant deeds of your youth. This, too, is evil in the eyes of the Lord. For while I boasted that the face of a beautiful woman had never allured me in the wars, and reviled my brother Reuben for his transgression with Bilhah, the spirit of passion and unchastity gained possession of me, and I took Bath-shua to wife, and trespassed with Tamar, though she was the affianced of my son. First I said to Bath-shua's father, 'I will take counsel with my father Jacob, to know whether I should marry thy daughter', but he was a king, and he showed me an untold heap of gold accredited to his daughter, and he adorned her with the magnificence of women, in gold and pearls, and he bade her pour the wine at the meal. The wine turned my eyes awry, and passion darkened my heart. In mad love for her, I violated the command of the Lord and the will of my father, and I took her to wife. The Lord gave me a recompense according to the counsel of my heart, for I had no joy in the sons she bore me.

"And now, my children, I pray you, do not intoxicate yourselves with wine, for wine twists the understanding away from the truth, and confuses the sight of the eyes. Wine led me astray, so that I felt no shame before the throngs of people in the city, and I turned aside and went in to Tamar in the presence of them, and committed a great sin. And though a man be a king, if he leads an unchaste life, he loses his kingship. I gave Tamar my staff, which is the stay of my tribe, and my girdle-cord, which is power, and my signet- diadem, which is the glory of my kingdom. I did penance for all this, and unto old age I drank no wine, and ate no flesh, and knew no sort of pleasure. Wine causes the secret things of God and man to be revealed unto the stranger. Thus did I disclose the commands of the Lord and the mysteries of my father Jacob to the Canaanite woman Bath-shua, though God had forbidden me to betray them. I also enjoin you not to love gold, and not to look upon the beauty of women, for through money and through beauty I was led astray to Bath-shua the Canaanite. I know that my stock will fall into misery through these two things, for even the wise men among my sons will be changed by them, and the consequence will be that the kingdom of Judah will be diminished, the domain that the Lord gave me as a reward for my obedient conduct toward my father, for never did I speak in contradiction of him, but I did all things according to his words. And Isaac, my father's father, blessed me with the blessing that I should be ruler in Israel, and I know that the kingdom will arise from me. In the books of Enoch the just I read all the evil that ye will do in the latter days. Only beware, my children, of unchastity and greed, for love of gold leads to idolatry, causing men to call them gods that are none, and dethroning the reason of man. On account of gold I lost my children, and had I not mortified my flesh, and humbled my soul, and had not my father Jacob offered up prayers for me, I had died childless. But the God of my fathers, the merciful and gracious One, saw that I had acted unwittingly, for the ruler of deception had blinded me, and I was ignorant, being flesh and blood, and corrupt through sins, and in the moment when I considered myself invincible, I recognized my weakness".

Then Judah revealed to his sons, in clear, brief words, the whole history of Israel until the advent of the Messiah, and his final speech was: "My children, observe the whole law of the Lord; in it is hope for all that keep His ways. I die this day at the age of one hundred and nineteen years before your eyes. None shall bury me in a costly garment, nor shall ye cut my body to embalm it, but ye shall carry me to Hebron".

Having spoken these words, Judah sank into death.

Issachar's Singleness of Heart

When Issachar felt his end approach, he summoned his sons, and he said to them: "Hearken, my children, unto your father Issachar, and listen to the words of him that is beloved of the Lord. I was born unto Jacob as his fifth son, as a reward for the dudaim. Reuben brought the dudaim from the field. They were fragrant apples, which grew in the land of Haran upon an eminence below a gully. Rachel met Reuben, and she took the dudaim away from him. The lad wept, and his cries brought his mother Leah to his side, and she addressed Rachel thus: 'Is it a small matter that thou hast taken away my husband? and wouldst thou take away my son's dudaim also?' And Rachel said, 'See, Jacob shall be thine to-night for thy son's dudaim'. But Leah insisted, 'Jacob is mine, and I am the wife of his youth', whereupon Rachel, 'Be not boastful and overweening. To me he was betrothed first, and for my sake he served our father fourteen years. Thou art not his wife, thou wast taken to him by cunning instead of me, for our father deceived me, and put me out of the way the night of thy nuptials, so that Jacob could not see me. Nevertheless, give me the dudaim, and thou mayest have Jacob for a night'".

"Then Leah bore me, and I was called Issachar, on account of the reward Rachel had given to my mother. At that time an angel of the Lord appeared to Jacob, and he spoke: 'Rachel will bear only two sons, for she rejected the espousal of her husband, and chose continence! But Leah bore six sons, for the Lord knew that she desired to be with her husband, not because she was prompted by the evil inclination, but for the sake of children. Rachel's prayer also was fulfilled, on account of the dudaim, for although she desired to eat of the apples, she did not touch them, but put them in the house of the Lord, and gave them to the priest of the Most High that was in those days."

"When I grew up, my children, I walked in the integrity of my heart, and I became a husbandman, cultivating the land for my father and my brethren, and I gathered the fruit from the fields in their due time. My father blessed me, because he saw that I walked in singleness of heart. I was not married to a wife until I was thirty years old, for the hard work I did consumed my strength, and I had no desire unto woman, but, overwhelmed by fatigue, I would sink into sleep. My father was well pleased at all times with my rectitude. If my work was crowned with good results, I brought the firstfruits of my labor to the priest of the Lord, the next harvest went to my father, and then I thought of myself. The Lord doubled the possessions in my hand, and Jacob knew that God aided me for the sake of my singleness of heart, for in my sincerity I gave of the produce of the land to the poor and the needy."

"And now hearken unto me, my children, and walk in singleness of heart, for upon it resteth the favor of the Lord at all times. The simple man longeth not for gold, he doth not defraud his neighbor, he hath no desire for meats and dainties of many kinds, he careth not for sumptuous dress, he hopeth not for long life, he waiteth only upon the will of God. The spirits of deception have no power over him, for he looketh not upon the beauty of woman, lest he defile his understanding with corruption. Jealousy cometh not into his thoughts, envy doth not sear his soul, and insatiable greed doth not make him look abroad for rich gain. Now, then, my children, observe the law of the Lord, attain to simplicity, and walk in singleness of heart, without meddling with the affairs of others. Love the Lord and love your neighbors, have pity upon the poor and the feeble, bow your backs to till the ground, occupy yourselves with work upon the land, and bring gifts unto the Lord in gratitude. For the Lord hath blessed you with the best of the fruits of the field, as he hath blessed all the saints from Abel down to our day."

"Know, my children, that in the latter time your sons will abandon the paths of probity, and will be ruled by greed. They will forsake rectitude and practice craft, they will depart from the commands of the Lord and follow after Beliar, they will give up husbandry and pursue their evil plans, they will be scattered among the heathen and serve their enemies. Tell this unto your children, so that, if they sin, they may repent speedily, and return to the Lord, for He is merciful, and He will take them out to bring them back unto their land."

"I am one hundred and twenty-two years old, and I can discern no sin in myself. Save my wife, I have known no woman. I was guilty of no unchastity through the lifting up of eyes. I drank no wine, that I might not be led astray, I did not covet what belonged to my neighbor, guile had no place in my heart, lies did not pass my lips. I sighed along with all that were heavy-laden, and to the poor I gave my bread. I loved the Lord with all my might, and mankind I also loved. Do ye likewise, my children, and all the spirits of Beliar will flee from you, no deed done by the wicked will have power over you, and ye will vanquish all the wild beasts, for ye have with you the Lord of heaven."

And Issachar bade his children carry him up to Hebron, and bury him there by his fathers in the Cave, and he stretched out his feet, and fell into the sleep of eternity, full of years, healthy of limb, and in the possession of all his faculties.

Zebulon Exhorts Unto Compassion

When Zebulon attained the age of one hundred and fourteen years, which was two years after the death of Joseph, he called his sons together, and admonished them, in these words, to lead a life of piety: "I am Zebulon, a precious gift for my parents, for when I was born, my father became very rich, by means of the streaked rods, in herds of sheep and herds of cattle. I am conscious of no sin in me, and I remember no wrong done by me, unless it be the unwitting sin committed against Joseph, in that I did not, out of consideration for my brethren, disclose to my father what had happened to his favorite son, though in secret I mourned exceedingly. I feared my brethren, because they had agreed that he who betrayed the secret should be slain with the sword. When they planned to kill Joseph, I besought them amid tears not to sin thus.

"And now, my children, hearken unto me. I exhort you to observe the commands of the Lord, and have mercy upon your neighbors, and act compassionately, not only toward men, but also toward dumb brutes. For on account of my mercifulness the Lord blessed me; all my brethren fell sick at one time or another, but I escaped without any illness. Also the sons of my brethren had to endure disease, and they were nigh unto death for the sake of Joseph, because they had no pity in their hearts. But my sons were preserved in perfect health, as ye well know. And when I was in Canaan, catching fish at the shores of the sea for my father Jacob, many were drowned in the waters of the sea, but I came away unharmed. For ye must know that I was the first to build a boat for rowing upon the sea, and I plied along the coasts in it, and caught fish for my father's household, until we went down into Egypt. Out of pity I would share my haul with the poor stranger, and if he was sick or well on in years, I would prepare a savory dish for him, and I gave unto each according to his needs, sympathizing with him in his distress and having pity upon him. Therefore the Lord brought numerous fish to my nets, for he that gives aught to his neighbor, receives it back from the Lord with great increase. For five years I fished in the summer, and in the winter I pastured the flocks with my brethren.

"Now, my children, have pity and compassion on all men, that the Lord may have pity and compassion on you, for in the measure in which man has mercy with his fellow-men, God has mercy with him. When we came down into Egypt, Joseph did not visit upon us the wrong he had suffered. Take him as your model, and remember not a wrong done unto you, else unity is rent asunder, and the bonds of kinship are torn, and the soul is disquieted. Observe the water! If it runs on undivided, it carries down stone, wood, and sand along with it. But if it is divided and flows through many channels, the earth sucks it up, and it loses its force. If you separate, one from the other, you will be like divided waters. Be not cleft into two heads, for all that the Lord hath made has but one head. He has given two shoulders unto his creatures, two hands, and two feet, but all these organs obey one head".

Zebulon ended his exhortation unto unity with an account of the divisions in Israel, whereof he had read in the writings of the fathers, that they would come about in future days, and bring sore suffering upon Israel. However, he spoke encouraging words to his children, saying: "Be not grieved over my death, and do not lose heart at my departure from you, for I shall arise again in the midst of you, and I shall live joyously among the people of my tribe, those who observe the law of the Lord. As for the godless, the Lord will bring everlasting fire down upon them, and exterminate them unto all generations. Now I hasten hence unto my eternal rest with my fathers. But ye, fear ye the Lord your God with all your might all the days of your life".

Having made an end of saying these words, he sank into the sleep of death, and his sons put him into a coffin, wherein they carried him up to Hebron later, to bury him there next to his fathers.

Dan's Confession

When Dan assembled his family at the last of his life, he spake: "I confess before you this day, my children, that I had resolved to kill Joseph, that good and upright man, and I rejoiced over his sale, for his father loved him more than he loved the rest of us. The spirit of envy and boastfulness goaded me on, saying, 'Thou, too, art the son of Jacob', and one of the spirits of Behar stirred me up, saying, 'Take this sword, and slay Joseph, for once he is dead thy father will love thee'. It was the spirit of anger that was seeking to persuade me to crush Joseph, as a leopard crunches a kid between its teeth. But the God of our father Jacob did not deliver him into my hand, to let me find him alone, and He did not permit me to execute this impious deed, that two tribes in Israel might not be destroyed.

"And now, my children, I am about to die, and I tell it unto you in truth, if you take not heed against the spirit of lies and anger, and if ye love not truth and generosity, you will perish. The spirit of anger casts the net of error around its victim, and it blinds his eyes, and the spirit of lies warps his mind, and clouds his vision. Evil is anger, it is the grave of the soul. Desist from anger and hate lies, that the Lord may dwell among you, and Behar flee from your presence. Speak the truth each unto his neighbor, and you will not fall into anger and trouble, but you will be at peace, and the Lord of peace you will have with you, and no war will vanquish you.

"I speak thus, for I know that in the latter days you will fall off from God, and you will kindle the wrath of Levi, and rise in rebellion against Judah, but you will not accomplish aught against them, for the angel of the Lord is their guide, and Israel will perish through them. And if you turn recreant to the Lord, you will execute every kind of evil thing, and do the abominations of the heathen, committing unchastity with the wives of the godless, while the tempter spirits are at work among you. Therefore you will be carried away into captivity, and in the lands of exile you will suffer all the plagues of Egypt and all the tribulations of the heathen. But when you return to the Lord, you will find mercy. He will take you into His sanctuary, and grant you peace.

"And now, my children, fear the Lord, and be on your guard against Satan and his spirits. Keep aloof from every evil deed, cast anger away from you and every sort of lie, love truth and forbearance, and what ye have heard from your father, tell unto your children. Avoid all manner of unrighteousness, cling to the integrity of the law of the Lord, and bury me near my fathers".

Having spoken these words, he kissed his children, and fell asleep.

Naphtali's Dreams of the Division of the Tribes

In the hundred and thirty-second year of his life, Naphtali invited all his children to a banquet. The next morning when he awoke, he told them that he was dying, but they would not believe him. He, however, praised the Lord, and assured them again that his death was due after the banquet of the day before. Then he addressed his last words to his children:

"I was born of Bilhah, and because Rachel had acted with cunning, and had given Jacob Bilhah instead of herself, I was called Naphtali. Rachel loved me, for I was born upon her knees, and while I was still very young, she was in the habit of kissing me and saying, 'O that I had a brother unto thee from mine own body, one in thine image'. Therefore Joseph resembled me in all respects, in accordance with Rachel's prayer. My mother Bilhah was a daughter of Rotheus, a brother of Deborah, Rebekah's nurse, and she was born the same day as Rachel. As for Rotheus, he was of the family of Abraham, a Chaldean, God-fearing, and a free man of noble birth, and when he was taken captive, he was bought by Laban and married to his slave Aina. She bore Rotheus a daughter, and he called her Zilpah, after the name of the village in which he was taken captive. His second daughter he called Bilhah, saying, 'My daughter is impetuous', for hardly was she born when she hastened to suckle."

"I was fleet of foot like a deer, and my father Jacob appointed me to be his messenger, and in his blessing he called me a hind let loose. As the potter knows the vessel he fashions, how much it is to hold, and uses clay accordingly, so the Lord makes the body in conformity with the soul, and to agree with the capacity of the body He plans the soul. The one corresponds to the other down to the third of a hair- breadth, for the whole of creation was made by weight, and measure, and rule. And as the potter knows the use of every vessel he fashions, so the Lord knows the body of His creature, unto what point it will be steadfast in the good, and at what point it will fall into evil ways. Now, then, my children, let your conduct be well-ordered unto good in the fear of God, do naught that is ill-regulated or untimely, for though ye tell your eye to hear, it yet cannot, and as little can ye do deeds of light while you abide in darkness."

Furthermore Naphtali said unto his children: "I give you no command concerning my silver, or my gold, or any other possession that I bequeath to you. And what I command you is not a hard matter, which you cannot do, but I speak unto you concerning an easy thing, which you can execute". Then his sons answered, and said, "Speak, father, for we are listening to thy words". Naphtali continued: "I give you no commandment except regarding the fear of God, that you should serve Him and follow after Him". Then the sons of Naphtali asked: "Wherefore does He require our service"? and he replied, saying: "He needs no creature, but all creatures need Him. Nevertheless He hath not created the world for naught, but that men should fear Him, and none should do unto his neighbor what he would not have others do unto him". His sons asked again, "Father, hast thou observed that we strayed from the ways of the Lord to the right or to the left"? Naphtali replied: "God is witness, and so am I witness for you, that it is as you say. But I fear regarding future times, that you may depart from the ways of the Lord, and follow after the idols of the stranger, and walk in the statutes of the heathen peoples, and join yourselves unto the sons of Joseph instead of the sons of Levi and Judah". The sons of Naphtali spoke, "What reason hast thou for commanding this thing unto us"? Naphtali: "Because I know that the sons of Joseph will one day turn recreant to the Lord, the God of their fathers, and it is they that will lead the sons of Israel into sin, and cause them to be driven away from their inheritance, their beautiful land, to a land that is not ours, even as it was Joseph that brought the Egyptian bondage down upon us.

"I will tell ye, my children, the vision I had while I was yet a shepherd of flocks. I saw my brethren pasturing the herds with me, and our father approached, and said: 'Up, my sons, each one take what he can in my presence!' We answered, and said to him, 'What shall we take? We see nothing but the sun, the moon, and the stars'. Then our father said: 'These shall ye take!' Levi, hearing this, snatched up an ox-goad, sprang up to the sun, sat upon him, and rode. Judah did likewise. He jumped up to the moon, and rode upon her. And the other nine tribes did the same, each rode upon his star or his planet in the heavens. Joseph remained behind alone on the earth, and our father Jacob said to him, 'My son, why hast thou not done like thy brethren?' Joseph answered, 'What right have men born of woman to be in the heavens, seeing that in the end they must stay on earth?' While Joseph was speaking thus, a tall steer appeared before him. He had great pinions like the wings of the stork, and his horns were as long as those of the reem. Jacob urged his son, 'Up, Joseph, mount the steer!' Joseph did as his father bade him, and Jacob went his way. For the space of two hours Joseph displayed himself upon the steer, sometimes galloping, sometimes flying, until he reached Judah. Then Joseph unfolded the standard in his hand, and began to rain blows down upon Judah with it, and when his brother demanded the reason for this treatment, he said, 'Because thou hast twelve rods in thine hand, and I have but one. Give thine to me, and peace shall prevail between us!' But Judah refused to do his bidding, and Joseph beat him until he dropped ten rods, and only two remained in his clutch. Joseph now invited his brethren to abandon Judah and follow after him. They all did thus, except Benjamin, who stayed true to Judah. Levi was grieved over the desertion of Judah, and he descended from the sun. Toward the end of the day a storm broke out, and it scattered the brethren, so that no two were together. When I gave an account of my vision to my father Jacob, he said, 'It is but a dream, it can neither help nor harm'."

"A short while thereafter another vision was revealed to me. I saw all of us together with our father at the shores of the sea, and a ship appeared in the midst of the sea, and it had neither sailors nor other crew. Our father spake, 'Do you see what I see?' And when we answered that we did, he commanded us to follow him. He took off his clothes, and sprang into the sea, and we sprang after him. Levi and Judah were the first to scale the side of the ship. Our father cried after them, 'See what is written upon the mast', for there is no ship that does not bear the name of the owner upon the mast. Levi and Judah scrutinized the writing, and what they read was this, 'This ship and all the treasures therein belong unto the son of Barachel'. Jacob thanked God for having blessed him, not only on land, but also upon the sea, and he said to us, 'Stretch forth your hands, and whatsoever each one seizes shall be his!' Levi caught hold of the big mast, Judah of the second mast, next to Levi's, and the other brethren, with the exception of Joseph, took the oars, and Jacob himself seized the two rudders, wherewith to guide the ship. He bade Joseph take an oar, too, but he refused to do his father's bidding, and Jacob gave him one of the rudders. After our father had instructed us each one in what we had to do, he disappeared, whereupon Joseph took possession of the second rudder, too. All went smoothly for a time, as long as Judah and Joseph acted together in harmony with each other, and Judah kept Joseph informed in what direction to steer. But a quarrel broke out between them, and Joseph did not guide the vessel in the way his father had commanded him, and Judah attempted to direct him, and the vessel was wrecked upon a rock. Levi and Judah descended from the masts, and likewise the other brethren left the ship and escaped to the shore. At this moment Jacob appeared, and he found us scattered in all directions, and we reported to him how Joseph had caused the vessel to run aground, because he had refused, out of jealousy of Judah and Levi, to steer it according to their instructions. Then Jacob asked us to show him the spot where we had lost the ship, of which only the masts were visible above the water. He emitted a whistle summoning us all, and he swam out into the water, and raised the vessel as before. Turning to Joseph, he spake thus, 'My son, never do that again, never permit jealousy of thy brethren to master thee. Nearly it happened that all thy brethren perished because of thee'."

"When I told my father what I had seen in this vision, he clasped his hands, and tears flowed from his eyes, and be said: 'My son, for that the vision was doubled unto thee twice, I am dismayed, and I shudder for my son Joseph. I loved him more than all of you, but by reason of his perverseness ye will be carried away into captivity, and scattered among the nations. Thy first and thy second vision had the same meaning, the vision is one'."

"Therefore, my sons, I command you not to join yourselves unto the sons of Joseph, but ye shall join yourselves unto the sons of Levi and Judah. I tell you, too, that my inheritance shall be of the best of Palestine, the middle of the earth. You will eat, and the delectable gifts of my portion will satisfy you. But I warn you not to kick in your prosperity and not to become perverse, resisting the commands of God, who satisfies you with the best of His land, and not to forget your God, whom your father Abraham chose when the families of the earth were divided in the days of Peleg. The Lord descended with seventy angels, at their head Michael, and he commanded them to teach the seventy languages unto the seventy families of Noah. The angels did according to the behest of God, and the holy Hebrew language remained only in the house of Shem and Eber, and in the house of their descendant Abraham. On this day of teaching languages, Michael came to each nation separately, and told it the message with which God had charged him, saying: 'I know the rebellion and the confusion ye have enacted against God. Now, make choice of him whom you will serve, and whom will you have as your mediator in heaven?' Then spake Nimrod the wicked, 'In my eyes there is none greater than he that taught me the language of Cush'. The other nations also answered in words like these, each one designated its angel. But Abraham said: 'I choose none other than Him that spake and the world was. In Him I will have faith, and my seed forever and ever'. Thenceforth God put every nation in the care of its angel, but Abraham and his seed He kept for Himself."

"Therefore I adjure you not to go astray and serve other gods beside Him whom our fathers made choice of. You can perceive somewhat of His power in the creation of man. From head to foot is man wonderfully made. With his ears he hears, with his eyes he sees, with his brain he comprehends, with his nose he smells, with the tubes of his throat he utters sounds, with his gullet he swallows food, with his tongue he articulates, with his mouth he forms words, with his hands he does his work, with his heart he meditates, with his spleen he laughs, with his liver he waxes angry, with his stomach he crushes his food, with his feet he walks, with his lungs he breathes, and with his kidneys he makes resolves, and none of his organs undergoes a change in function, each performs its own. Therefore it behooves man to take to heart who it is that hath created him, and who hath developed him from a foul-smelling drop in the womb of woman, who hath brought him to the light of the world, who hath given sight to his eyes, and who hath bestowed the power of motion upon his feet, who maketh him to stand upright, who hath infused the breath of life into him, and who hath imparted of His own pure spirit unto him. Happy the man, therefore, that polluteth not the holy spirit of God within him by doing evil deeds, and well for him if he returns it to his Creator as he received it."

After Naphtali had charged his children thus, and with many other lessons like these, he enjoined them to carry his remains to Hebron, to be buried there near his fathers. Then he ate and drank with rejoicing, covered his face, and died, and his sons did according to all that their father Naphtali had commanded them.

Gad's Hatred

In the hundred and twenty-fifth year of his life Gad assembled his sons, and he spake to them: "I am the ninth son of Jacob, and I was a valiant shepherd of the flocks. I guarded the herds, and when a lion or any other wild beast approached, I pursued it, gripped it by the foot, flung it a stone's throw from me, and killed it thus. Once, for a space of thirty days, Joseph tended the flocks with us, and when he returned to our father, he told him that the sons of Zilpah and Bilhah slaughtered the best of the herds, and used the flesh without the knowledge of Reuben and Judah. He had seen me snatch a lamb out of the jaws of a bear, kill the bear, and slaughter the lamb, for it was too badly injured to live. I was wroth with Joseph for his talebearing, until he was sold into Egypt. I would neither look upon him nor hear aught about him, for to our very faces he, blamed us, because we had eaten the lamb without seeking the permission of Judah first. And whatever Joseph told our father, he believed.

"Now I confess my sin, that ofttimes I longed to kill him, for I hated him from the bottom of my heart, and on account of his dreams I hated him still more, and I desired to destroy him from off the land of the living. But Judah sold him by stealth to the Ishmaelites. Thus the God of our fathers saved him out of our hands, and He did not permit us to commit an abominable outrage in Israel."

"Hear now, my children, the words of truth, that ye may practice justice and the whole law of the Most High, and permit yourselves not to be tempted by the spirit of hatred. Evil is hatred, for it is the constant companion of deception, it always contradicts the truth. A little thing it magnifies into a great thing, light it takes for darkness, the sweet it calls bitter, and it teaches slander, enkindles anger, brings on war and violence, and fills the heart with devilish poison. I tell you my own experience, my children, that ye may drive hatred out of your hearts, and cleave to the love of the Lord. Righteousness banishes hatred, and humility kills it, for he that fears to give umbrage to the Lord, desires not to do wrong even in his thoughts. This is what I recognized at the last, after I had done penance on account of Joseph, for true atonement, pleasing to God, enlightens the eyes, illumines the soul with knowledge, and creates a counsel of salvation. My penance came in consequence of a sickness of the liver that God inflicted upon me. Without the prayers of my father Jacob, my spirit would have departed from me, for through the organ wherewith man transgresses, he is punished. As my liver had felt no mercy for Joseph, unmerciful suffering was caused unto me by my liver. My judgment lasted eleven months, as long as my enmity toward Joseph."

"And now, my children, each of you shall love his brother, and ye shall uproot hatred from your hearts by loving one another in word and deed and the thoughts of the soul. For I spake peaceably with Joseph in the presence of our father, but when I went out from before him, the spirit of hatred darkened my understanding, and stirred up my soul to murder him. If you see one that hath more good fortune than you, do not grieve, but pray for him, that his happiness may be perfect, and if one of the wicked even should grow rich in substance, like Esau, my father's brother, do not envy him. Wait for the end of the Lord."

"This also tell unto your children, that they shall honor Judah and Levi, for from them the Lord will cause a savior to arise unto Israel. For I know that in the end your children will fall off from God, and they will take part in all wickedness, malice, and corruptness, before the Lord."

After Gad had rested a little while, he spake again, "My children, hearken unto your father, and bury me with my fathers". Then he drew up his feet, and slept in peace. After five years, his sons carried his remains to Hebron unto his fathers.

Asher's Last Words

In the hundred and twenty-fifth year of his life, while be was still robust in health, Asher summoned his children unto him, and admonished them to walk in the ways of virtue and the fear of God. He spake: "Hearken, ye sons of Asher, unto your father, and I will show you all that is right before God. Two ways hath God put before the children of men, and two inclinations hath He bestowed upon them, two kinds of actions and two aims. Therefore all things are in twos, the one opposite to the other. But ye, my children, ye shall not be double, pursuing both goodness and wickedness. Ye shall cling only to the ways of goodness, for the Lord taketh delight in them, and men yearn after them. And flee from wickedness, for thus you will destroy the evil inclination. Heed well the commands of the Lord, by following truth with a single mind. Observe the law of the Lord, and have not the same care for wicked things as for good things. Rather keep your eyes upon what is truly good, and guard it through all the commands of the Lord. The end of man, when he meets the messengers of God and of Satan, shows whether he was righteous or unrighteous in his life. If his soul goes out with agitation, she will be plagued by the evil spirit, whom she served with her lusts and her evil deeds; but if she departs tranquilly, the angel of peace will lead her to life eternal.

"Be not like Sodom, my children, which recognized not the angels of the Lord, that ye be not delivered into the hands of your enemies, and your land be cursed, and your sanctuary destroyed, and you be scattered to the four corners of the earth, and scorned in the confusion like stale water, until the Most High shall visit the earth, and break the heads of the dragons in the waters. Tell this, my sons, unto your children, that they be not disobedient toward God, for I read in the tablets of the heavens that you will be contumacious and act impiously toward Him, in that you will have no care for the law of God, but you will heed human laws, and they are corrupted by reason of man's godlessness. Therefore ye will be dispersed abroad like unto Gad and Dan, my brethren, and you will not know either your land, or your tribe, or your tongue. Nevertheless the Lord will gather you in His faithfulness, for the sake of His gracious mercy, and for the sake of Abraham, Isaac, and Jacob."

And when he had made an end of saying these words, he commanded them to bury him in Hebron. And he sank into sweet sleep, and died. His sons did as he had commanded, and they carried him up and buried him with his fathers.

Benjamin Extols Joseph

Benjamin was one hundred and twenty-five years old, and he called his children to come to him. When they appeared, he kissed them, and spake: "As Isaac was born unto Abraham in his old age, so was I born unto Jacob when he was stricken in years. Therefore I was called Benjamin, 'the son of days'. My mother Rachel died at my birth, and Bilhah her slave suckled me. Rachel had no children for twelve years after bearing Joseph. Therefore she prayed to God, and fasted twelve days, and she conceived and bare me. Our father loved Rachel fondly, and he had longed greatly to have two sons by her.

"When I came down to Egypt, and my brother Joseph recognized me, he asked me, 'What said my brethren to my father regarding me?' And I told him that they had sent Jacob his coat stained with blood, and had said, 'Know now whether this be thy son's coat or not'. And Joseph said: 'This is what happened to me. Canaanitish merchantmen stole me away with violence, and on the way they wanted to hide my coat, to make it seem as though a wild beast had met me and slain me. But he who was about to conceal it, was torn by a lion, whereupon his companions, in great fear, sold me to the Ishmaelites. My brethren, thou seest, did not deceive my father with a lie'. In this wise Joseph tried to keep the deed of our brethren a secret from me. He also summoned my brethren, and enjoined them not to make known to our father what they had done to him, and bade them repeat the tale he had told me."

"Now, my children, love ye the Lord, the God of heaven and earth, and observe His commandments, taking that good and pious man Joseph as your model. Until the day of his death he would not have divulged what his brethren had done to him, and although God revealed their action to Jacob, he continued to deny it. Only after many efforts, when Jacob adjured him to confess the truth, he was induced to speak out. Even then he besought our father Jacob to pray for our brethren, that God account not the evil they had done to him as a sin. And Jacob exclaimed, 'O my good child Joseph, thou hast shown thyself more merciful than I was'!"

"My children, have you observed the mercy of the good man? Imitate it with pure intention, that ye, too, may wear crowns of glory. A good man has not an envious eye, he has mercy with all, even with sinners, though their evil designs be directed against him, and by his good deeds he conquers the evil, since it was ordained of God. If you do good, the unclean spirits will depart from you, and even the wild beasts will stand in fear of you. The inclination of a good man lies not in the power of the tempter spirit Behar, for the angel of peace guides his soul. Flee before the malice of Beliar, whose sword is drawn to slay all that pay him obedience, and his sword is the mother of seven evils, bloodshed, corruptness, error, captivity, hunger, panic, and devastation. Therefore God surrendered Cain to seven punishments. Once in a hundred years the Lord brought a castigation upon him. His afflictions began when he was two hundred years old, and in his nine hundredth year he was destroyed by the deluge, for having slain his righteous brother Abel. And those who are like unto Cain will be chastised forever with the same punishments as his."

"Know now, my children, that I am about to die. Practice truth and righteousness, and observe the law of the Lord and also His commandments. This I bequeath unto you as your sole heritage, and you shall leave it to your children as an eternal possession. Thus Abraham, Isaac, and Jacob did, they transmitted it unto us, saying, 'Observe the commands of God, until the Lord shall reveal His salvation in the sight of all the heathen'. Then you will see Enoch, Noah, Shem, Abraham, Isaac, and Jacob rise up with rejoicing to new life at the right hand of God, and we brethren, the sons of Jacob, will arise also, each of us at the head of his tribe, and we will pay homage to the King of the heavens."

After Benjamin had made an end of speaking thus, he said: "I command you, my children, to carry my bones up out of Egypt and bury me near my fathers".

And when he had made an end of saying these things, he fell asleep at a good old age, and they put his body into a coffin, and in the ninety-first year of their sojourning in Egypt, his sons and the sons of his brethren brought up the bones of their father, in secret, and buried them in Hebron, at the feet of their fathers. Then they returned from the land of Canaan, and they dwelt in Egypt until the day of the exodus from the land.

III. Job

Job and the Patriarchs

Job, the most pious Gentile that ever lived, one of the few to bear the title of honor "the servant of God", was of double kin to Jacob. He was a grandson of Jacob's brother Esau, and at the same time the son-in-law of Jacob himself, for lie had married Dinah as his second wife. He was entirely worthy of being a member of the Patriarch's family, for he was perfectly upright, one that feared God, and eschewed evil. Had he not wavered in his resignation to the Divine will during the great trial to which he was subjected, and murmured against God, the distinction would have been conferred upon him of having his name joined to the Name of God in prayer, and men would have called upon the God of Job as they now call upon the God of Abraham, Isaac, and Jacob. But he was not found steadfast like the three Fathers, and he forfeited the honor God had intended for him.

The Lord remonstrated with him for his lack of patience, saying: "Why didst thou murmur when suffering came upon thee? Dost thou think thyself of greater worth than Adam, the creation of Mine own hands, upon whom together with his descendants I decreed death on account of a single transgression? And yet Adam murmured not. Thou art surely not more worthy than Abraham, whom I tempted with many trials, and when he asked, 'Whereby shall I know that I shall inherit the land?' and I replied, 'Know of a surety that thy seed will be a stranger in a land that is not theirs, and shall serve them; and they shall afflict them four hundred years', he yet murmured not. Thou dost not esteem thyself more worthy than Moses, dost thou? Him I would not grant the favor of entering the promised land, because he spake the words, 'Hear now, ye rebels; shall we bring you forth water out of this rock?' And yet he murmured not. Art thou more worthy than Aaron, unto whom I showed greater honor than unto any created being, for I sent the angels themselves out of the Holy of Holies when he entered the place? Yet when his two sons died, he murmured not".

The contrast between Job and the Patriarchs appears from words spoken by him and words spoken by Abraham. Addressing God, Abraham said, "That be far from Thee to do after this manner, to slay the righteous with the wicked, that so the righteous should be as the wicked", and Job exclaimed against God, "It is all one; therefore I say, He destroyeth the perfect and the wicked". They both received their due recompense, Abraham was rewarded and Job was punished.

Convinced that his suffering was undeserved and unjust, Job had the audacity to say to God: "O Lord of the world, Thou didst create the ox with cloven feet and the ass with unparted hoof, Thou hast created Paradise and hell, Thou createst the righteous and also the wicked. There is none to hinder, Thou canst do as seemeth good in Thy sight". The friends of Job replied: "It is true, God hath created the evil inclination, but He hath also given man the Torah as a remedy against it. Therefore the wicked cannot roll their guilt from off their shoulders and put it upon God".

The reason Job did not shrink from such extravagant utterances was because he denied the resurrection of the dead. He judged of the prosperity of the wicked and the woes of the pious only by their earthly fortunes. Proceeding from this false premise, he held it to be possible that the punishment falling to his share was not at all intended for him. God had slipped into an error, He imposed the suffering upon him that had been appointed unto a sinner. But God spake to him, saying: "Many hairs have I created upon the head of man, yet each hair hath its own sac, for were two hairs to draw their nourishment from the same sac, man would lose the sight of his eyes. It hath never happened that a sac hath been misplaced. Should I, then, have mistaken Job for another? I let many drops of rain descend from the heavens, and for each drop there is a mould in the clouds, for were two drops to issue from the same mould, the ground would be made so miry that it could not bring forth any growth. It hath never happened that a mould hath been misplaced. Should I, then, have mistaken Job for another? Many thunderbolts I hurl from the skies, but each one comes from its own path, for were two to proceed from the same path, they would destroy the whole world. It hath never happened that a path hath been misplaced. Should I, then, have mistaken Job for another? The gazelle gives birth to her young on the topmost point of a rock, and it would fall into the abyss and be crushed to death, if I did not send an eagle thither to catch it up and carry it to its mother. Were the eagle to appear a minute earlier or later than the appointed time, the little gazelle would perish. It hath never happened that the proper minute of time was missed. Should I, then, have mistaken Job for another? The hind has a contracted womb, and would not be able to bring forth her young, if I did not send a dragon to her at the right second, to nibble at her womb and soften it, for then she can bear. Were the dragon to come a second before or after the right time, the hind would perish. It hath never happened that I missed the right second. Should I, then, have mistaken Job for another"?

Notwithstanding Job's unpardonable words, God was displeased with his friends for passing harsh judgment upon him. "A man may not be held responsible for what he does in his anguish", and Job's agony was great, indeed.

Job's Wealth and Benefactions

Job was asked once what he considered the severest affliction that could strike him, and he replied, "My enemies' joy in my misfortune, and when God demanded to know of him, after the accusations made by Satan, what he preferred, poverty or physical suffering, he chose pain, saying, "O Lord of the whole world, chastise my body with suffering of all kinds, only preserve me from poverty". Poverty seemed the greater scourge, because before his trials he had occupied a brilliant position on account of his vast wealth. God graciously granted him this foretaste of the Messianic time. The harvest followed close upon the ploughing of his field; no sooner were the seeds strewn in the furrows, than they sprouted and grew and ripened produce. He was equally successful with his cattle. His sheep killed wolves, but were themselves never harmed by wild beasts. Of sheep he had no less than one hundred and thirty thousand, and he required eight hundred dogs to keep guard over them, not to mention the two hundred dogs needed to secure the safety of his house. Besides, his herds consisted of three hundred and forty thousand asses and thirty-five hundred pairs of oxen. All these possessions were not used for self- indulgent pleasures, but for the good of the poor and the needy, whom he clothed, and fed, and provided with all things necessary. To do all this, he even had to employ ships that carried supplies to all the cities and the dwelling- places of the destitute. His house was furnished with doors on all its four sides, that the poor and the wayfarer might enter, no matter from what direction they approached. At all times there were thirty tables laden with viands ready in his house, and twelve besides for widows only, so that all who came found what they desired. Job's consideration for the poor was so delicate that he kept servants to wait upon them constantly. His guests, enraptured by his charitableness, frequently offered themselves as attendants to minister to the poor in his house, but Job always insisted upon paying them for their services. If he was asked for a loan of money, to be used for business purposes, and the borrower promised to give a part of his profits to the poor, he would demand no security beyond a mere signature. And if it happened that by some mischance or other the debtor was not able to discharge his obligation, Job would return the note to him, or tear it into bits in his presence.

He did not rest satisfied at supplying the material needs of those who applied to him. He strove also to convey the knowledge of God to them. After a meal he was in the habit of having music played upon instruments, and then he would invite those present to join him in songs of praise to God. On such occasions he did not consider himself above playing the cithern while the musicians rested.

Most particularly Job concerned himself about the weal and woe of widows and orphans. He was wont to pay visits to the sick, both rich and poor, and when it was necessary, he would bring a physician along with him. If the case turned out to be hopeless, he would sustain the stricken family with advice and consolation. When the wife of the incurably sick man began to grieve and weep, he would encourage her with such words as these: "Trust always in the grace and lovingkindness of God. He hath not abandoned thee until now, and He will not forsake thee henceforth. Thy husband will be restored to health, and will be able to provide for his family as heretofore. But if--which may God forefend--thy husband should die, I call Heaven to witness that I shall provide sustenance for thee and thy children". Having spoken thus, he would send for a notary, and have him draw up a document, which he signed in the presence of witnesses, binding himself to care for the family, should it be bereaved of its head. Thus he earned for himself the blessing of the sick man and the gratitude of the sorrowing wife.

Sometimes, in case of necessity, Job could be severe, too, especially when it was a question of helping a poor man obtain his due. If one of the parties to a suit cited before his tribunal was known to be a man of violence, he would surround himself with his army and inspire him with fear, so that the culprit could not but show himself amenable to his decision.

He endeavored to inculcate his benevolent ways upon his children, by accustoming them to wait upon the poor. On the morrow after a feast he would sacrifice bountifully to God, and together with the pieces upon the altar his offerings would be divided among the needy. He would say: "Take and help yourselves, and pray for my children. It may be that they have sinned, and renounced God, saying in the presumption of their hearts: 'We are the children of this rich man. All these things are our possessions. Why should we be servants to the poor'?".

Satan and Job

The happy, God-pleasing life led by Job for many years excited the hatred of Satan, who had an old grudge against him. Near Job's house there was an idol worshipped by the people. Suddenly doubts assailed the heart of Job, and he asked himself: "Is this idol really the creator of heaven and earth? How can I find out the truth about it"? In the following night he perceived a voice calling: "Jobab! Jobab! Arise, and I will tell thee who he is whom thou desirest to know. This one to whom the people offer sacrifices is not God, he is the handiwork of the tempter, wherewith he deceives men". When he heard the voice, Job threw himself on the ground, and said: "O Lord, if this idol is the handiwork of the tempter, then grant that I may destroy it. None can hinder me, for I am the king of this land".

Job, or, as he is sometimes called, Jobab, was, indeed, king of Edom, the land wherein wicked plans are concocted against God, wherefore it is called also Uz, "counsel".

The voice continued to speak. It made itself known as that of an archangel of God, and revealed to Job that he would bring down the enmity of Satan upon himself by the destruction of the idol, and much suffering with it. However, if he remained steadfast under them, God would change his troubles into joys, his name would become celebrated throughout the generations of mankind, and he would have a share in the resurrection to eternal life. Job replied to the voice: "Out of love of God I am ready to endure all things unto the day of my death. I will shrink back from naught". Now Job arose, and accompanied by fifty men he repaired to the idol, and destroyed it.

Knowing that Satan would try to approach him, he ordered his guard not to give access to any one, and then he withdrew to his chamber. He had guessed aright. Satan appeared at once, in the guise of a beggar, and demanded speech with Job. The guard executed his orders, and forbade his entering. Then the mendicant asked him to intercede for him with Job for a piece of bread. Job knew it was Satan, and he sent word to him as follows, "Do not expect to eat of my bread, for it is prohibited unto thee", at the same time putting a piece of burnt bread into the hand of the guard for Satan. The servant was ashamed to give a beggar burnt bread, and he substituted a good piece for it. Satan, however, knowing that the servant had not executed his master's errand, told him so to his face, and he fetched the burnt bread and handed it to him, repeating the words of Job. Thereupon Satan returned this answer, "As the bread is burnt, so I will disfigure thy body". Job replied: "Do as thou desirest, and execute thy plan. As for me, I am ready to suffer whatever thou bringest down upon me".

Now Satan betook himself to God, and prayed Him to put Job into his power, saying: "I went to and fro in the earth, and walked up and down in it, and I saw no man as pious as Abraham. Thou didst promise him the whole land of Palestine, and yet he did not take it in ill part that he had not so much as a burial-place for Sarah. As for Job, it is true, I found none that loveth Thee as he does, but if Thou wilt put him into my hand, I shall succeed in turning his heart away from Thee". But God spake, "Satan, Satan, what hast thou a mind to do with my servant Job, like whom there is none in the earth"? Satan persisted in his request touching Job, and God granted it, He gave him full power over Job's possessions.

This day of Job's accusation was the New Year's Day, whereon the good and the evil deeds of man are brought before God.

Job's Suffering

Equipped with unlimited power, Satan endeavored to deprive Job of all he owned. He burnt part of his cattle, and the other part was carried off by enemies. What pained Job more than this was that recipients of his bounty turned against him, and took of his belongings.

Among the adversaries that assailed him was Lilith, the queen of Sheba. She lived at a great distance from his residence, it took her and her army three years to travel from her home to his. She fell upon his oxen and his asses, and took possession of them, after slaying the men to whose care Job had entrusted them. One man escaped alone. Wounded and bruised, he had only enough life in him to tell Job the tale of his losses, and then he fell down dead. The sheep, which had been left unmolested by the queen of Sheba, were taken away by the Chaldeans. Job's first intention was to go to war against these marauders, but when he was told that some of his property had been consumed by fire from heaven, he desisted, and said, "If the heavens turn against me, I can do nothing".

Dissatisfied with the result, Satan disguised himself as the king of Persia, besieged the city of Job's residence, took it, and spoke to the inhabitants, saying: "This man Job hath appropriated all the goods in the world, leaving naught for others, and he hath also torn down the temple of our god, and now I will pay him back for his wicked deeds. Come with me and let us pillage his house". At first the people refused to hearken to the words of Satan. They feared that the sons and daughters of Job might rise up against them later, and avenge their father's wrongs. But after Satan had pulled down the house wherein the children of Job were assembled, and they lay dead in the ruins, the people did as he bade them, and sacked the house of Job.

Seeing that neither the loss of all he had nor the death of his children could change his pious heart, Satan appeared before God a second time, and requested that Job himself, his very person, be put into his hand. God granted Satan's plea, but he limited his power to Job's body, his soul he could not touch. In a sense Satan was worse off than Job. He was in the position of the slave that has been ordered by his master to break the pitcher and not spill the wine.

Satan now caused a terrific storm to burst over the house of Job. He was cast from his throne by the reverberations, and he lay upon the floor for three hours. Then Satan smote his body with leprosy from the sole of his foot unto his crown. This plague forced Job to leave the city, and sit down outside upon an ash-heap, for his lower limbs were covered with oozing boils, and the issue flowed out upon the ashes. The upper part of his body was encrusted with dry boils, and to ease the itching they caused him, he used his nails, until they dropped off together with his fingertips, and he took him a potsherd to scrape himself withal. His body swarmed with vermin, but if one of the little creatures attempted to crawl away from him, he forced it back, saying, "Remain on the place whither thou wast sent, until God assigns another unto thee". His wife, fearful that he would not bear his horrible suffering with steadfastness, advised him to pray to God for death, that lie might be sure of going hence an upright man. But he rejected her counsel, saying, "If in the days of good fortune, which usually tempts men to deny God, I stood firm, and did not rebel against Him, surely I shall be able to remain steadfast under misfortune, which compels men to be obedient to God". And Job stuck to his resolve in spite of all suffering, while his wife was not strong enough to bear her fate with resignation to the will of God.

Her lot was bitter, indeed, for she had had to take service as a water-carrier with a common churl, and when her master learnt that she shared her bread with Job, he dismissed her. To keep her husband from starving, she cut off her hair, and purchased bread with it. It was all she had to pay the price charged by the bread merchant, none other than Satan himself, who wanted to put her to the test. He said to her, "Hadst thou not deserved this great misery of thine, it had not come upon thee". This speech was more than the poor woman could bear. Then it was that she came to her husband, and amid tears and groans urged him to renounce God and die. Job, however, was not perturbed by her words, because he divined at once that Satan stood behind his wife, and seduced her to speak thus. Turning to the tempter, he said: "Why dost thou not meet me frankly? Give up thy underhand ways, thou wretch". Thereupon Satan appeared before Job, admitted that he had been vanquished, and went away abashed.

The Four Friends

The friends of Job lived in different places, at intervals of three hundred miles one from the other. Nevertheless they all were informed of their friend's misfortune at the same time, in this way: Each one had the pictures of the others set in his crown, and as soon as any one of them met with reverses, it showed itself in his picture. Thus the friends of Job learnt simultaneously of his misfortune, and they hastened to his assistance.

The four friends were related to one another, and each one was related to Job. Eliphaz, king of Teman, was a son of Esau; Bildad, Zophar, and Elihu were cousins, their fathers, Shuah, Naamat, and Barachel, were the sons of Buz, who was a brother of Job and a nephew of Abraham.

When the four friends arrived in the city in which Job lived, the inhabitants took them outside the gates, and pointing to a figure reclining upon an ash-heap at some distance off, they said, "Yonder is Job". At first the friends would not give them credence, and they decided to look more closely at the man, to make sure of his identity. But the foul smell emanating from Job was so strong that they could not come near to him. They ordered their armies to scatter perfumes and aromatic substances all around. Only after this had been done for hours, they could approach the outcast close enough to recognize him.

Eliphaz was the first to address Job, "Art thou indeed Job, a king equal in rank with ourselves"? And when Job said Aye, they broke out into lamentations and bitter tears, and all together they sang an elegy, the armies of the three kings, Eliphaz, Bildad, and Zophar, joining in the choir. Again Eliphaz began to speak, and he bemoaned Job's sad fortune, and depicted his friend's former glory, adding the refrain to each sentence, "Whither hath departed the splendor of thy throne"?

After listening long to the wailing and lamenting of Eliphaz and his companions, Job spake, saying: "Silence, and I will show you my throne and the splendor of its glory. Kings will perish, rulers disappear, their pride and lustre will pass like a shadow across a mirror, but my kingdom will persist forever and ever, for glory and magnificence are in the chariot of my Father".These words aroused the wrath of Eliphaz, and he called upon his associates to abandon Job to his fate and go their way. But Bildad appeased his anger, reminding him that some allowance ought to be made for one so sorely tried as Job. Bildad put a number of questions to the sufferer in order to establish his sanity. He wanted to elicit from Job how it came about that God, upon whom he continued to set his hopes, could inflict such dire suffering. Not even a king of flesh and blood would allow a guardsman of his that had served him loyally to come to grief. Bildad desired to have information from Job also concerning the movements of the heavenly bodies.

Job had but one answer to make to these questions: man cannot comprehend Divine wisdom, whether it reveal itself in inanimate and brute nature or in relation to human beings. "But", continued Job, "to prove to you that I am in my right mind, listen to the question I shall put to you. Solid food and liquids combine inside of man, and they separate again when they leave his body. Who effects the separation"? And when Bildad conceded that he could not answer the question, Job said, "If thou canst not comprehend the changes in thy body, how canst thou hope to comprehend the movements of the planets"?

Zophar, after Job had spoken thus to Bildad, was convinced that his suffering had had no effect upon his mind, and he asked him whether he would permit himself to be treated by the physicians of the three kings, his friends. But Job rejected the offer, saying, "My healing and my restoration come from God, the Creator of all physicians".

While the three kings were conversing thus with Job, his wife Zitidos made her appearance clad in rags, and she threw herself at the feet of her husband's friends, and amid tears she spoke, saying: "O Eliphaz, and ye other friends of Job, remember what I was in other days, and how I am now changed, coming before you in rags and tatters". The sight of the unhappy woman touched them so deeply that they could only weep, and not a word could they force out of their mouths. Eliphaz, however, took his royal mantle of purple, and laid it about the shoulders of the poor woman. Zitidos asked only one favor, that the three kings should order their soldiers to clear away the ruins of the building under which her children lay entombed, that she might give their remains decent burial. The command was issued to the soldiers accordingly, but Job said, "Do not put yourselves to trouble for naught. My children will not be found, for they are safely bestowed with their Lord and Creator". Again his friends were sure that Job was bereft of his senses. He arose, however, prayed to God, and at the end of his devotions, he bade his friends look eastward, and when they did his bidding, they beheld his children next to the Ruler of heaven, with crowns of glory upon their heads. Zitidos prostrated herself, and said, "Now I know that my memorial resides with the Lord". And she returned to the house of her master, whence she had absented herself for some time against his will. He had forbidden her to leave it, because he had feared that the three kings would take her with them.

In the evening she lay down to sleep next to the manger for the cattle, but she never rose again, she died there of exhaustion. The people of the city made a great mourning for her, and the elegy composed in her honor was set down in writing and recorded.

Job Restored

More and more the friends of Job came to the conclusion that he had incurred Divine punishment on account of his sins, and as he asseverated his innocence again and again, they prepared angrily to leave him to his fate. Especially Elihu was animated by Satan to speak scurrilous words against

Job, upbraiding him for his unshakable confidence in God. Then the Lord appeared to them, first unto Job, and revealed to him that Elihu was in the wrong, and his words were inspired by Satan. Next he appeared unto Eliphaz, and to him He spake thus: "Thou and thy friends Bildad and Zophar have committed a sin, for ye did not speak the truth concerning my servant Job. Rise up and let him bring a sin offering for you. Only for his sake do I refrain from destroying you".

The sacrifice offered by Job in behalf of his friends was accepted graciously by God, and Eliphaz broke out into a hymn of thanksgiving to the Lord for having pardoned the transgression of himself and his two friends. At the same time he announced the damnation of Elihu, the instrument of Satan.

God appeared to Job once more, and gave him a girdle composed of three ribands, and he bade him tie it around his waist. Hardly had he put it on when all his pain disappeared, his very recollection of it vanished, and, more than this, God made him to see all that ever was and all that shall ever be.

After suffering sevenfold pain for seven years Job was restored to strength. With his three friends he returned to the city, and the inhabitants made a festival in his honor and unto the glory of God. All his former friends joined him again, and he resumed his old occupation, the care of the poor, for which he obtained the means from the people around. He said to them, "Give me, each one of you, a sheep for the clothing of the poor, and four silver or gold drachmas for their other needs". The Lord blessed Job, and in a few days his wealth had increased to double the substance he had owned before misfortune overtook him. Zitidos having died during the years of his trials, he married a second wife, Dinah, the daughter of Jacob, and she bore him seven sons and three daughters. He had never had more than one wife at a time, for he was wont to say, "If it had been intended that Adam should have ten wives, God would have given them to him. Only one wife was bestowed upon him, whereby God indicated that he was to have but one, and therefore one wife suffices for me, too".

When Job, after a long and happy life, felt his end approaching, he gathered his ten children around him, and told them the tale of his days. Having finished the narrative, he admonished them in these words: "See, I am about to die, and you will stand in my place. Forsake not the Lord, be generous toward the poor, treat the feeble with consideration, and do not marry with the women of the Gentiles".

Thereupon he divided his possessions among his sons, and to his daughters he gave what is more precious than all earthly goods, to each of them one riband of the celestial girdle he had received from God. The magic virtue of these ribands was such that no sooner did their possessors tie them around their waists than they were transformed into higher beings, and with seraphic voices they broke out into hymns after the manner of the angels.

For three days Job lay upon his bed, sick though not suffering, for the celestial girdle made him proof against pain. On the fourth day he saw the angels descend to fetch his soul. He arose from his bed, handed a cithern to his oldest daughter Jemimah, "Day", a censer to the second one, Keziah, "Perfume", and a cymbal to the third, Amaltheas, "Horn", and bade them welcome the angels with the sound of music. They played and sang and praised the Lord in the holy tongue. Then he appeared that sits in the great chariot, kissed Job, and rode away bearing his soul with him eastward. None saw them depart except the three daughters of Job.

The grief of the people, especially the poor, the widows, and the orphans, was exceeding great. For three days they left the corpse unburied, because they could not entertain the thought of separating themselves from it.

As the name of Job will remain imperishable unto all time, by reason of the man's piety, so his three friends were recompensed by God for their sympathy with him in his distress. Their names were preserved, the punishment of hell was remitted unto them, and, best of all, God poured out the holy spirit over them. But Satan, the cause of Job's anguish, the Lord cast down from heaven, for he had been vanquished by Job, who amid his agony had thanked and praised God for all He had done unto him.

IV. Moses in Egypt

The Beginning of the Egyptian Bondage

As soon as Jacob was dead, the eyes of the Israelites were closed, as well as their hearts. They began to feel the dominion of the stranger, although real bondage did not enslave them until some time later. While a single one of the sons of Jacob was alive, the Egyptians did not venture to approach the Israelites with evil intent. It was only when Levi, the last of them, had departed this life that their suffering commenced. A change in the relation of the Egyptians toward the Israelites had, indeed, been noticeable immediately after the death of Joseph, but they did not throw off their mask completely until Levi was no more. Then the slavery of the Israelites supervened in good earnest.

The first hostile act on the part of the Egyptians was to deprive the Israelites of their fields, their vineyards, and the gifts that Joseph had sent to his brethren. Not content with these animosities, they sought to do them harm in, other ways. The reason for the hatred of the Egyptians was envy and fear. The Israelites had increased to a miraculous degree. At the death of Jacob the seventy persons he had brought down with him bad grown to the number of six hundred thousand, and their physical strength and heroism were extraordinary and therefore alarming to the Egyptians. There were many occasions at that time for the display of prowess. Not long after the death of Levi occurred that of the Egyptian king Magron, who had been bred up by Joseph, and therefore was not wholly without grateful recollection of what he and his family had accomplished for the welfare of Egypt. But his son and successor Malol, together with his whole court, knew not the sons of Jacob and their achievements, and they did not scruple to oppress the Hebrews.

The final breach between them and the Egyptians took place during the wars waged by Malol against Zepho, the grandson of Esau. In the course of it, the Israelites had saved the Egyptians from a crushing defeat, but instead of being grateful they sought only the undoing of their benefactors, from fear that the giant strength of the Hebrews might be turned against them.

Pharaoh's Cunning

The counsellors and elders of Egypt came to Pharaoh, and spake unto him, saying: "Behold, the people of the children of Israel are greater and mightier than we. Thou hast seen their strong power, which they have inherited from their fathers, for a few of them stood up against a people as many as the sand of the sea, and not one hath fallen. Now, therefore, give us counsel what to do with them, until we shall gradually destroy them from among us, lest they become too numerous in the land, for if they multiply, and there falleth out any war, they will also join themselves with their great strength unto our enemies, and fight against us, destroy us from the land, and get them up out of the land".

The king answered the elders, saying: "This is the plan advised by me against Israel, from which we will not depart. Behold, Pithom and Raamses are cities not fortified against battle. It behooves us to fortify them. Now, go ye and act cunningly against the children of Israel, and proclaim in Egypt and in Goshen, saying: 'All ye men of Egypt, Goshen, and Pathros! The king has commanded us to build Pithom and Raamses and fortify them against battle. Those amongst you in all Egypt, of the children of Israel and of all the inhabitants of the cities, who are willing to build with us, shall have their wages given to them daily at the king's order'.

"Then go ye first, and begin to build Pithom and Raamses, and cause the king's proclamation to be made daily, and when some of the children of Israel come to build, do ye give them their wages daily, and after they shall have built with you for their daily wages, draw yourselves away from them day by day, and one by one, in secret. Then you shall rise up and become their taskmasters and their officers, and you shall have them afterward to build without wages. And should they refuse, then force them with all your might to build. If you do this, it will go well with us, for we shall cause our land to be fortified after this manner, and with the children of Israel it will go ill, for they will decrease in number on account of the work, because you will prevent them from being with their wives."

The elders, the counsellors, and the whole of Egypt did according to the word of the king. For a month the servants of Pharaoh built with Israel, then they withdrew themselves gradually, while the children of Israel continued to work, receiving their daily wages, for some men of Egypt were still carrying on the work with them. After a time all the Egyptians had withdrawn, and they had turned to become the officers and taskmasters of the Israelites. Then they refrained from giving them any pay, and when some of the Hebrews refused to work without wages, their taskmasters smote them, and made them return by force to labor with their brethren. And the children of Israel were greatly afraid of the Egyptians, and they came again and worked without pay, all except the tribe of Levi, who were not employed in the work with their brethren. The children of Levi knew that the proclamation of the king was made to deceive Israel, therefore they refrained from listening to it, and the Egyptians did not molest them later, since they had not been with their brethren at the beginning, and though the Egyptians embittered the lives of the other Israelites with servile labor, they did not disturb the children of Levi. The Israelites called Malol, the king of Egypt, Maror, "Bitterness", because in his days the Egyptians embittered their lives with all manner of rigorous service.

But Pharaoh did not rest satisfied with his proclamation and the affliction it imposed upon the Israelites. He suspended a brick-press from his own neck, and himself took part in the work at Pithom and Raamses. After this, whenever a Hebrew refused to come and help with the building, alleging that he was not fit for such hard service, the Egyptians would retort, saying, "Dost thou mean to make us believe thou art more delicate than Pharaoh"?

The king himself urged the Israelites on with gentle words, saying, "My children, I beg you to do this work and erect these little buildings for me. I will give you great reward therefor". By means of such artifices and wily words the Egyptians succeeded in overmastering the Israelites, and once they had them in their power, they treated them with undisguised brutality. Women were forced to perform men's work, and men women's work.

The building of Pithom and Raamses turned out of no advantage to the Egyptians, for scarcely were the structures completed, when they collapsed, or they were swallowed by the earth, and the Hebrew workmen, besides having to suffer hardships during their erection, lost their lives by being precipitated from enormous heights, when the buildings fell in a heap.

But the Egyptians were little concerned whether or not they derived profit from the forced labor of the children of Israel. Their main object was to hinder their increase, and Pharaoh therefore issued an order, that they were not to be permitted to sleep at their own homes, that so they might be deprived of the opportunity of having intercourse with their wives. The officers executed the will of the king, telling the Hebrews that the reason was the loss of too much time in going to and fro, which would prevent them from completing the required tale of bricks. Thus the Hebrew husbands were kept apart from their wives, and they were compelled to sleep on the ground, away from their habitations.

But God spake, saying: "Unto their father Abraham I gave the promise, that I would make his children to be as numerous as the stars in the heavens, and you contrive plans to prevent them from multiplying. We shall see whose word will stand, Mine or yours". And it came to pass that the more the Egyptians afflicted them, the more they multiplied, and the more they spread abroad. And they continued to increase in spite of Pharaoh's command, that those who did not complete the required tale of bricks were to be immured in the buildings between the layers of bricks, and great was the number of the Israelites that lost their lives in this way. Many of their children were, besides, slaughtered as sacrifices to the idols of the Egyptians. For this reason God visited retribution upon the idols at the time of the going forth of the Israelites from Egypt. They had caused the death of the Hebrew children, and in turn they were shattered, and they crumbled into dust".

The Pious Midwives

When now, in spite of all their tribulations, the children of Israel continued to multiply and spread abroad, so that the land was full of them as with thick underbrush--for the women brought forth many children at a birth--the Egyptians appeared before Pharaoh again, and urged him to devise some other way of ridding the land of the Hebrews, seeing that they were increasing mightily, though they were made to toil and labor hard. Pharaoh could invent no new design; he asked his counsellors to give him their opinion of the thing. Then spake one of them, Job of the land of Uz, which is in Aram-naharaim, as follows: "The plan which the king invented, of putting a great burden of work upon the Israelites, was good in its time, and it should be executed henceforth, too, but to secure us against the fear that, if a war should come to pass, they may overwhelm us by reason of their numbers, and chase us forth out of the land, let the king issue a decree, that every male child of the Israelites shall be killed at his birth. Then we need not be afraid of them if we should be overtaken by war. Now let the king summon the Hebrew midwives, that they come hither, and let him command them in accordance with this plan".

Job's advice found favor in the eyes of Pharaoh and the Egyptians". They preferred to have the midwives murder the innocents, for they feared the punishment of God if they laid hands upon them themselves. Pharaoh cited the two midwives of the Hebrews before him, and commanded them to slay all men children, but to save the daughters of the Hebrew women alive", for the Egyptians were as much interested in preserving the female children as in bringing about the death of the male children. They were very sensual, and were desirous of having as many women as possible at their service".

However, the plan, even if it had been carried into execution, was not wise, for though a man may marry many wives, each woman can marry but one husband. Thus a diminished number of men and a corresponding increase in the number of women did not constitute so serious a menace to the continuance of the nation of the Israelites as the reverse case would have been.

The two Hebrew midwives were Jochebed, the mother of Moses, and Miriam, his sister. When they appeared before Pharaoh, Miriam exclaimed: "Woe be to this man when God visits retribution upon him for his evil deeds". The king would have killed her for these audacious words, had not Jochebed allayed his wrath by saying: "Why dost thou pay heed to her words? She is but a child, and knows not what she speaks". Yet, although Miriam was but five years old at the time, she nevertheless accompanied her mother, and helped her with her offices to the Hebrew women, giving food to the new-born babes while Jochebed washed and bathed them.

Pharaoh's order ran as follows: "At the birth of the child, if it be a man child, kill it; but if it be a female child, then you need not kill it, but you may save it alive". The midwives returned: "How are we to know whether the child is male or female"? for the king had bidden them kill it while it was being born. Pharaoh replied: "If the child issues forth from the womb with its face foremost, it is a man child, for it looks to the earth, whence man was taken; but if its feet appear first, it is a female, for it looks up toward the rib of the mother, and from a rib woman was made".

The king used all sorts of devices to render the midwives amenable to his wishes. He approached them with amorous proposals, which they both repelled, and then he threatened them with death by fire. But they said within themselves: "Our father Abraham opened an inn, that he might feed the wayfarers, though they were heathen, and we should neglect the children, nay, kill them? No, we shall have a care to keep them alive". Thus they failed to execute what Pharaoh had commanded. Instead of murdering the babes, they supplied all their needs. If a mother that had given birth to a child lacked food and drink, the midwives went to well-to-do women, and took up a collection, that the infant might not suffer want. They did still more for the little ones. They made supplication to God, praying: "Thou knowest that we are not fulfilling the words of Pharaoh, but it is our aim to fulfil Thy words. O that it be Thy will, our Lord, to let the child come into the world safe and sound, lest we fall under the suspicion that we tried to slay it, and maimed it in the attempt". The Lord hearkened to their prayer, and no child born under the ministrations of Shiphrah and Puah, or Jochebed and Miriam, as the midwives are also called, came into the world lame or blind or afflicted with any other blemish.

Seeing that his command was ineffectual, he summoned the midwives a second time, and called them to account for their disobedience. They replied: "This nation is compared unto one animal and another, and, in sooth, the Hebrews are like the animals. As little as the animals do they need the offices of midwives". These two God-fearing women were rewarded in many ways for their good deeds. Not only that Pharaoh did them no harm, but they were made the ancestors of priests and Levites, and kings and princes. Jochebed became the mother of the priest Aaron and of the Levite Moses, and from Miriam's union with Caleb sprang the royal house of David. The hand of God was visible in her married life. She contracted a grievous sickness, and though it was thought by all that saw her that death would certainly overtake her, she recovered, and God restored her youth, and bestowed unusual beauty upon her, so that renewed happiness awaited her husband, who had been deprived of the pleasures of conjugal life during her long illness. His unexpected joys were the reward of his piety and trust in God. And another recompense was accorded to Miriam: she was privileged to bring forth Bezalel, the builder of the Tabernacle, who was endowed with celestial wisdom.

The Three Counsellors

In the one hundred and thirtieth year after Israel's going down to Egypt Pharaoh dreamed that he was sitting upon his throne, and he lifted up his eyes, and he beheld an old man before him with a balance in his hand, and he saw him taking all the elders, nobles, and great men of Egypt, tying them together, and laying them in one scale of the balance, while he put a tender kid into the other. The kid bore down the pan in which it lay until it hung lower than the other with the bound Egyptians. Pharaoh arose early in the morning, and called together all his servants and his wise men to interpret his dream, and the men were greatly afraid on account of his vision. Balaam the son of Beor then spake, and said: "This means nothing but that a great evil will spring up against Egypt, for a son will be born unto Israel, who will destroy the whole of our land and all its inhabitants, and he will bring forth the Israelites from Egypt with a mighty hand. Now, therefore, O king, take counsel as to this matter, that the hope of Israel be frustrated before this evil arise against Egypt".

The king said unto Balaam: "What shall we do unto Israel? We have tried several devices against this people, but we could not prevail over it. Now let me hear thy opinion".

At Balaam's instance, the king sent for his two counsellors, Reuel the Midianite and Job the Uzite, to hear their advice. Reuel spoke: "If it seemeth good to the king, let him desist from the Hebrews, and let him not stretch forth his hand against them, for the Lord chose them in days of old, and took them as the lot of His inheritance from amongst all the nations of the earth, and who is there that hath dared stretch forth his hand against them with impunity, but that their God avenged the evil done unto them"? Reuel then proceeded to enumerate some of the mighty things God had performed for Abraham, Isaac, and Jacob, and he closed his admonition with the words: "Verily, thy grandfather, the Pharaoh of former days, raised Joseph the son of Jacob above all the princes of Egypt, because he discerned his wisdom, for through his wisdom he rescued all the inhabitants of the land from the famine, after which he invited Jacob and his sons to come down to Egypt, that the land of Egypt and the land of Goshen be delivered from the famine through their virtues. Now, therefore, if it seem good in thine eyes, leave off from destroying the children of Israel, and if it be not thy will that they dwell in Egypt, send them forth from here, that they may go to the land of Canaan, the land wherein their ancestors sojourned".

When Pharaoh heard the words of Jethro-Reuel, he was exceedingly wroth with him, and he was dismissed in disgrace from before the king, and he went to Midian.

The king then spoke to Job, and said: "What sayest thou, Job, and what is thy advice respecting the Hebrews"? Job replied: "Behold, all the inhabitants of the land are in thy power. Let the king do as seemeth good in his eyes".

Balaam was the last to speak at the behest of the king, and he said: "From all that the king may devise against the Hebrews, they will be delivered. If thou thinkest to diminish them by the flaming fire, thou wilt not prevail over them, for their God delivered Abraham their father from the furnace in which the Chaldeans cast him. Perhaps thou thinkest to destroy them with a sword, but their father Isaac was delivered from being slaughtered by the sword. And if thou thinkest to reduce them through hard and rigorous labor, thou wilt also not prevail, for their father Jacob served Laban in all manner of hard work, and yet he prospered. If it please the king, let him order all the male children that shall be born in Israel from this day forward to be thrown into the water. Thereby canst thou wipe out their name, for neither any of them nor any of their fathers was tried in this way.

The Slaughter of the Innocents

Balaam's advice was accepted by Pharaoh and the Egyptians. They knew that God pays measure for measure, therefore they believed that the drowning of the men children would be the safest means of exterminating the Hebrews, without incurring harm themselves, for the Lord had sworn unto Noah never again to destroy the world by water. Thus, they assumed, they would be exempt from punishment, wherein they were wrong, however. In the first place, though the Lord had sworn not to bring a flood upon men, there was nothing in the way of bringing men into a flood. Furthermore, the oath of God applied to the whole of mankind, not to a single nation. The end of the Egyptians was that they met their death in the billows of the Red Sea. "Measure for measure"--as they had drowned the men children of the Israelites, so they were drowned.

Pharaoh now took steps looking to the faithful execution of his decree. He sent his bailiffs into the houses of the Israelites, to discover all new-born children, wherever they might be. To make sure that the Hebrews should not succeed in keeping the children hidden, the Egyptians hatched a devilish plan. Their women were to take their little ones to the houses of the Israelitish women that were suspected of having infants. When the Egyptian children began to cry or coo, the Hebrew children that were kept in hiding would join in, after the manner of babies, and betray their presence, whereupon the Egyptians would seize them and bear them off.

Furthermore, Pharaoh commanded that the Israelitish women employ none but Egyptian midwives, who were to secure precise information as to the time of their delivery, and were to exercise great care, and let no male child escape their vigilance alive. If there should be parents that evaded the command, and preserved a new-born boy in secret, they and all belonging to them were to be killed.

Is it to be wondered at, then, that many of the Hebrews kept themselves away from their wives? Nevertheless those who put trust in God were not forsaken by Him. The women that remained united with their husbands would go out into the field when their time of delivery arrived, and give birth to their children and leave them there, while they themselves returned home. The Lord, who had sworn unto their ancestors to multiply them, sent one of His angels to wash the babes, anoint them, stretch their limbs, and swathe them. Then he would give them two smooth pebbles, from one of which they sucked milk, and from the other honey. And God caused the hair of the infants to grow down to their knees and serve them as a protecting garment, and then He ordered the earth to receive the babes, that they be sheltered therein until the time of their growing up, when it would open its mouth and vomit forth the children, and they would sprout up like the herb of the field and the grass of the forest. Thereafter each would return to his family and the house of his father.

When the Egyptians saw this, they went forth, every man to his field, with his yoke of oxen, and they ploughed up the earth as one ploughs it at seed time. Yet they were unable to do harm to the infants of the children of Israel that had been swallowed up and lay in the bosom of the earth. Thus the people of Israel increased and waxed exceedingly. And Pharaoh ordered his officers to go to Goshen, to look for the male babes of the children of Israel, and when they discovered one, they tore him from his mother's breast by force, and thrust him into the river". But no one is so valiant as to be able to foil God's purposes, though he contrive ten thousand subtle devices unto that end. The child foretold by Pharaoh's dreams and by his astrologers was brought up and kept concealed from the king's spies. It came to pass after the following manner.

The Parents of Moses

When Pharaoh's proclamation was issued, decreeing that the men children of the Hebrews were to be cast into the river, Amram, who was the president of the Sanhedrin, decided that in the circumstances it was best for husbands to live altogether separate from their wives. He set the example. He divorced his wife, and all the men of Israel did likewise, for he occupied a place of great consideration among his people, one reason being that he belonged to the tribe of Levi, the tribe that was faithful to its God even in the land of Egypt, though the other tribes wavered in their allegiance, and attempted to ally themselves with the Egyptians, going so far as to give up Abraham's sign of the covenant. To chastise the Hebrews for their impiety, God turned the love of the Egyptians for them into hatred, so that they resolved upon their destruction. Mindful of all that he and his people owed to Joseph's wise rule, Pharaoh refused at first to entertain the malicious plans proposed by the Egyptians against the Hebrews. He spoke to his people, "You fools, we are indebted to these Hebrews for whatever we enjoy, and you desire now to rise up against them"? But the Egyptians could not be turned aside from their purpose of ruining Israel. They deposed their king, and incarcerated him for three months, until he declared himself ready to execute with determination what they had resolved upon, and he sought to bring about the ruin of the children of Israel by every conceivable means. Such was the retribution they had drawn down upon themselves by their own acts.

As for Amram, not only did he belong to the tribe of Levi, distinguished for its piety, but by reason of his extraordinary piety he was prominent even among the pious of the tribe. He was one of the four who were immaculate, untainted by sin, over whom death would have had no power, had mortality not been decreed against every single human being on account of the fall of the first man and woman. The other three that led the same sinless life were Benjamin, Jesse the father of David, and Chileab the son of David. If the Shekinah was drawn close again to the dwelling-place of mortals, it was due to Amram's piety. Originally the real residence of the Shekinah was among men, but when Adam committed his sin, she withdrew to heaven, at first to the lowest of the seven heavens. Thence she was banished by Cain's crime, and she retired to the second heaven. The sins of the generation of Enoch removed her still farther off from men, she took up her abode in the third heaven; then, successively, in the fourth, on account of the malefactors in the generation of the deluge; in the fifth, during the building of the tower of Babel and the confusion of tongues; in the sixth, by reason of the wicked Egyptians at the time of Abraham; and, finally, in the seventh, in consequence of the abominations of the inhabitants of Sodom. Six righteous men, Abraham,

Isaac, Jacob, Levi, Kohath, and Amram, drew the Shekinah back, one by one, from the seventh to the first heaven, and through the seventh righteous man, Moses, she was made to descend to the earth and abide among men as aforetime.

Amram's sagacity kept pace with his piety and his learning. The Egyptians succeeded in enslaving the Hebrews by seductive promises. At first they gave them a shekel for every brick they made, tempting them to superhuman efforts by the prospect of earning much money. Later, when the Egyptians forced them to work without wages, they insisted upon having as many bricks as the Hebrews had made when their labor was paid for, but they could demand only a single brick daily from Amram, for he had been the only one whom they had not led astray by their artifice. He had been satisfied with a single shekel daily, and had therefore made only a single brick daily, which they had to accept afterward as the measure of his day's work.

As his life partner, Amram chose his aunt Jochebed, who was born the same day with him. She was the daughter of Levi, and she owed her name, "Divine Splendor", to the celestial light that radiated from her countenance. She was worthy of being her husband's helpmeet, for she was one of the midwives that had imperilled their own lives to rescue the little Hebrew babes. Indeed, if God had not allowed a miracle to happen, she and her daughter Miriam would have been killed by Pharaoh for having resisted his orders and saved the Hebrew children alive. When the king sent his hangmen for the two women, God caused them to become invisible, and the bailiffs bad to return without accomplishing their errand.

The first child of the union between Amram and Jochebed, his wife, who was one hundred and twenty-six years old at the time of her marriage, was a girl, and the mother called her Miriam, "Bitterness", for it was at the time of her birth that the Egyptians began to envenom the life of the Hebrews. The second child was a boy, called Aaron, which means, "Woe unto this pregnancy"! because Pharaoh's instructions to the midwives, to kill the male children of the Hebrews, was proclaimed during the months before Aaron's birth.

The Birth of Moses

When Amram separated from his wife on account of the edict published against the male children of the Hebrews, and his example was followed by all the Israelites, his daughter Miriam said to him: "Father, thy decree is worse than Pharaoh's decree. The Egyptians aim to destroy only the male children, but thou includest the girls as well. Pharaoh deprives his victims of life in this world, but thou preventest children from being born, and thus thou deprivest them of the future life, too. He resolves destruction, but who knows whether the intention of the wicked can persist? Thou art a righteous man, and the enactments of the righteous are executed by God, hence thy decree will be upheld".

Amram recognized the justice of her plea, and he repaired to the Sanhedrin, and put the matter before this body. The members of the court spoke, and said: "It was thou that didst separate husbands and wives, and from thee should go forth the permission for re-marriage". Amram then made the proposition that each of the members of the Sanhedrin return to his wife, and wed her clandestinely, but his colleagues repudiated the plan, saying, "And who will make it known unto the whole of Israel"?

Accordingly, Amram stood publicly under the wedding canopy with his divorced wife Jochebed, while Aaron and Miriam danced about it, and the angels proclaimed, "Let the mother of children be joyful"! His re-marriage was solemnized with great ceremony, to the end that the men that bad followed his example in divorcing their wives might imitate him now in taking them again unto themselves. And so it happened.

Old as Jochebed was, she regained her youth. Her skin became soft, the wrinkles in her face disappeared, the warm tints of maiden beauty returned, and in a short time she became pregnant.

Amram was very uneasy about his wife's being with child; he knew not what to do. He turned to God in prayer, and entreated Him to have compassion upon those who had in no wise transgressed the laws of His worship, and afford them deliverance from the misery they endured, while He rendered abortive the hope of their enemies, who yearned for the destruction of their nation. God had mercy on him, and He stood by him in his sleep, and exhorted him not to despair of His future favors. He said further, that He did not forget their piety, and He would always reward them for it, as He had granted His favor in other days unto their forefathers. "Know, therefore", the Lord continued to speak, "that I shall provide for you all together what is for your good, and for thee in particular that which shall make thee celebrated; for the child out of dread of whose nativity the Egyptians have doomed the Israelite children to destruction, shall be this child of thine, and be shall remain concealed from those who watch to destroy him, and when he has been bred up, in a miraculous way, he shall deliver the Hebrew nation from the distress they are under by reason of the Egyptians. His memory shall be celebrated while the world lasts, and not only among the Hebrews, but among strangers also. And all this shall be the effect of My favor toward thee and thy posterity. Also his brother shall be such that he shall obtain My priesthood for himself, and for his posterity after him, unto the end of the world".

After he had been informed of these things by the vision, Amram awoke, and told all unto his wife Jochebed.

His daughter Miriam likewise had a prophetic dream, and she related it unto her parents, saying: "In this night I saw a man clothed in fine linen. 'Tell thy father and thy mother', he said, 'that he who shall be born unto them, shall be cast into the waters, and through him the waters shall become dry, and wonders and miracles shall be performed through him, and he shall save My people Israel, and be their leader forever'".

During her pregnancy, Jochebed observed that the child in her womb was destined for great things. All the time she suffered no pain, and also she suffered none in giving birth to her son, for pious women are not included in the curse pronounced upon Eve, decreeing sorrow in conception and in childbearing.

At the moment of the child's appearance, the whole house was filled with radiance equal to the splendor of the sun and the moon. A still greater miracle followed. The infant was not yet a day old when he began to walk and speak with his parents, and as though he were an adult, he refused to drink milk from his mother's breast.

Jochebed gave birth to the child six months after conception. The Egyptian bailiffs, who kept strict watch over all pregnant women in order to be on the spot in time to carry off their new-born boys, had not expected her delivery for three months more. These three months the parents succeeded in keeping the babe concealed, though every Israelitish house was guarded by two Egyptian women, one stationed within and one without. At the end of this time they determined to expose the child, for Amram was afraid that both he and his son would be devoted to death if the secret leaked out, and he thought it better to entrust the child's fate to Divine Providence. He was convinced that God would protect the boy, and fulfil His word in truth.

Moses Rescued from the Water

Jochebed accordingly took an ark fashioned of bulrushes, daubed it with pitch on the outside, and lined it with clay within. The reason she used bulrushes was because they float on the surface of the water, and she put pitch only on the outside, to protect the child as much as possible against the annoyance of a disagreeable odor. Over the child as it lay in the ark she spread a tiny canopy, to shade the babe, with the words, "Perhaps I shall not live to see him under the marriage canopy". And then she abandoned the ark on the shores of the Red Sea. Yet it was not left unguarded. Her daughter Miriam stayed near by, to discover whether a prophecy she had uttered would be fulfilled. Before the child's birth, his sister had foretold that her mother would bring forth a son that should redeem Israel. When he was born, and the house was filled with brilliant light, Amram kissed her on her head, but when he was forced into the expedient of exposing the child, he beat her on her head, saying, "My daughter, what hath become of thy prophecy"? Therefore Miriam stayed, and strolled along the shore, to observe what would be the fate of the babe, and what would come of her prophecy concerning him.

The day the child was exposed was the twenty-first of the month of Nisan, the same on which the children of Israel later, under the leadership of Moses, sang the song of praise and gratitude to God for the redemption from the waters of the sea. The angels appeared before God, and spoke: "O Lord of the world, shall he that is appointed to sing a song of praise unto Thee on this day of Nisan, to thank Thee for rescuing him and his people from the sea, shall he find his death in the sea to-day"? The Lord replied: "Ye know well that I see all things. The contriving of man can do naught to change what bath been resolved in My counsel. Those do not attain their end who use cunning and malice to secure their own safety, and endeavor to bring ruin upon their fellow-men. But he who trusts Me in his peril will be conveyed from profoundest distress to unlooked-for happiness. Thus My omnipotence will reveal itself in the fortunes of this babe.

At the time of the child's abandonment, God sent scorching heat to plague the Egyptians, and they all suffered with leprosy and smarting boils. Thermutis, the daughter of Pharaoh, sought relief from the burning pain in a bath in the waters of the Nile. But physical discomfort was not her only reason for leaving her father's palace. She was determined to cleanse herself as well of the impurity of the idol worship that prevailed there.

When she saw the little ark floating among the flags on the surface of the water, she supposed it to contain one of the little children exposed at her father's order, and she commanded her handmaids to fetch it. But they protested, saying, "O our mistress, it happens sometimes that a decree issued by a king is unheeded, yet it is observed at least by his children and the members of his household, and dost thou desire to transgress thy father's edict"? Forthwith the angel Gabriel appeared, seized all the maids except one, whom he permitted the princess to retain for her service, and buried them in the bowels of the earth.

Pharaoh's daughter now proceeded to do her own will. She stretched forth her arm, and although the ark was swimming at a distance of sixty ells, she succeeded in grasping it, because her arm was lengthened miraculously. No sooner had she touched it than the leprosy afflicting her departed from her. Her sudden restoration led her to examine the contents of the ark, and when she opened it, her amazement was great. She beheld an exquisitely beautiful boy, for God bad fashioned the Hebrew babe's body with peculiar care, and beside it she perceived the Shekinah. Noticing that the boy bore the sign of the Abrahamic covenant, she knew that he was one of the Hebrew children, and mindful of her father's decree concerning the male children of the Israelites, she was about to abandon the babe to his fate. At that moment the angel Gabriel came and gave the child a vigorous blow, and he began to cry aloud, with a voice like a young man's. His vehement weeping and the weeping of Aaron, who was lying beside him, touched the princess, and in her pity she resolved to save him. She ordered an Egyptian woman to be brought, to nurse the child, but the little one refused to take milk from her breast, as he refused to take it from one after the other of the Egyptian women fetched thither. Thus it had been ordained by God, that none of them might boast later on, and say, "I suckled him that holds converse now with the Shekinah". Nor was the mouth destined to speak with God to draw nourishment from the unclean body of an Egyptian woman.

Now Miriam stepped into the presence of Thermutis, as though she had been standing there by chance to look at the child, and she spoke to the princess, saying, "It is vain for thee, O queen, to call for nurses that are in no wise of kin to the child, but if thou wilt order a woman of the Hebrews to be brought, he may accept her breast, seeing that she is of his own nation". Thermutis therefore bade Miriam fetch a Hebrew woman, and with winged steps, speeding like a vigorous youth, she hastened and brought back her own mother, the child's mother, for she knew that none present was acquainted with her. The babe, unresisting, took his mother's breast, and clutched it tightly. The princess committed the child to Jochebed's care, saying these words, which contained an unconscious divination: "Here is what is thine". Nurse the boy henceforth, and I will give thee two silver pieces as thy wages.

The return of her son, safe and sound, after she had exposed him, was Jochebed's reward from God for her services as one of the midwives that had bidden defiance to Pharaoh's command and saved the Hebrew children alive.

By exposing their son to danger, Amram and Jochebed had effected the withdrawal of Pharaoh's command enjoining the extermination of the Hebrew men children. The day Moses was set adrift in the little ark, the astrologers had come to Pharaoh and told him the glad tidings, that the danger threatening the Egyptians on account of one boy, whose doom lay in the water, had now been averted. Thereupon Pharaoh cried a halt to the drowning of the boys of his empire. The astrologers had seen something, but they knew not what, and they announced a message, the import of which they did not comprehend. Water was, indeed, the doom of Moses, but that did not mean that he would perish in the waters of the Nile. It had reference to the waters of Meribah, the waters of strife, and how they would cause his death in the desert, before he had completed his task of leading the people into the promised land. Pharaoh, misled by the obscure vision of his astrologers, thought that the future redeemer of Israel was to lose his life by drowning, and to make sure that the boy whose appearance was foretold by the astrologers might not escape his fate, he had ordered all boys, even the children of the Egyptians, born during a period of nine months to be cast into the water.

On account of the merits of Moses, the six hundred thousand men children of the Hebrews begotten in the same night with him, and thrown into the water on the same day, were rescued miraculously together with him, and it was therefore not an idle boast, if he said later, "The people that went forth out of the water on account of my merits are six hundred thousand men".

The Infancy of Moses

For two years the child rescued by Pharaoh's daughter stayed with his parents and kindred. They gave him various names. His father called him Heber, because it was for this child's sake that he had been "reunited" with his wife. His mother's name for him was Jekuthiel, "because", she said, "I set my hope upon God, and He gave him back to me". To his sister Miriam he was Jered, because she had "descended" to the stream to ascertain his fate. His brother Aaron called him Abi Zanoah, because his father, who had "cast off" his mother, had taken her back for the sake of the child to be born. His grandfather Kohath knew him as Abi Gedor, because the Heavenly Father had "built up" the breach in Israel, when He rescued him, and thus restrained the Egyptians from throwing the Hebrew men children into the water. His nurse called him Abi Soco, because he had been kept concealed in a "tent" for three months, escaping the pursuit of the Egyptians. And Israel called him Shemaiah ben Nethanel, because in his day God would "hear" the sighs of the people, and deliver them from their oppressors, and through him would He "give" them His own law.

His kindred and all Israel knew that the child was destined for great things, for he was barely four months old when he began to prophesy, saying, "In days to come I shall receive the Torah from the flaming torch".

When Jochebed took the child to the palace at the end of two years, Pharaoh's daughter called him Moses, because she had "drawn" him out of the water, and because he would "draw" the children of Israel out of the land of Egypt in a day to come. And this was the only name whereby God called the son of Amram, the name conferred upon him by Pharaoh's daughter. He said to the princess: "Moses was not thy child, yet thou didst treat him as such. For this I will call thee My daughter, though thou art not My daughter", and therefore the princess, the daughter of Pharaoh, bears the name Bithiah, "the daughter of God". She married Caleb later on, and he was a suitable husband for her. As she stood up against her father's wicked counsels, so Caleb stood up against the counsel of his fellow-messengers sent to spy out the land of Canaan. For rescuing Moses and for her other pious deeds, she was permitted to enter Paradise alive.

That Moses might receive the treatment at court usually accorded to a prince, Bithiah pretended that she was with child for some time before she had him fetched away from his parents' house". His royal foster-mother caressed and kissed him constantly, and on account of his extraordinary beauty she would not permit him ever to quit the palace. Whoever set eyes on him, could not leave off from looking at him, wherefore Bithiah feared to allow him out of her sight.

Moses' understanding was far beyond his years; his instructors observed that he disclosed keener comprehension than is usual at his age. All his actions in his infancy promised greater ones after he should come to man's estate, and when he was but three years old, God granted him remarkable size. As for his beauty, it was so attractive that frequently those meeting him as he was carried along on the road were obliged to turn and stare at him. They would leave what they were about, and stand still a great while, looking after him, for the loveliness of the child was so wondrous that it held the gaze of the spectator. The daughter of Pharaoh, perceiving Moses to be an extraordinary lad, adopted him as her son, for she had no child of her own. She informed her father of her intention concerning him, in these words: "I have brought up a child, who is divine in form and of an excellent mind, and as I received him through the bounty of the river in a wonderful way, I have thought it proper to adopt him as my son and as the heir of thy kingdom". And when she had spoken thus, she put the infant between her father's hands, and he took him and hugged him close to his breast.

Moses Rescued by Gabriel

When Moses was in his third year, Pharaoh was dining one day, with the queen Alfar'anit at his right hand, his daughter Bithiah with the infant Moses upon her lap at his left, and Balaam the son of Beor together with his two sons and all the princes of the realm sitting at table in the king's presence. It happened that the infant took the crown from off the king's head, and placed it on his own. When the king and the princes saw this, they were terrified, and each one in turn expressed his astonishment. The king said unto the princes, "What speak you, and what say you, O ye princes, on this matter, and what is to be done to this Hebrew boy on account of this act"?

Balaam spoke, saying: "Remember now, O my lord and king, the dream which thou didst dream many days ago, and how thy servant interpreted it unto thee. Now this is a child of the Hebrews in whom is the spirit of God. Let not my lord the king imagine in his heart that being a child he did the thing without knowledge. For he is a Hebrew boy, and wisdom and understanding are with him, although he is yet a child, and with wisdom has he done this, and chosen unto himself the kingdom of Egypt. For this is the manner of all the Hebrews, to deceive kings and their magnates, to do all things cunningly in order to make the kings of the earth and their men to stumble.

"Surely thou knowest that Abraham their father acted thus, who made the armies of Nimrod king of Babel and of Abimelech king of Gerar to stumble, and he possessed himself of the land of the children of Heth and the whole realm of Canaan. Their father Abraham went down into Egypt, and said of Sarah his wife, She is my sister, in order to make Egypt and its king to stumble.

"His son Isaac did likewise when he went to Gerar, and he dwelt there, and his strength prevailed over the army of Abimelech, and he intended to make the kingdom of the Philistines to stumble, by saying that Rebekah his wife was his sister."

"Jacob also dealt treacherously with his brother, and took his birthright and his blessing from him. Then he went to Paddan-aram, to Laban, his mother's brother, and he obtained his daughters from him cunningly, and also his cattle and all his belongings, and he fled away and returned to the land of Canaan, to his father."

"His sons sold their brother Joseph, and he went down into Egypt and became a slave, and he was put into prison for twelve years, until the former Pharaoh delivered him from the prison, and magnified him above all the princes of Egypt on account of his interpreting the king's dreams. When God caused a famine to descend upon the whole world, Joseph sent for his father, and he brought him down into Egypt his father, his brethren, and all his father's household, and he supplied them with food without pay or reward, while he acquired Egypt, and made slaves of all its inhabitants."

"Now, therefore, my lord king, behold, this child has risen up in their stead in Egypt, to do according to their deeds and make sport of every man, be he king, prince, or judge. If it please the king, let us now spill his blood upon the ground, lest he grow up and snatch the government from thine hand, and the hope of Egypt be cut off after he reigns. Let us, moreover, call for all the judges and the wise men of Egypt, that we may know whether the judgment of death be due to this child, as I have said, and then we will slay him."

Pharaoh sent and called for all the wise men of Egypt, and they came, and the angel Gabriel was disguised as one of them. When they were asked their opinion in the matter, Gabriel spoke up, and said: "If it please the king, let him place an onyx stone before the child, and a coal of fire, and if he stretches out his hand and grasps the onyx stone, then shall we know that the child hath done with wisdom all that he bath done, and we will slay him. But if he stretches out his hand and grasps the coal of fire, then shall we know that it was not with consciousness that he did the thing, and he shall live".

The counsel seemed good in the eyes of the king, and when they had placed the stone and the coal before the child, Moses stretched forth his hand toward the onyx stone and attempted to seize it, but the angel Gabriel guided his hand away from it and placed it upon the live coal, and the coal burnt the child's hand, and he lifted it up and touched it to his mouth, and burnt part of his lips and part of his tongue, and for all his life he became slow of speech and of a slow tongue.

Seeing this, the king and the princes knew that Moses had not acted with knowledge in taking the crown from off the king's head, and they refrained from slaying him. God Himself, who protected Moses, turned the king's mind to grace, and his foster-mother snatched him away, and she had him educated with great care, so that the Hebrews depended upon him, and cherished the hope that great things would be done by him. But the Egyptians were suspicious of what would follow from such an education as his.

At great cost teachers were invited to come to Egypt from neighboring lands, to educate the child Moses. Some came of their own accord, to instruct him in the sciences and the liberal arts. By reason of his admirable endowments of mind, he soon excelled his teachers in knowledge. His learning seemed a process of mere recollecting, and when there was a difference of opinion among scholars, he selected the correct one instinctively, for his mind refused to store up anything that was false.

But he deserves more praise for his unusual strength of will than for his natural capacity, for he succeeded in transforming an originally evil disposition into a noble, exalted character, a change that was farther aided by his resolution, as he himself acknowledged later. After the wonderful exodus of the Israelites from Egypt, a king of Arabia sent an artist to Moses, to paint his portrait, that he might always have the likeness of the divine man before him. The painter returned with his handiwork, and the king assembled his wise men, those in particular who were conversant with the science of physiognomy. He displayed the portrait before them, and invited their judgment upon it. The unanimous opinion was that it represented a man covetous, haughty, sensual, in short, disfigured by all possible ugly traits. The king was indignant that they should pretend to be masters in physiognomy, seeing that they declared the picture of Moses, the holy, divine man, to be the picture of a villain. They defended themselves by accusing the painter in turn of not having produced a true portrait of Moses, else they would not have fallen into the erroneous judgment they had expressed. But the artist insisted that his work resembled the original closely.

Unable to decide who was right, the Arabian king went to see Moses, and he could not but admit that the portrait painted for him was a masterpiece. Moses as he beheld him in the flesh was the Moses upon the canvas. There could be no doubt but that the highly extolled knowledge of his physiognomy experts was empty twaddle. He told Moses what had happened, and what he thought of it. He replied: "Thy artist and thy experts alike are masters, each in his line. If my fine qualities were a product of nature, I were no better than a log of wood, which remains forever as nature produced it at the first. Unashamed I make the confession to thee that by nature I possessed all the reprehensible traits thy wise men read in my picture and ascribed to me, perhaps to a greater degree even than they think. But I mastered my evil impulses with my strong will, and the character I acquired through severe discipline has become the opposite of the disposition with which I was born. Through this change, wrought in me by my own efforts, I have earned honor and commendation upon earth as well as in heaven".

The Youth of Moses

One day--it was after he was grown up, and had passed beyond the years of childhood--Moses went to the land of Goshen, in which lived the children of Israel. There he saw the burdens under which his people were groaning, and he inquired why the heavy service had been put upon them. The Israelites told him all that had befallen, told him of the cruel edict Pharaoh had issued shortly before his birth, and told him of the wicked counsels given by Balaam against themselves as well as against his person when he was but a little boy and had set Pharaoh's crown upon his head. The wrath of Moses was kindled against the spiteful adviser, and he tried to think out means of rendering him harmless. But Balaam, getting wind of his ill-feeling, fled from

Egypt with his two sons, and betook himself to the court of Kikanos king of Ethiopia.

The sight of his enslaved people touched Moses unto tears, and he spoke, saying: "Woe unto me for your anguish! Rather would I die than see you suffer so grievously". He did not disdain to help his unfortunate brethren at their heavy tasks as much as lay in his power. He dismissed all thought of his high station at court, shouldered a share of the burdens put upon the Israelites, and toiled in their place. The result was that he not only gave relief to the heavily-laden workmen, but he also gained the favor of Pharaoh, who believed that Moses was taking part in the labor in order to promote the execution of the royal order. And God said unto Moses: "Thou didst relinquish all thy other occupations, and didst join thyself unto the children of Israel, whom thou dost treat as brethren; therefore will I, too, put aside now all heavenly and earthly affairs, and hold converse with thee".

Moses continued to do all he could to alleviate the suffering of his brethren to the best of his ability. He addressed encouraging words to them, saying: "My dear brethren, bear your lot with fortitude! Do not lose courage, and let not your spirit grow weary with the weariness of your body. Better times will come, when tribulation shall be changed into joy. Clouds are followed by sunshine, storms by calm, all things in the world tend toward their opposites, and nothing is more inconstant than the fortunes of man".

The royal favor, which the king accorded him in ever- increasing measure, he made use of to lighten the burden laid upon the children of Israel. One day he came into the presence of Pharaoh, and said: "O my lord, I have a request to make of thee, and my hope is that thou wilt not deny it". "Speak", replied the king. "It is an admitted fact", said Moses, "that if a slave is not afforded rest at least one day in the week, he will die of overexertion. Thy Hebrew slaves will surely perish, unless thou accordest them a day of cessation from work". Pharaoh fulfilled the petition preferred by Moses, and the king's edict was published in the whole of Egypt and in Goshen, as follows: "To the sons of Israel! Thus saith the king: Do your work and perform your service for six days, but on the seventh day you shall rest; on it ye shall do no labor. Thus shall ye do unto all times, according to the command of the king and the command of Moses the son of Bithiah". And the day appointed by Moses as the day of rest was Saturday, later given by God to the Israelites as the Sabbath day.

While Moses abode in Goshen, an incident of great importance occurred. To superintend the service of the children of Israel, an officer from among them was set over every ten, and ten such officers were under the surveillance of an Egyptian taskmaster. One of these Hebrew officers, Dathan by name, had a wife, Shelomith, the daughter of Dibri, of the tribe of Dan, who was of extraordinary beauty, but inclined to be very loquacious. Whenever the Egyptian taskmaster set over her husband came to their house on business connected with his office, she would approach him pleasantly and enter into conversation with him. The beautiful Israelitish woman enkindled a mad passion in his breast, and he sought and found a cunning way of satisfying his lustful desire. One day he appeared at break of dawn at the house of Dathan, roused him from his sleep, and ordered him to hurry his detachment of men to their work. The husband scarcely out of sight, he executed the villainy he had planned, and dishonored the woman, and the fruit of this illicit relation was the blasphemer of the Name whom Moses ordered to execution on the march through the desert.

At the moment when the Egyptian slipped out of Shelomith's chamber, Dathan returned home. Vexed that his crime had come to the knowledge of the injured husband, the taskmaster goaded him on to work with excessive vigor, and dealt him blow after blow with the intention to kill him. Young Moses happened to visit the place at which the much-abused and tortured Hebrew was at work. Dathan hastened toward him, and complained of all the wrong and suffering the Egyptian had inflicted upon him. Full of wrath, Moses, whom the holy spirit had acquainted with the injury done the Hebrew officer by the Egyptian taskmaster, cried out to the latter, saying: "Not enough that thou hast dishonored this man's wife, thou aimest to kill him, too"? And turning to God, he spoke further: "What will become of Thy promise to Abraham, that his posterity shall be as numerous as the stars, if his children are given over to death? And what will become of the revelation on Sinai, if the children of Israel are exterminated"?

Moses wanted to see if someone would step forward, and, impelled by zeal for the cause of God and for God's law, would declare himself ready to avenge the outrage. He waited in vain. Then he determined to act himself. Naturally enough he hesitated to take the life of a human being. He did not know whether the evil-doer might not be brought to repentance, and then lead a life of pious endeavor. He also considered, that there would perhaps be some among the descendants to spring from the Egyptian for whose sake their wicked ancestor might rightfully lay claim to clemency. The holy spirit allayed all his doubts. He was made to see that not the slightest hope existed that good would come either from the malefactor himself or from any of his offspring. Then Moses was willing to requite him for his evil deeds. Nevertheless he first consulted the angels, to hear what they had to say, and they agreed that the Egyptian deserved death, and Moses acted according to their opinion.

Neither physical strength nor a weapon was needed to carry out his purpose. He merely pronounced the Name of God, and the Egyptian was a corpse. To the bystanders, the Israelites, Moses said: "The Lord compared you unto the sand of the sea-shore, and as the sand moves noiselessly from place to place, so I pray you to keep the knowledge of what hath happened a secret within yourselves. Let nothing be heard concerning it".

The wish expressed by Moses was not honored. The slaying of the Egyptian remained no secret, and those who betrayed it were Israelites, Dathan and Abiram, the sons of Pallu, of the tribe of Reuben, notorious for their effrontery and contentiousness. The day after the thing with the Egyptians happened, the two brothers began of malice aforethought to scuffle with each other, only in order to draw Moses into the quarrel and create an occasion for his betrayal. The plan succeeded admirably. Seeing Dathan raise his hand against Abiram, to deal him a blow, Moses exclaimed, "O thou art a villain, to lift up thy hand against an Israelite, even if he is no better than thou". Dathan replied: "Young man, who hath made thee to be a judge over us, thou that hast not yet attained to years of maturity? We know very well that thou art the son of Jochebed, though people call thee the son of the princess Bithiah, and if thou shouldst attempt to play the part of our master and judge, we will publish abroad the thing thou didst unto the Egyptian. Or, peradventure, thou harborest the intention to slay us as thou didst slay him, by pronouncing the Name of God"?

Not satisfied with these taunts, the noble pair of brothers betook themselves to Pharaoh, and spoke before him, "Moses dishonoreth thy royal mantle and thy crown", to which Pharaoh returned, saying, "Much good may it do him"! But they pursued the subject. "He helps thine enemies, Pharaoh", they continued, whereupon he replied, as before, "Much good may it do him"! Still they went on, "He is not the son of thy daughter". These last words did not fail of making an impression upon Pharaoh. A royal command was issued for the arrest of Moses, and he was condemned to death by the sword.

The angels came to God, and said, "Moses, the familiar of Thine house, is held under restraint", and God replied, "I will espouse his cause". "But", the angels urged, "his verdict of death has been pronounced--yes, they are leading him to execution", and again God made reply, as before, "I will espouse his cause".

Moses mounted the scaffold, and a sword, sharp beyond compare, was set upon his neck ten times, but it always slipped away, because his neck was as hard as ivory. And a still greater miracle came to pass. God sent down the angel Michael, in the guise of a hangman, and the human hangman charged by Pharaoh with the execution was changed into the form of Moses. This spurious Moses the angel killed with the very sword with which the executioner had purposed to slay the intended victim. Meantime Moses took to flight. Pharaoh ordered his pursuit, but it was in vain. The king's troops were partly stricken with blindness partly with dumbness. The dumb could give no information about the abiding-place of Moses, and the blind, though they knew where it was, could not get to it.

The Flight

An angel of God took Moses to a spot removed forty days' journey from Egypt, so far off that all fear was banished from his mind. Indeed, his anxiety had never been for his own person, but only on account of the future of Israel. The subjugation of his people had always been an unsolved enigma to him. Why should Israel, he would ask himself, suffer more than all the other nations? But when his personal straits initiated him in the talebearing and back- biting that prevailed among the Israelites, then he asked himself, Does this people deserve to be redeemed? The religious conditions among the children of Israel were of such kind at that time as not to permit them to hope for Divine assistance. They refused to give ear to Aaron and the five sons of Zerah, who worked among them as prophets, and admonished them unto the fear of God. It was on account of their impiety that the heavy hand of Pharaoh rested upon them more and more oppressively, until God had mercy upon them, and sent Moses to deliver them from the slavery of Egypt.

When he succeeded in effecting his escape from the hands of the hangman, Moses had no idea that a royal throne awaited him. It was nevertheless so. A war broke out at this time between Ethiopia and the nations of the East that had been subject to it until then. Kikanos, the king, advanced against the enemy with a great army. He left Balaam and Balaam's two sons, Jannes and Jambres, behind, to keep guard over his capital and take charge of the people remaining at home. The absence of the king gave Balaam the opportunity of winning his subjects over to his side, and he was put upon the throne, and his two sons were set over the army as generals. To cut Kikanos off from his capital, Balaam and his sons invested the city, so that none could enter it against their will. On two sides they made the walls higher, on the third they dug a network of canals, into which they conducted the waters of the river girding the whole land of Ethiopia, and on the fourth side their magic arts collected a large swarm of snakes and scorpions. Thus none could depart, and none could enter.

Meantime Kikanos succeeded in subjugating the rebellious nations. When he returned at the head of his victorious army, and espied the high city wall from afar, he and his men said: "The inhabitants of the city, seeing that the war detained us abroad for a long time, have raised the walls and fortified them, that the kings of Canaan may not be able to enter". On approaching the city gates, which were barred, they cried out to the guards to open them, but by Balaam's instructions they were not permitted to pass through. A skirmish ensued, in which Kikanos lost one hundred and thirty men. On the morrow the combat was continued, the king with his troops being stationed on the thither bank of the river. This day he lost his thirty riders, who, mounted on their steeds, had attempted to swim the stream. Then the king ordered rafts to be constructed for the transporting of his men. When the vessels reached the canals, they were submerged, and the waters, swirling round and round as though driven by mill wheels, swept away two hundred men, twenty from each raft. On the third day they set about assaulting the city from the side on which the snakes and scorpions swarmed, but they failed to reach it, and the reptiles killed one hundred and seventy men. The king desisted from attacking the city, but for the space of nine years he surrounded it, so that none could come out or go in.

While the siege was in progress, Moses appeared in the king's camp on his flight before Pharaoh, and at once found favor with Kikanos and his whole army. He exercised an attraction upon all that saw him, for he was slender like a palm-tree, his countenance shone as the morning sun, and his strength was equal to a lion's. So deep was the king's affection for him that he appointed him to be commander-in-chief of his forces.

At the end of the nine years Kikanos fell a prey to a mortal disease, and he died on the seventh day of his illness. His servants embalmed him, buried him opposite to the city gate toward the land of Egypt, and over his grave they erected a magnificent structure, strong and high, upon the walls whereof they engraved all the mighty deeds and battles of the dead king.

Now, after the death of Kikanos, his men were greatly grieved on account of the war. One said unto the other, "Counsel us, what shall we do at this time? We have been abiding in the wilderness, away from our homes, for nine years. If we fight against the city, many of us will fall dead; and if we remain here besieging it, we shall also die. For now all the princes of Aram and of the children of the East will hear that our king is dead, and they will attack us suddenly, and they will fight with us until not a remnant will be left. Now, therefore, let us go and set a king over us, and we will remain here besieging the city until it surrenders unto us".

The King of Ethiopia

They could find none except Moses fit to be their king. They hastened and stripped off each man his upper garment, and cast them all in a heap upon the ground, making a high place, on top of which they set Moses. Then they blew with trumpets, and called out before him: "Long live the king! Long live the king"! And all the people and the nobles swore unto him to give him

Adoniah for wife, the Ethiopian queen, the widow of Kikanos. And they made Moses king over them on that day.

They also issued a proclamation, commanding every man to give Moses of what he possessed, and upon the high place they spread a sheet, wherein each one cast something, this one a gold nose ring, that one a coin, and onyx stones, bdellium, pearls, gold, and silver in great abundance.

Moses was twenty-seven years old when he became king over Ethiopia, and he reigned for forty years. On the seventh day of his reign, all the people assembled and came before him, to ask his counsel as to what was to be done to the city they were besieging. The king answered them, and said: "If you will hearken to my words, the city will be delivered into our hands. Proclaim with a loud voice throughout the whole camp, unto all the people, saying: 'Thus saith the king! Go to the forest and fetch hither of the young of the stork, each man one fledgling in his hand. And if there be any man that transgresseth the word of the king, not to bring a bird, he shall die, and the king shall take all belonging to him'. And when you have brought them, they shall be in your keeping. You shall rear them until they grow up, and you shall teach them to fly as the hawk flieth".

All the people did according to the word of Moses, and after the young storks had grown to full size, he ordered them to be starved for three days. On the third day the king said unto them, "Let every man put on his armor and gird his sword upon him. Each one shall mount his horse, and each shall set his stork upon his hand, and we will rise up and fight against the city opposite to the place of the serpents".

When they came to the appointed spot, the king said to them, "Let each man send forth his young stork, to descend upon the serpents". Thus they did, and the birds swooped down and devoured all the reptiles and destroyed them. After the serpents were removed in this way, the men fought against the city, subdued it, and killed all its inhabitants, but of the people besieging it there died not one.

When Balaam saw that the city had fallen into the hands of the besiegers, he exercised his magic arts, which enabled him to fly through the air, and he carried with him his two sons, Jannes and Jambres, and his eight brothers, and they all took refuge in Egypt.

Seeing that they had been saved by the king, and the city had been taken by his good counsel, the people became more than ever attached to him. They set the royal crown upon his head, and gave him Adoniah, the widow of Kikanos to wife. But Moses feared the stern God of his fathers, and he went not in unto Adoniah, nor did he turn his eyes toward her, for he remembered how Abraham had made his servant Eliezer swear, saying unto him, "Thou shalt not take a wife for my son of the daughters of the Canaanites, among whom I dwell". He also remembered what Isaac did when Jacob fled before his brother Esau, how he commanded his son, saying, "Thou shalt not take a wife from the daughters of Canaan, nor ally thyself by marriage with any of the children of Ham, for the Lord our God gave Ham the son of Noah and all his seed as slaves to the children of Shem and Japheth forever".

At that time Aram and the children of the East heard that Kikanos the king of Ethiopia had died, and they rose up against the Ethiopians, but Moses went forth with a mighty army to fight against the rebellious nations, and he subdued them, first the children of the East and then Aram.

Moses continued to prosper in his kingdom. He conducted the government in justice, righteousness, and integrity, and his people loved and feared him.

In the fortieth year of his reign, while he was sitting upon his throne one day, surrounded by all the nobles, Adoniah the queen, who was seated before him, rose up, and spake: "What is this thing which you, the people of Ethiopia, have done these many days? Surely you know that during the forty years this man bath reigned over you, he hath not approached me, nor hath he worshipped the gods of Ethiopia. Now, therefore, let this man reign over you no more, for he is not of our flesh. Behold, Monarchos my son is grown up, let him reign over you. It is better for you to serve the son of your lord than a stranger, a slave of the king of Egypt".

A whole day the people and the nobles contended with one another, whether to pay heed to the words of the queen. The officers of the army remained faithful to Moses, but the people of the cities were in favor of crowning the son of their former lord as king. The following morning they rose up and made Monarchos, the son of Kikanos, king over them, but they were afraid to stretch forth their hand against Moses, for the Lord was with him. They also remembered the oath they had sworn unto Moses, and therefore they did him no harm. Moreover, they gave many presents to him, and dismissed him with great honor.

When Moses left Ethiopia, in the sixty-seventh year of his age, it was the time appointed by God in the days of old to bring Israel forth from the affliction of the children of Ham. But fearing to return to Egypt on account of Pharaoh, Moses journeyed to Midian.

Jethro

In the city of Midian, named thus for a son of Abraham by Keturah, the man Jethro had lived for many years, doing a priest's service before the idols. As time went on, he grew more and more convinced of the vanity of idol worship. His priesthood became repugnant to him, and he resolved to give up his, charge. He stood before his townsmen, and said, "Until now I performed your service before the idols, but I have grown too old for the duties of the office. Choose, therefore, whomever you would choose in my place". Speaking thus, he delivered to the people all the paraphernalia appertaining to the idol worship, and bade them transfer them to the one to whom in their discretion they should entrust his position. Suspecting Jethro's hidden motives, the people put him under the ban, and none might venture to do him the slightest service. Not even would the shepherds pasture his flocks, and there was nothing for him to do but impose this work upon his seven daughters.

Jethro's transformation from an idolatrous priest into a God-fearing man is conveyed by his seven names. He was called Jether, because the Torah contains an "additional" section about him; Jethro, he "overflowed" with good deeds. Hobab, "the beloved son of God"; Reuel, "the friend of God"; Heber, "the associate of God"; Putiel, "he that hath renounced idolatry"; and Keni, he that was "zealous" for God, and "acquired" the Torah.

In consequence of the hostile relation between Jethro and the inhabitants of the city, his daughters were in the habit of making their appearance at the watering troughs before the other shepherds came thither. But the ruse was not successful. The shepherds would drive them away, and water their own flocks at the troughs that the maidens had filled. When Moses arrived in Midian, it was at the well that he made halt, and his experience was the same as Isaac's and Jacob's. Like them he found his helpmeet there. Rebekah had been selected by Eliezer as the wife of Isaac, while she was busy drawing water for him; Jacob had seen Rachel first, while she was watering her sheep, and at this well in Midian Moses met his future wife Zipporah.

The rudeness of the shepherds reached its climax the very day of Moses' arrival. First they deprived the maidens of the water they had drawn for themselves, and attempted to do violence to them, and then they threw them into the water with intent to kill them. At this moment Moses appeared, dragged the maidens out of the water, and gave the flocks to drink, first Jethro's and then the flocks of the shep- herds, though the latter did not deserve his good offices. True, he did them the service with but little trouble to himself, for he had only to draw a bucketful, and the water flowed so copiously that it sufficed for all the herds, and it did not cease to flow until Moses withdrew from the well, --the same well at which Jacob had met

Rachel, his future wife, and the same well that God created at the beginning of the world, the opening of which He made in the twilight of the first Sabbath eve.

Jethro's daughters thanked Moses for the assistance he had afforded them. But Moses warded off their gratitude, saying, "Your thanks are due to the Egyptian I killed, on account of whom I had to flee from Egypt. Had it not been for him, I should not be here now".

Moses Marries Zipporah

One of the seven maidens whom Moses saw at the well attracted his notice in particular on account of her modest demeanor, and he made her a proposal of marriage. But Zipporah repulsed him, saying, "My father has a tree in his garden with which he tests every man that expresses a desire to marry one of his daughters, and as soon as the suitor touches the tree, he is devoured by it".

Moses: "Whence has he the tree"?

Zipporah: "It is the rod that the Holy One, blessed be He, created in the twilight of the first Sabbath eve, and gave to Adam. He transmitted it to Enoch, from him it descended to Noah, then to Shem, and Abraham, and Isaac, and finally to Jacob, who brought it with him to Egypt, and gave it to his son Joseph. When Joseph died, the Egyptians pillaged his house, and the rod, which was in their booty, they brought to Pharaoh's palace. At that time my father was one of the most prominent of the king's sacred scribes, and as such he had the opportunity of seeing the rod. He felt a great desire to possess it, and he stole it and took it to his house. On this rod the Ineffable Name is graven, and also the ten plagues that God will cause to visit the Egyptians in a future day. For many years it lay in my father's house. One day he was walking in his garden carrying it, and he stuck it in the ground. When he attempted to draw it out again, he found that it had sprouted, and was putting forth blossoms. That is the rod with which he tries any that desire to marry his daughters. He insists that our suitors shall attempt to pull it out of the ground, but as soon as they touch it, it devours them".

Having given him this account of her father's rod, Zipporah went home, accompanied by her sisters, and Moses followed them.

Jethro was not a little amazed to see his daughters return so soon from the watering troughs. As a rule, the chicanery they had to suffer from the shepherds detained them until late. No sooner had he heard their report about the wonder- working Egyptian than he exclaimed, "Mayhap he is one of the descendants of Abraham, from whom issueth blessing for the whole world". He rebuked his daughters for not having invited the stranger that had done them so valuable a service to come into their house, and he ordered them to fetch him, in the hope that he would take one of his daughters to wife.

Moses had been standing without all this time, and had allowed Jethro's daughters to describe him as an Egyptian, without protesting and asserting his Hebrew birth. For this God punished him by causing him to die outside of the promised land. Joseph, who had proclaimed in public that he was a Hebrew, found his last resting-place in the land of the Hebrews, and Moses, who apparently had no objection to being considered an Egyptian, had to live and die outside of that land.

Zipporah hastened forth to execute her father's wish, and no sooner had she ushered him in than Moses requested her hand in marriage. Jethro replied, "If thou canst bring me the rod in my garden, I will give her to thee". Moses went out, found the sapphire rod that God had bestowed upon Adam when he was driven forth from Paradise, the rod that had reached Jethro after manifold vicissitudes, and which he had planted in the garden. Moses uprooted it and carried it to Jethro, who conceived the idea at once that he was the prophet in Israel concerning whom all the wise men of Egypt had foretold that he would destroy their land and its inhabitants. As soon as this thought struck him, he seized Moses, and threw him into a pit, in the expectation that he would meet with death there.

And, indeed, he would have perished, if Zipporah had not devised a stratagem to save his life. She said to her father: "Would it were thy will to hearken unto my counsel. Thou hast no wife, but only seven daughters. Dost thou desire my six sisters to preside over thy household? Then shall I go abroad with the sheep. If not, let my sisters tend the flocks, and I shall take care of the house". Her father said: "Thou hast spoken well. Thy six sisters shall go forth with the sheep, and thou shalt abide in the house and take care of it, and all that belongeth to me therein".

Now Zipporah could provide Moses with all sorts of dainties as he lay in the pit, and she did it for the space of seven years. At the expiration of this period, she said to her father: "I recollect that once upon a time thou didst cast into yonder pit a man that had fetched thy rod from the garden for thee, and thou didst commit a great trespass thereby. If it seemeth well to thee, uncover the pit and look into it. If the man is dead, throw his corpse away, lest it fill the house with stench. But should he be alive, then thou oughtest to be convinced that he is one of those who are wholly pious, else he had died of hunger".

The reply of Jethro was: "Thou hast spoken wisely. Dost thou remember his name"? And Zipporah rejoined, "I remember he called himself Moses the son of Amram". Jethro lost no time, he opened the pit, and called out, "Moses! Moses"! Moses replied, and said: "Here am I"! Jethro drew him up out of the pit, kissed him, and said: "Blessed be God, who guarded thee for seven years in the pit. I acknowledge that He slayeth and reviveth, that thou art one of the wholly pious, that through thee God will destroy Egypt in time to come, lead His people out of the land, and drown Pharaoh and his whole army in the sea".

Thereupon Jethro gave much money to Moses, and he bestowed his daughter Zipporah upon him as wife, giving her to him under the condition that the children born of the marriage in Jethro's house should be divided into two equal classes, the one to be Israelitish, the other Egyptian. When Zipporah bore him a son, Moses circumcised him, and called him Gershom, as a memorial of the wonder God had done for him, for although he lived in a "strange" land, the Lord had not refused him aid even "there".

Zipporah nursed her first child for two years, and in the third year she bore a second son. Remembering his compact with Jethro, Moses realized that his father-in-law would not permit him to circumcise this one, too, and he determined to return to Egypt, that he might have the opportunity of bringing up his second son as an Israelite. On the journey thither, Satan appeared to him in the guise of a serpent, and swallowed Moses down to his extremities. Zipporah knew by this token that the thing had happened because her second son had not been circumcised, and she hastened to make good the omission. As soon as she sprinkled the blood of the circumcision on her husband's feet, a heavenly voice was heard to cry to the serpent, commanding him, "Spew him out"! and Moses came forth and stood upon his feet. Thus Zipporah saved Moses' life twice, first from the pit and then from the serpent.

When Moses arrived in Egypt, he was approached by Dathan and Abiram, the leaders of the Israelites, and they spake: "Comest thou hither to slay us, or dost thou purpose to do the same with us as thou didst with the Egyptian"? This drove Moses straightway back to Midian, and there he remained two years more, until God revealed Himself at Horeb, and said to him, "Go and bring forth My children out of the land of Egypt.

A Bloody Remedy

The latter years of Israel's bondage in Egypt were the worst. To punish Pharaoh for his cruelty toward the children of Israel, God afflicted him with a plague of leprosy, which covered his whole body, from the crown of his bead to the soles of his feet. Instead of being chastened by his disease, Pharaoh remained stiffnecked, and he tried to restore his health by murdering Israelitish children. He took counsel with his three advisers, Balaam, Jethro, and Job, how he might be healed of the awful malady that had seized upon him. Balaam spoke, saying, "Thou canst regain thy health only if thou wilt slaughter Israelitish children and bathe in their blood". Jethro, averse from having a share in such an atrocity, left the king and fled to Midian. Job, on the other hand, though he also disapproved of Balaam's counsel, kept silence, and in no wise protested against it, wherefor God punished him with a year's suffering. But afterward He loaded him down with all the felicities of this life, and granted him many years, so that this pious Gentile might be rewarded in this world for his good deeds and not have the right to urge a claim upon the beatitude of the future life.

In pursuance of the sanguinary advice given by Balaam, Pharaoh had his bailiffs snatch Israelitish babes from their mothers' breasts, and slaughter them, and in the blood of these innocents he bathed. His disease afflicted him for ten years, and every day an Israelitish child was killed for him. It was all in vain; indeed, at the end of the time his leprosy changed into boils, and he suffered more than before.

While he was in this agony, the report was brought to him that the children of Israel in Goshen were careless and idle in their forced labor. The news aggravated his suffering, and he said: "Now that I am ill, they turn and scoff at me. Harness my chariot, and I will betake myself to Goshen, and see the derision wherewith the children of Israel deride me". And they took and put him upon a horse, for he was not able to mount it himself. When he and his men had come to the border between Egypt and Goshen, the king's steed passed into a narrow place. The other horses, running rapidly through the pass, pressed upon each other until the king's horse fell while he sate upon it, and when it fell, the chariot turned over on his face, and also the horse lay upon him. The king's flesh was torn from him, for this thing was from the Lord, He had heard the cries of His people and their affliction. The king's servants carried him upon their shoulders, brought him back to Egypt, and placed him on his bed.

He knew that his end was come to die, and the queen Alfar'anit and his nobles gathered about his bed, and they wept a great weeping with him.

The princes and his counsellors advised the king to make choice of a successor, to reign in his stead, whomsoever he would choose from among his sons. He had three sons and two daughters by the queen Alfar'anit, beside children from concubines. The name of his first-born was Atro, the name of the second Adikam, and of the third Moryon. The name of the older daughter was Bithiah, and of the other, Akuzit. The first-born of the sons of the king was an idiot, precipitate and heedless in all his actions. Adikam, the second son, was a cunning and clever man, and versed in all the wisdom of Egypt, but ungainly in appearance, fleshy and short of stature; his height was a cubit and a space, and his beard flowed down to his ankles.

The king resolved that Adikam should reign in his stead after his death. When this second son of his was but ten years old, he had given him Gedidah, the daughter of Abilat, to wife, and she bore him four sons. Afterward Adikam went and took three other wives, and begot eight sons and three daughters.

The king's malady increased upon him greatly, and his flesh emitted a stench like a carcass cast into the field in summer time in the heat of the sun. When he saw that his disorder bad seized upon him with a strong grip, he commanded his son Adikam to be brought to him, and they made him king over the land in his place.

At the end of three years the old king died in shame and disgrace, a loathing to all that saw him, and they buried him in the sepulchre of the kings of Egypt in Zoan, but they did not embalm him, as was usual with kings, for his flesh was putrid, and they could not approach his body on account of the stench, and they buried him in haste. Thus the Lord requited him with evil for the evil he had done in his days to Israel, and he died in terror and shame after having reigned ninety-four years.

Adikam was twenty years old when he succeeded his father, and he reigned four years. The people of Egypt called him Pharaoh, as was their custom with all their kings, but his wise men called him Akuz, for Akuz is the word for "short" in the Egyptian language, and Adikam was exceedingly awkward and undersized. The new Pharaoh surpassed his father Malol and all the former kings in wickedness, and he made heavier the yoke upon the children of Israel. He went to Goshen with his servants, and increased their labor, and he said unto them, "Complete your work, each day's task, and let not your hands slacken from the work from this day forward, as you did in the day of my father". He placed officers over them from amongst the children of Israel, and over these officers he placed taskmasters from amongst his servants. And he put before them a measure for bricks, according to the number they were to make day by day, and whenever any deficiency was discovered in the measure of their daily bricks, the taskmasters of Pharaoh would go to the women of the children of Israel, and take their infants from them, as many as the number of bricks lacking in the measure, and these babes they put into the building instead of the missing bricks. The taskmasters forced each man of the Israelites to put his own child in the building. The father would place his son in the wall, and cover him over with mortar, all the while weeping, his tears running down upon his child.

The children of Israel sighed every day on account of their dire suffering, for they had thought that after Pharaoh's death his son would lighten their toil, but the new king was worse than his father. And God saw the burden of the children of Israel, and their heavy work, and He determined to deliver them.

However, it was not for their own sake that God resolved upon the deliverance of the children of Israel, for they were empty of good deeds, and the Lord foreknew that, once they were redeemed, they would rise up against Him, and even worship the golden calf. Yet He took mercy upon them, for He remembered His covenant with the Fathers, and He looked upon their repentance for their sins, and accepted their promise, to fulfil the word of God after their going forth from Egypt even before they should hear it.

After all, the children of Israel were not wholly without merits. In a high degree they possessed qualities of extraordinary excellence. There were no incestuous relations among them, they were not evil-tongued, they did not change their names, they clung to the Hebrew language, never giving it up, and great fraternal affection prevailed among them. If one happened to finish the tale of his bricks before his neighbors, he was in the habit of helping the others. Therefore God spake, "They deserve that I should have mercy upon them, for if a man shows mercy unto another, I have mercy upon him".

The Faithful Shepherd

When Jethro bestowed his daughter Zipporah upon Moses as his wife, he said to his future son-in-law: "I know that thy father Jacob took his wives, the daughters of Laban, and went away with them against their father's will. Now take an oath that thou wilt not do the same unto me", and Moses swore not to leave him without his consent, and he remained with Jethro, who made him the shepherd of his flocks. By the way he tended the sheep, God saw his fitness to be the shepherd of His people, for God never gives an exalted office to a man until He has tested him in little things. Thus Moses and David were tried as shepherds of flocks, and only after they had proved their ability as such, He gave them dominion over men.

Moses watched over the flocks with loving care. He led the young animals to pasture first, that they might have the tender, juicy grass for their food; the somewhat older animals he led forth next, and allowed them to graze off the herbs suitable for them; and finally came the vigorous ones that had attained their full growth, and to them he gave the hard grass that was left, which the others could not eat, but which afforded good food for them. Then spake

God, “He that understandeth how to pasture sheep, providing for each what is good for it, he shall pasture My people”.

Once a kid escaped from the flock, and when Moses followed it, he saw how it stopped at all the water courses, and he said to it: “Poor kid, I knew not that thou wast thirsty, and wast running after water! Thou art weary, I ween”, and he carried it back to the herd on his shoulder. Then said God: “Thou hast compassion with a flock belonging to a man of flesh and blood! As thou livest, thou shalt pasture Israel, My flock”.

Not only did Moses take heed that no harm should come to the herds under his charge, but he was also careful that they cause no injury to men. He always chose an open meadow as his pasturing place, to prevent his sheep from grazing in private estates.

Jethro had no reason to be dissatisfied with the services rendered to him by his son-in-law. During the forty years Moses acted as his shepherd not one sheep was attacked by wild beasts, and the herds multiplied to an incredible degree. Once he drove the sheep about in the desert for forty days, without finding a pasturing place for them. Nevertheless he did not lose a single sheep.

Moses’ longing for the desert was irresistible. His prophetic spirit caused him to foresee that his own greatness and the greatness of Israel would manifest themselves there. In the desert God’s wonders would appear, though it would be at the same time the grave of the human herd to be entrusted to him in the future, and also his own last resting- place. Thus he had a presentiment at the very beginning of his career that the desert would be the scene of his activity, which not only came true in the present order of things, but also will be true in the latter days, when he will appear in the desert again, to lead into the promised land the generation, arisen from their graves, that he brought forth from Egyptian bondage.

Wandering through the desert, he reached Mount Horeb, which is called by six names, each conveying one of its distinctions. It is “the mountain of God”, wherein the Lord revealed His law; “Basban”, for God “came there”; “a mountain of humps”, for the Lord declared all the other mountains unfit for the revelation, as “crookbackt” animals are declared unfit for sacrifices; “mountain of abode”, because it is the mountain that God desired for His “abode”; Sinai, because the “hatred” of God against the heathen began at the time when Israel received the law thereon; and Horeb, “sword”, because there the sword of the law was drawn upon the sinners.

The Burning Thorn-Bush

When Moses drew near to Mount Horeb, he was aware at once that it was a holy place, for he noticed that passing birds did not alight upon it. At his approach the mountain began to move, as though to go forward and meet him, and it settled back into quietude only when his foot rested upon it. The first thing Moses noticed was the wonderful burning bush, the upper part of which was a blazing flame, neither consuming the bush, nor preventing it from bearing blossoms as it burnt, for the celestial fire has three peculiar qualities: it produces blossoms, it does not consume the object around which it plays, and it is black of color. The fire that Moses saw in the bush was the appearance of the angel Michael, who had descended as the forerunner of the Shekinah herself to come down presently. It was the wish of God to hold converse with Moses, who, however, was not inclined to permit any interruption of the work under his charge. Therefore God startled him with the wonderful phenomenon of the burning thorn-bush. That brought Moses to a stop, and then God spoke with him.

There were good reasons for selecting the thorn-bush as the vessel for a Divine vision. It was "clean", for the heathen could not use it to make idols. God's choosing to dwell in the stunted thorn-bush conveyed the knowledge to Moses that He suffers along with Israel. Furthermore, Moses was taught that there is nothing in nature, not even the insignificant thorn-bush, that can exist without the presence of the Shekinah. Besides, the thorn-bush may be taken as the symbol for Israel in several respects. As the thorn- bush is the lowliest of all species of trees, so the condition of Israel in the exile is the lowliest as compared with that of all the other nations, but as the thorn-bush releases no bird that alights upon it without lacerating its wings, so the nations that subjugate Israel will be punished. Also, as a garden hedge is made of the thorn-bush, so Israel forms the hedge for the world, the garden of God, for without Israel the world could not endure. Furthermore, as the thorn- bush bears thorns and roses alike, so Israel has pious and impious members, and as the thorn-bush requires ample water for its growth, so Israel can prosper only through the Torah, the celestial water. And the thorn-bush, the leaf of which consists of five leaflets, was to indicate to Moses that God had resolved to redeem Israel only for the sake of the merits of five pious men, Abraham, Isaac, Jacob, Aaron, and Moses. The numbers represented by the letters composing the Hebrew word for thorn-bush, Seneh, add up to one hundred and twenty, to convey that Moses would reach the age of one hundred and twenty years, and that the Shekinah would rest on Mount Horeb for one hundred and twenty days. Finally, in order to give Moses an illustration of His modesty, God descended from the exalted heavens and spake to him from a lowly thorn-bush instead of the summit of a lofty mountain or the top of a stately cedar tree.

The Ascension of Moses

The vision of the burning bush appeared to Moses alone; the other shepherds with him saw nothing of it. He took five steps in the direction of the bush, to view it at close range, and when God beheld the countenance of Moses distorted by grief and anxiety over Israel's suffering, He spake, "This one is worthy of the office of pasturing My people".

Moses was still a novice in prophecy, therefore God said to Himself, "If I reveal Myself to him in loud tones, I shall alarm him, but if I reveal Myself with a subdued voice, he will hold prophecy in low esteem", whereupon he addressed him in his father Amram's voice. Moses was overjoyed to hear his father speak, for it gave him the assurance that. he was still alive. The voice called his name twice, and he answered, "Here am I! What is my father's wish"? God replied, saying, "I am not thy father. I but desired to refrain from terrifying thee, therefore I spoke with thy father's voice. I am the God of thy father, the God of Abraham, the God of Isaac, and the God of Jacob". These words rejoiced Moses greatly, for not only was his father Amram's name pronounced in the same breath with the names of the three Patriarchs, but it came before theirs, as though he ranked higher than they.

Moses said not a word. In silent reverence before the Divine vision he covered his face, and when God disclosed the mission with which He charged him, of bringing the Israelites forth from the land of Egypt, he answered with humility, "Who am I, that I should go unto Pharaoh, and bring forth the children of Israel out of Egypt"? Thereupon spake God, "Moses, thou art meek, and I will reward thee for thy modesty. I will deliver the whole land of Egypt into thine hand, and, besides, I will let thee ascend unto the throne of My glory, and look upon all the angels of the heavens".

Hereupon God commanded Metatron, the Angel of the Face, to conduct Moses to the celestial regions amid the sound of music and song, and He commanded him furthermore to summon thirty thousand angels, to serve as his body-guard, fifteen thousand to right of him and fifteen thousand to left of him. In abject terror Moses asked Metatron, "Who art thou"? and the angel replied, "I am Enoch, the son of Jared, thy ancestor, and God has charged me to accompany thee to His throne". But Moses demurred, saying, "I am but flesh and blood, and I cannot look upon the countenance of an angel", whereupon Metatron changed Moses' flesh into torches of fire, his eyes into Merkabah wheels, his strength into an angel's, and his tongue into a flame, and he took him to heaven with a retinue of thirty thousand angels, one half moving to right of them and one half to left of them.

In the first heaven Moses saw streams upon streams of water, and he observed that the whole heaven consisted of windows, at each of which angels were stationed. Metatron named and pointed out all the windows of heaven to him: the window of prayer and the window of supplication; of weeping and of joy; plenitude and starvation; wealth and poverty; war and peace; conception and birth; showers and soft rains; sin and repentance; life and death; pestilence and healing; sickness and health; and many windows more.

In the second heaven Moses saw the angel Nuriel, standing three hundred parasangs high, with his retinue of fifty myriads of angels, all fashioned out of water and fire, and all keeping their faces turned toward the Shekinah while they sang a song of praise to God. Metatron explained to Moses, that these were the angels set over the clouds, the winds, and the rains, who return speedily, as soon as they have executed the will of their Creator, to their station in the second of the heavens, there to proclaim the praise of God.

In the third heaven Moses saw an angel, so tall it would take a human being five hundred years to climb to his height. He had seventy thousand heads, each head having as many mouths, each mouth as many tongues, and each tongue as many sayings, and he together with his suite of seventy thousand myriads of angels made of white fire praised and extolled the Lord. "These", said Metatron to Moses, "are called Erelim, and they are appointed over the grass, the trees, the fruits, and the grain, but as soon as they have done the will of their Creator, they return to the place assigned to them, and praise God".

In the fourth heaven Moses saw a Temple, the pillars thereof made of red fire, the staves of green fire, the thresholds of white fire, the boards and clasps of flaming fire, the gates of carbuncles, and the pinnacles of rubies. Angels were entering the Temple and giving praise to God there. In response to a question from Moses Metatron told him that they presided over the earth, the sun, the moon, the stars, and the other celestial bodies. and all of them intone songs before God. In this heaven Moses noticed also the two great planets, Venus and Mars, each as large as the whole earth, and concerning these he asked unto what purpose they had been created. Metatron explained thereupon, that Venus lies upon the sun to cool him off in summer, else he would scorch the earth, and Mars lies upon the moon, to impart warmth to her, lest she freeze the earth.

Arrived in the fifth heaven, Moses saw hosts of angels, whose nether parts were of snow and their upper parts of fire, and yet the snow did not melt nor was the fire extinguished, for God had established perfect harmony between the two elements. These angels, called Ishim, have had nothing to do since the day of their creation but praise and extol the Lord.

In the sixth of the heavens were millions and myriads of angels praising God, they were called 'Irin and kadishim, "Watchers" and "Holy Ones", and their chief was made of hail, and he was so tall, it would take five hundred years to walk a distance equal to his height.

In the last heaven Moses saw two angels, each five hundred parasangs in height, forged out of chains of black fire and red fire, the angels Af, "Anger", and Hemah, "Wrath", whom God created at the beginning of the world, to execute His will. Moses was disquieted when he looked upon them, but Metatron embraced him, and said, "Moses, Moses, thou favorite of God, fear not, and be not terrified", and Moses became calm. There was another angel in the seventh heaven, different in appearance from all the others, and of frightful mien. His height was so great, it would have taken five hundred years to cover a distance equal to it, and from the crown of his head to the soles of his feet he was studded with glaring eyes, at the sight of which the beholder fell prostrate in awe. "This one", said Metatron, addressing Moses, "is Samael, who takes the soul away from man". "Whither goes he now"? asked Moses, and Metatron replied, "To fetch the soul of Job the pious". Thereupon Moses prayed to God in these words, "O may it be Thy will, my God and the God of my fathers, not to let me fall into the hands of this angel".

Here, in the highest heaven, he saw also the seraphim with their six wings. With two they cover their face, that they gaze not upon the Shekinah; and with two their feet, which, being like a calf's feet, they hide, to keep secret Israel's transgression of the golden calf. With the third pair of wings they fly and do the service of the Lord, all the while exclaiming, "Holy, holy, holy is the Lord of hosts; the whole earth is full of His glory". The wings of these angels are of prodigious size, it would take a man five hundred years to traverse their length and their breadth, as from one end of the earth to the other.

And Moses saw in the seventh heaven the holy Hayyot, which support the throne of God; and he beheld also the angel Zagzagel, the prince of the Torah and of wisdom, who teaches the Torah in seventy languages to the souls of men, and thereafter they cherish the precepts contained therein as laws revealed by God to Moses on Sinai. From this angel with the horns of glory Moses himself learnt all the ten mysteries".

Having seen what there is in the seven heavens, he spoke to God, saying, "I will not leave the heavens unless Thou grantest me a gift", and God replied, "I will give thee the Torah, and men shall call it the Law of Moses".

Moses Visits Paradise and Hell

When Moses was on the point of departing from heaven, a celestial voice announced: "Moses, thou camest hither, and thou didst see the throne of My glory. Now thou shalt see also Paradise and hell", and God dispatched Gabriel on the errand of showing hell to him. Terrified by its fires, when he caught sight of them as he entered the portals of hell, Moses refused to go farther. But the angel encouraged him, saying, "There is a fire that not only burns but also consumes, and that fire will protect thee against hell fire, so that thou canst step upon it, and yet thou wilt not be seared".

As Moses entered hell, the fire withdrew a distance of five hundred parasangs, and the Angel of Hell, Nasargiel, asked him, "Who art thou"? and he answered, "I am Moses, the son of Amram".

Nasargiel: "This is not thy place, thou belongest in Paradise".

Moses: "I came hither to see the manifestation of the power of God".

Then said God to the Angel of Hell, "Go and show hell unto Moses, and how the wicked are treated there". Immediately he went with Moses, walking before him like a pupil before his master, and thus they entered hell together, and Moses saw men undergoing torture by the Angels of Destruction: some of the sinners were suspended by their eyelids, some by their ears, some by their hands, and some by their tongues, and they cried bitterly. And women were suspended by their hair and by their breasts, and in other ways, all on chains of fire. Nasargiel explained: "These hang by their eyes, because they looked lustfully upon the wives of their neighbors, and with a covetous eye upon the possessions of their fellow-men. These hang by their ears because they listened to empty and vain speech, and turned their ear away from hearing the Torah. These hang by their tongues, because they talked slander, and accustomed their tongue to foolish babbling. These hang by their feet, because they walked with them in order to spy upon their fellow-men, but they walked not to the synagogue, to offer prayer unto their Creator. These hang by their hands, because with them they robbed their neighbors of their possessions, and committed murder. These women hang by their hair and their breasts, because they uncovered them in the presence of young men, so that they conceived desire unto them, and fell into sin".

Moses heard hell cry with a loud and a bitter cry, saying to Nasargiel: "Give me something to eat, I am hungry".-- Nasargiel: "What shall I give thee"?-- Hell: "Give me the souls of the pious".--Nasargiel: "The Holy One, blessed be He, will not deliver the souls of the pious unto thee".

Moses saw the place called Alukah, where sinners were suspended by their feet, their heads downward, and their bodies covered with black worms, each five hundred parasangs long. They lamented, and cried: "Woe unto us for the punishment of hell. Give us death, that we may die"! Nasargiel explained: "These are the sinners that swore falsely, profaned the Sabbath and the holy days, despised the sages, called their neighbors by unseemly nicknames, wronged the orphan and the widow, and bore false witness. Therefore bath God delivered them to these worms".

Moses went thence to another place, and there he saw sinners prone on their faces, with two thousand scorpions lashing, stinging, and tormenting them, while the tortured victims cried bitterly. Each of the scorpions had seventy thousand heads, each head seventy thousand mouths, each mouth seventy thousand stings, and each sting seventy thousand pouches of poison and venom, which the sinners are forced to drink down, although the anguish is so racking that their eyes melt in their sockets. Nasargiel explained: "These are the sinners who caused the Israelites to lose their money, who exalted themselves above the community, who put their neighbors to shame in public, who delivered their fellow-Israelites into the hands of the Gentiles, who denied the Torah of Moses, and who maintained that God is not the Creator of the world".

Then Moses saw the place called Tit ba-Yawen, in which the sinners stand in mud up to their navels, while the Angels of Destruction lash them with fiery chains, and break their teeth with fiery stones, from morning until evening, and during the night they make their teeth grow again, to the length of a parasang, only to break them anew the next morning. Nasargiel explained: "These are the sinners who ate carrion and forbidden flesh, who lent their money at usury, who wrote the Name of God on amulets for Gentiles, who used false weights, who stole money from their fellow-Israelites, who ate on the Day of Atonement, who ate forbidden fat, and animals and reptiles that are an abomination, and who drank blood".

Then Nasargiel said to Moses: "Come and see how the sinners are burnt in hell", and Moses answered, "I cannot go there", but Nasargiel replied, "Let the light of the Shekinah precede thee, and the fire of hell will have no power over thee". Moses yielded, and he saw how the sinners were burnt, one half of their bodies being immersed in fire and the other half in snow, while worms bred in their own flesh crawled over them, and the Angels of Destruction beat them incessantly. Nasargiel explained: "These are the sinners who committed incest, murder, and idolatry, who cursed their parents and their teachers, and who, like Nimrod and others, called themselves gods". In this place, which is called Abaddon, he saw the sinners taking snow by stealth and putting it in their armpits, to relieve the pain inflicted by the scorching fire, and he was convinced that the saying was true, "The wicked mend not their ways even at the gate of hell".

As Moses departed from hell, he prayed to God, "May it be Thy will, O Lord my God and God of my fathers, to save me and the people of Israel from the places I have seen in hell". But God answered him, and said, "Moses, before Me there is no respecting of persons and no taking of gifts. Whoever doeth good deeds entereth Paradise, and he that doeth evil must go to hell".

At the command of God, Gabriel now led Moses to Paradise. As he entered, two angels came toward him, and they said to him, "Thy time is not yet arrived to leave the world", and Moses made answer, "What ye say is true, but I have come to see the reward of the pious in Paradise". Then the angels extolled Moses, saying: "Hail, Moses, servant of God! Hail, Moses, born of woman, that hast been found worthy to ascend to the seven heavens! Hail to the nation to which thou belongest"!

Under the tree of life Moses saw the angel Shamshiel, the prince of Paradise, who led him through it, and showed him all there is therein. He saw seventy thrones made of precious stones, standing on feet of fine gold, each throne surrounded by seventy angels. But one of them was larger than all the others, and it was encircled by one hundred and twenty angels. This was the throne of Abraham, and when Abraham beheld Moses, and heard who he was, and what his purpose was in visiting Paradise, he exclaimed, "Praise ye the Lord, for He is good, for His mercy endureth forever".

Moses asked Shamshiel about the size of Paradise, but not even he who is the prince thereof could answer the question, for there is none that can gauge it. It can neither be measured nor fathomed nor numbered. But Shamshiel explained to Moses about the thrones, that they were different one from the other, some being of silver, some of gold, some of precious stones and pearls and rubies and carbuncles. The thrones made of pearls are for the scholars that study the Torah day and night for her own sake; those of precious stones are for the pious, those of rubies for the just, those of gold for the repentant sinners, and those of silver for the righteous proselytes. "The greatest of them all", continued Shamshiel, "is the throne of Abraham, the next in size the thrones of Isaac and Jacob, then come the thrones of the prophets, the saints, and the righteous, each in accordance with a man's worth, and his rank, and the good deeds he has performed in his lifetime". Moses asked then for whom the throne of copper was intended, and the angel answered, "For the sinner that has a pious son. Through the merits of his son he receives it as his share".

Again Moses looked, and he beheld a spring of living water welling up from under the tree of life and dividing into four streams, which passed under the throne of glory, and thence encompassed Paradise from end to end. He also saw four rivers flowing under each of the thrones of the pious, one of honey, the second of milk, the third of wine, and the fourth of pure balsam.

Beholding all these desirable and pleasant things, Moses felt great joy, and he said, "Oh, how great is Thy goodness, which Thou hast laid up for them that fear Thee, which Thou hast wrought for them that put their trust in Thee, before the sons of men"! And Moses left Paradise, and returned to the earth.

At the moment of his departure, a heavenly voice cried aloud: "Moses, servant of the Lord, thou that art faithful in His house, even as thou hast seen the reward that is laid up for the pious in the world to come, so also thou wilt be worthy of seeing the life of the world that shall be in the future time. Thou and all Israel, ye shall see the rebuilding of the Temple and the advent of the Messiah, behold the beauty of the Lord, and meditate in His Temple".

In the world to come Moses, beside sharing the joys of Israel, will continue his activity as the teacher of Israel, for the people will go before Abraham and request him to instruct them in the Torah. He will send them to Isaac, saying, "Go to Isaac, he hath studied more of the Torah than ever I studied", but Isaac, in turn, will send them to Jacob, saying, "Go to Jacob, he hath had more converse with the sages than ever I had". And Jacob will send them to Moses, saying, "Go to Moses, he was instructed in the Torah by God Himself".

In the Messianic time, Moses will be one of the seven shepherds that shall be the leaders of Israel with the Messiah.

Moses Declines the Mission

When Moses turned aside to see the great sight, that the bush was not consumed, he heard a voice calling to him, "Draw not nigh hither". These words were to convey that the dignity to be conferred upon him God intended for Moses personally, not for his descendants, and further he was warned not to arrogate honors appointed for others, as the priesthood, which was to belong to Aaron and Aaron's descendants, or royalty, which was to appertain to David and the house of David.

Again the voice spake: "Put off thy shoes from off thy feet, for the place whereon thou standest is holy ground". These words conveyed the desire of God that he cut asunder every bond uniting him with earthly concerns, he was even to give up his conjugal life. Hereupon the angel Michael spoke to God: "O Lord of the world, can it be Thy purpose to destroy mankind? Blessing can prevail only if male and female are united, and yet Thou biddest Moses separate from his wife". God answered, saying, "Moses has begot children, he has done his duty toward the world. I desire him to unite himself now with the Shekinah, that she may descend upon earth for his sake".

God spake furthermore, addressing Moses, "Thou seest only what is to happen in the near future, that Israel is to receive the Torah on Mount Sinai, but I behold what cometh after, bow the people will worship the steer, the figure of which they will see upon My chariot, even while My revelation will be made on Sinai. Thus they will excite My wrath. Nevertheless, though I know all the perverseness of their hearts, wherein they will rebel against Me in the desert, I will redeem them now, for I accord unto man the treatment he merits for his present actions, not what he will deserve in the future. I promised their father Jacob, 'I will go down with thee into Egypt, and I will also surely bring thee up again', and now I will betake myself thither, to bring Israel up in accordance with My words unto Jacob, and bear them to the land I swore unto their fathers, that their seed should inherit it. So long as the time of affliction that I had appointed unto his seed in My revelation to Abraham was not past, I hearkened not to the supplication and the groaning of his children, but now the end hath come. Therefore, go before Pharaoh, that he dismiss My people. If thou dost not bring about the redemption, none other will, for there is none other that can do it. In thee doth Israel hope, and upon thee doth Israel wait. The matter lieth in thine hands alone".

Moses, however, refused to take the mission upon himself. He said to God, "Thy promise unto Jacob was, 'I will surely bring thee up again out of Egypt'. Thou didst undertake to do it Thyself, and now it is Thy purpose to send me thither. And how, indeed, were it possible for me to accomplish this great matter, to bring the children of Israel up out of Egypt? How could I provide them with food and drink? Many are the women in childbirth among them, many are the pregnant women and the little children. Whence shall I procure dainties for those who have borne babes, whence sweetmeats for the pregnant, and whence tidbits for the little ones? And how may I venture to go among the Egyptian brigands and murderers? for Thou art bidding me to go to mine enemies, to those who lie in wait to take my life. Why should I risk the safety of my person, seeing that I know not whether Israel possesses merits making them worthy of redemption?' I have reckoned up the years with care, and I have found that but two hundred and ten have elapsed since the covenant of the pieces made with Abraham, and at that time Thou didst ordain four hundred years of oppression for his seed".

But God overturned all his objections. He spake to Moses, saying: "I will be with thee. Whatever thou desirest I will do, so that the redemption will in very truth be realized through Me, in accordance with My promise to Jacob. The little ones that Israel will carry up out of Egypt I will provide with food for thirty days. This shall prove to thee in what manner I will supply the needs of all. And as I will be at thy side, thou hast no need to fear any man.

Respecting thy doubt, whether Israel deserves to be redeemed, this is My answer: they will be permitted to go forth from Egypt on account of the merits they will acquire at this mountain, whereon they will receive the Torah through thee. And thy reckoning of the end is not correct, for the four hundred years of bondage began with the birth of Isaac, not with the going down of Jacob into Egypt. Therefore the appointed end hath come".

Persuaded now of God's unalterable resolve to use him as His instrument in the redemption of Israel from Egypt, Moses entreated God to impart to him the knowledge of His Great Name, that he be not confounded if the children of Israel ask for it. God answered, saying: "Thou desirest to know My Name? My Name is according to My acts. When I judge My creatures, I am called Elohim, "judge"; when I rise up to do battle against the sinners, I am Lord Zebaot, "the Lord of hosts"; when I wait with longsuffering patience for the improvement of the sinner, My name is El Shaddai; when I have mercy upon the world, I am Adonai. But unto the children of Israel shalt thou say that I am He that was, that is, and that ever will be, and I am He that is with them in their bondage now, and He that shall be with them in the bondage of the time to come".

In reply to the latter words of God, Moses said, "Sufficient unto the day is the evil thereof", and God assented thereto. He admitted that it was not proper to force the knowledge of future suffering upon Israel in a present that was itself full of evil and sorrow. And the Lord said to Moses: "My words about the future were meant for thee alone, not also for them. Tell the children of Israel, besides, that at My behest an angel can stretch his hand from heaven and touch the earth with it, and three angels can find room under one tree, and My majesty can fill the whole world, for when it was My will, it appeared to Job in his hair, and, again, when I willed otherwise, it appeared in a thorn-bush".

But the most important communication from God to Moses concerning the Divine Names were the words to follow: "In mercy I created the world; in mercy I guide it; and with mercies I will return to Jerusalem. But unto the children of Israel thou shalt say that My mercy upon them is for the sake of the merits of Abraham, Isaac, and Jacob".

When Moses heard these words, he spoke to God, saying, "Are there men that transgress after death"? and when God assured him that it was not possible for the dead to sin, Moses asked again, "Why, then, is it that Thou didst reveal Thyself to me at the first as the God of my father, and now Thou passest him over"? Whereupon God said, "In the beginning it was My purpose to address thee with flattering words, but now thou hearest the whole and exact truth, I am only the God of Abraham, the God of Isaac, and the God of Jacob".

Moses prayed to God, entreating Him to reveal His Great and Holy Name unto him, so that he might call upon Him with it and secure the fulfilment of all his wishes. The Lord granted the prayer of Moses, and when the celestials knew that He had revealed the secret of the Ineffable Name, they cried out, "Blessed art Thou, O Lord, gracious Giver of knowledge"!

God is always regardful of the honor of the elders of a people, and He bade Moses assemble those of Israel and announce the approaching redemption to them. And as God knew beforehand how Pharaoh's obduracy would display itself, He made it known to Moses at once, lest he reproach God later with the Egyptian king's frowardness.

Moses Punished for His Stubbornness

In spite of all these safeguards, Moses was not yet ready to accept the mission God wished to impose upon him. He persisted in urging his fears, saying: "But, behold, they will not believe me, nor hearken unto my voice, for they will say, 'The Lord hath not appeared unto thee.[] And the Lord said unto him, "What is that in thine hand"? And he said, "A rod". And the Lord said: "Thou deservest to be castigated with it. If thou didst not intend to take My mission upon thyself, thou shouldst have said so in the beginning. Instead, thou didst hold back with thy refusal, until I revealed to thee the great secret of the Ineffable Name, that thou mightest know it if the children of Israel should ask thee concerning it. And now thou sayest, I will not go. Now, therefore, if thou wilt not execute My charge to thee, it will be executed by this rod. It was My wish to distinguish thee and make thee My instrument for doing many miracles. But thou deservest a punishment for having suspected My children of lack of faith. The children of Israel are believers and sons of believers, but thou wilt show thyself of little faith in thy career, and as thou followest the example of the slanderous serpent, so shalt thou be punished with leprosy, wherewith the serpent was punished".

The Lord now bade Moses put his hand into his bosom and take it out again, and when he took it out, behold, his hand was leprous, as white as snow. And God bade him put his hand into his bosom again, and it turned again as his other flesh. Beside being a chastisement for his hasty words, the plague on his hand was to teach him that as the leper defiles, so the Egyptians defiled Israel, and as Moses was healed of his uncleanness, so God would cleanse the children of Israel of the pollution the Egyptians had brought upon them.

The second wonder connected with the rod of Moses likewise conveyed a double meaning, in that it pointed to the coming redemption of Israel, and taught Moses a specific lesson. At the bidding of God, Moses cast his rod on the ground, and it became a serpent, to show him that when he traduced Israel, he was following the example of the abusive serpent, and also to show him that the great dragon that lieth in the midst of the rivers of Egypt, though he was now hacking into Israel with his teeth, would be rendered harmless like the rod of wood, which has no power to bite.

And, again, through the third miracle he was bidden to perform, God conveyed to Moses what would happen in the latter years of his own life. The sign He gave him was to make known to him that, before the water came, blood would flow from the rock at Meribah, when Moses should strike it after uttering the hasty, impatient words that were destined to bring death down upon him.

For seven days God urged Moses to undertake the mission He desired him to execute. He resorted to persuasion, that the heathen might not say, that He abused His power as the Ruler of the world, forcing men to do His service against their will. But Moses remained obdurate, he could not be won over. He said: "Thou doest a wrong unto me in sending me to Pharaoh. In the palace of the Egyptian king there are persons that know how to speak the seventy languages of the world. No matter what language a man may use, there is someone that understands him. If I should come as Thy representative, and they should discover that I am not able to converse in the seventy languages, they will mock at me, and say, 'Behold this man, he pretends to be the ambassador of the Creator of the world, and he cannot speak the seventy languages'. " To this God made reply, as follows: "Adam, who was taught by none, could give names to the beasts in the seventy languages. Was it not I that made him to speak"?

Moses was not yet satisfied, he continued to urge objections, and he said: "O Lord of the world, Thou wouldst charge me with the task of chastising Egypt and redeeming Israel, and I am ready to be Thy messenger. But is it seemly that a man should execute two errands at once? Nay, my Lord, for this two men are needed". God made answer, and said, "Moses, I know well whom thou hast in mind with thy request, to be thy companion in the mission I assign to thee. Know, therefore, that the holy spirit hath already come upon thy brother Aaron, and even now he is awaiting thee on the way of Egypt, and when his eyes rest upon thee he will rejoice".

Furthermore God spake to Moses, saying, "When I appeared unto thee the first time, thou wast meek, and didst hide thy face, not to see the vision. Whence cometh now this effrontery of thine, that thou addressest Me as a servant his master? Thou speakest too many words by far. Perchance thou thinkest I have no messengers, hosts, seraphim, ofanim, ministering angels, and Merkabah wheels, to send to Egypt, to bring My children thence, that thou sayest, 'Send by the hand of him whom Thou wilt send'. In sooth, thou deservest severe chastisement. But what can I do, seeing that I am the Master of mercy? If thou escapest unpunished, thou owest it to thy father Amram, who rendered great services in behalf of the preservation of the Israelitish people in Egypt".

But Moses replied: "O Lord of the world, I a prophet and the son of a prophet obeyed Thy words only after much hesitation, and I cannot expect Pharaoh, a wicked man and the son of a wicked man, and the Egyptians, a disobedient people and the sons of a disobedient people, to give ear to my words. O Lord of the world, Thou dost send me to Egypt to redeem sixty myriads of Thy people from the oppression of the Egyptians. If it were a question of delivering a couple of hundred men, it were a sufficiently difficult enterprise. How much severer is the task of freeing sixty myriads from the dominion of Pharaoh! If Thou hadst called upon the Egyptians to give up their evil ways soon after they began to enslave Israel, they might have heeded Thy admonitions. But if I should go and speak to them now, after they have been ruling over Israel these two hundred and ten years, Pharaoh would say, 'If a slave has served his master for ten years, and no protest has made itself heard from any quarter, how can a man conceive the idea suddenly of having him set at liberty?' Verily, O Lord of the world, the task Thou puttest upon me is too heavy for my strength".

Moses said furthermore: "I am not an eloquent man, nor can I see of what avail words can be in this matter. Thou art sending me to one that is himself a slave, to Pharaoh of the tribe of Ham, and a slave will not be corrected by words. I consent to go on Thy errand only if Thou wilt invest me with the power of chastising Pharaoh with brute force". To these words spoken by Moses, God made reply: "Let it not fret thee that thou art not an eloquent speaker. It is I that made the mouth of all that speak, and I that made men dumb. One I make to see, another I make blind; one I make to hear, another I make deaf. Had I willed it so, thou hadst been a man of ready speech. But I desired to show a wonder through thee. Whenever I will it, the words I cast into thy mouth shall come forth without hesitation. But what thou sayest about a slave, that he cannot be corrected by words, is true, and therefore I give thee My rod for Pharaoh's castigation".

But Moses still stood his ground. He raised other objections. "His grandchild", he said, "is closer to a man than his nephew. Nevertheless when Lot was taken captive, Thou didst send angels to the aid of Abraham's nephew. But now, when the life of sixty myriads of Abraham's lineal descendants is at stake, Thou sendest me, and not the angels. When the Egyptian bondwoman Hagar was in distress, Thou didst dispatch five angels to stand by her, and to redeem sixty myriads of the children of Sarah Thou dost dispatch me. O Lord, send, I pray Thee, by the hand of him whom Thou wilt send in days to come". To this God answered, saying, "I said not that I would send thee to Israel, but to Pharaoh, and that one whom thou madest mention of, I will send to Israel at the end of days--Elijah will appear to them before the great and terrible day".

If Moses refused to do the errand of the Lord, there was a reason. God had revealed to him the treasures of the Torah, of wisdom, and of knowledge, and the whole world's future. Now he beheld in the inner chamber of God rows of scholars and judges interpreting the Torah in forty- nine different ways as they sat in the court of hewn stones; and he saw, besides, Rabbi Akiba explaining the meaning of the crowns upon the letters. Then said Moses: "I do not care to be God's messenger. Let Him rather send one of these great scholars". Then God ordered the Angel of Wisdom to carry Moses to a place of myriads of scholars, all interpreting the Torah, and all making use of the formula: This is a Halakah revealed to Moses on Mount Sinai. Now Moses recognized that even the greatest scholars of future generations would be dependent upon him, and then, at last, he was ready to execute the mission God desired to lay upon him.

But Moses had to pay dear for having hesitated in the execution of the Divine bidding. God said to him: "It was appointed that thou shouldst be priest, and Aaron should be the Levite. Because thou hast refused to execute My will, thou shalt be the Levite, and Aaron shall be priest",--a punishment that did not fall upon Moses personally, but only upon his descendants, all of whom are Levites. As for himself, he performed a priest's service in the Tabernacle.

Moses had said to God, "Thou hast been speaking to me now these many days, nevertheless I am still slow of speech and of a slow tongue". For this he received another punishment. God said to him: "I might change thee into a new man, and heal thee of thy imperfect speech, but because thou hast uttered such words, I refrain from curing thee".

The Return to Egypt

When Moses finally gave in, and declared himself ready to go to Egypt as God's messenger, his acceptance was still conditional upon the promise of God to fulfil all his wishes, and God granted whatsoever he desired, except immortality and entering the Holy Land. God also allayed his fears regarding the danger that threatened him from his whilom enemies Dathan and Abiram, on account of whom he had had to flee from Egypt. He told him that they had sunk to the estate of poor and insignificant men, bereft of the power of doing him harm.

Moses was loyal to the oath he had given his father-in-law Jethro, never to return to Egypt without securing his consent. His first concern therefore was to go back to Midian and obtain his permission, which Jethro gave freely. Then Moses could set out on his journey. He tarried only to take his wife and his children with him, which made his father- in-law say, "Those who are in Egypt are to leave it, and thou desirest to take more thither"? Moses replied: "Very soon the slaves held in bondage in Egypt will be redeemed, and they will go forth from the land, and gather at Mount Sinai, and hear the words, 'I am the Lord thy God', and should my sons not be present there"? Jethro acknowledged the justice of Moses' words, and he said to him, "Go in peace, enter Egypt in peace, and leave the land in peace".

At last Moses sallied forth upon his journey to Egypt, accompanied by his wife and his children. He was mounted upon the very ass that had borne Abraham to the Akedah on Mount Moriah, the ass upon which the Messiah will appear riding at the end of days. Even now, his journey begun, Moses was but half-hearted about his mission. He travelled leisurely, thinking: "When I arrive in Egypt and announce to the children of Israel that the end of the term of Egyptian slavery has come, they will say, 'We know very well that our bondage must last four hundred years, and the end is not yet', but if I were to put this objection before God, He would break out in wrath against me. It is best for me to consume as much time as possible on the way thither".

God was ill pleased with Moses for this artifice, and He spake to him, saying, "Joseph prophesied long ago that the oppression of Egypt would endure only two hundred and ten years". For his lack of faith Moses was punished while he was on the road to Egypt. The angels Af and Hemah appeared and swallowed his whole body down to his feet, and they gave him up only after Zipporah, nimble as a "bird", circumcised her son Gershom, and touched the feet of her husband with the blood of the circumcision. The reason why their son had remained uncircumcised until then was that Jethro had made the condition, when he consented to the marriage of his daughter with Moses, that the first son of their union should be brought up as a Gentile.

When Moses was released by the angels, he attacked them, and he slew Hemah, whose host of angels, however, held their own before the assailant.The Divine voice heard by Moses in Midian telling him to return to his brethren in Egypt fell at the same time upon the ear of Aaron, dwelling in Egypt, and it bade him "go into the wilderness to meet Moses". God speaketh marvellously with His voice, and therefore the same revelation could be understood one way in Midian and another way in Egypt.

The greeting of the two brothers was very cordial. Envy and jealousy bad no place between them. Aaron was rejoiced that God had chosen his younger brother to be the redeemer of Israel, and Moses was rejoiced that his older brother had been divinely appointed the high priest in Israel. God knew their hearts, for at the time when He charged him with the Egyptian mission, Moses had said, “All these years Aaron has been active as a prophet in Israel, and should I now encroach upon his province and cause him vexation”? But God reassured him, saying, “Moses, thy brother Aaron will surely not be vexed, he will rather rejoice at thy mission, yea, he will come forth and meet thee”.

Aaron showed his joy freely at seeing his brother once more, after their separation of many years. As for his joy in the distinction accorded to Moses, it was too great to be expressed in all its depth and extent. For his kind, generous spirit, he received a reward from God, in that he was permitted to bear the Urim and Thummim upon his heart, “for”, God said, “the heart that rejoiced at the exalting of a brother shall wear the Urim and Thummim”.

Aaron ran to meet his brother, and embraced him, and asked where he had spent all the years of their separation. When he was told in Midian, he continued to question him, saying, “Who are these that are travelling with thee”?

Moses: “My wife and my sons”.

Aaron: “Whither goest thou with them”?

Moses: “To Egypt”.

Aaron: “What! Great enough is our sorrow through those who have been in Egypt from the beginning, and thou takest more to the land”?

Moses recognized that Aaron was right, and he sent his wife and his sons back to his father-in-law Jethro.

He was no less magnanimous than Aaron. If the elder brother felt no envy on account of the younger brother’s dignity, the younger brother did not withhold from the other the teachings and revelations he had received. Immediately after meeting with Aaron, Moses told him all that God had taught him, even the awful secret of the Ineffable Name communicated to him on Mount Horeb.

In obedience to the command of God, the elders of the people were assembled, and before them Moses performed the wonders that were to be his credentials as the redeemer sent to deliver the people. Nevertheless, the deeds he did were not so potent in convincing them of the reality of the mission as the words wherein God had announced the approaching redemption to him, which he repeated in their ears. The elders knew that

Jacob had imparted to Joseph the secret mark designating the redeemer, and Joseph had in turn confided it to his brethren before his death. The last surviving one of the brethren, Asher, had revealed it to his daughter Serah, in the following words: "He that will come and proclaim the redemption with the words of God, 'I have surely visited you, and seen that which is done to you in Egypt', he is the true redeemer". Serah was still alive at Moses' return, and the elders betook themselves to her, and told her the words of Moses announcing the redemption. When she heard that his words had been the same as those Asher had quoted, she knew that he was the promised redeemer, and all the people believed in him.

Thereupon Moses invited the elders to go to Pharaoh with him, but they lacked the courage to appear before the king. Though they started out with Moses, they dropped off stealthily on the way, one by one, and when Moses and Aaron stood in the presence of the king, they found themselves alone, deserted by all the others. The elders did not go out free. Their punishment was that God did not permit them to ascend the holy mountain with Moses. They durst accompany him on the way to God only as far as they had accompanied him on the way to Pharaoh, and then they had to tarry until he came again.

Moses and Aaron Before Pharaoh

The day Moses and Aaron made their appearance before Pharaoh happened to be the anniversary of his birth, and he was surrounded by many kings, for he was the ruler of the whole world, and this was the occasion on which the kings of the earth came to do him homage. When the attendants announced Moses and Aaron, Pharaoh inquired whether the two old men had brought him crowns, and, receiving a negative reply, he ordered that they were not to be admitted to his presence, until he had seen and dismissed all the others desirous of paying him their respects.

Pharaoh's palace was surrounded by a vast army. It was built with four hundred entrances, one hundred on each side, and each of them guarded by sixty thousand soldiers. Moses and Aaron were overawed by this display of power, and they were afraid. But the angel Gabriel appeared, and he led them into the palace, observed by none of the guards, and Pharaoh decreed severe punishment upon the inattentive sentinels for having admitted the old men without his permission. They were dismissed, and others put in their places. But the same thing happened the next day. Moses and Aaron were within the palace, and the new guard had not been able to hinder their passing. Pharaoh questioned his servants, how it had been possible for the two old men to enter, and they said: "We know it not! Through the doors they did not come. Surely, they must be magicians".

Not enough that the palace was guarded by a host, at each entrance two lions were stationed, and in terror of being torn to pieces none dared approach the doors, and none could go within until the lion tamer came and led the beasts away. Now Balaam and all the other sacred scribes of Egypt advised that the keepers loose the lions at the approach of Moses and Aaron. But their advice availed naught. Moses had but to raise his rod, and the lions bounded toward him joyously, and followed at his feet, gambolling like dogs before their master on his return home.

Within the palace, Moses and Aaron found seventy secretaries busy with Pharaoh's correspondence, which was carried on in seventy languages. At the sight of the messengers of Israel, they started up in great awe, for the two men resembled angels. In stature they were as the cedars of Lebanon, their countenances radiated splendor like the sun, the pupils of their eyes were like the sphere of the morning star, their beards like palm branches, and their mouths emitted flames when they opened them for speech. In their terror, the secretaries flung down pen and paper, and prostrated themselves before Moses and Aaron.

Now the two representatives of the children of Israel stepped before Pharaoh, and they spake, "The God of the Hebrews hath met with us; let us go, we pray thee, three days' journey into the wilderness, and sacrifice unto the Lord our God, lest He fall upon us with pestilence or with the sword". But Pharaoh answered, saying: "What is the name of your God? Wherein doth His strength consist, and His power? How many countries, how many provinces, how many cities hath He under His dominion? In how many campaigns was He victorious? How many lands did He make subject to Himself? How many cities did He capture? When He goeth to war, how many warriors, riders, chariots, and charioteers doth He lead forth"? Whereto Moses and Aaron replied: "His strength and His power fill the whole world. His voice heweth out flames of fire; His words break mountains in pieces. The heaven is His throne, and the earth His footstool. His bow is fire, His arrows are flames, His spears torches, His shield clouds, and His sword lightning flashes. He created the mountains and the valleys, He brought forth spirits and souls, He stretched out the earth by a word, He made the mountains with His wisdom, He forms the embryo in the womb of the mother, He covers the heavens with clouds, at His word the dew and the rain descend earthward, He causes plants to grow from the ground, He nourishes and sustains the whole world, from the horns upon the rem down to the eggs of vermin. Every day He causes men to die, and every day He calls men into life".

Pharaoh answered, and said: "I have no need of Him. I have created myself, and if ye say that He causes dew and rain to descend, I have the Nile, the river that hath its source under the tree of life, and the ground impregnated by its waters bears fruit so huge that it takes two asses to carry it. and it is palatable beyond description, for it has three hundred different tastes".

Then Pharaoh sent to fetch the books of the chronicles of his kingdom from his archives, wherein are recorded the names of the gods of all the nations, to see whether the name of the God of the Hebrews was among them. He read off: "The gods of Moab, the gods of Ammon, the gods of Zidon--I do not find your God inscribed in the archives"! Moses and Aaron exclaimed: "O thou fool! Thou seekest the Living in the graves of the dead. These which thou didst read are the names of dumb idols, but our God is the God of life and the King of eternal life".

When Pharaoh said the words, "I know not the Lord", God Himself made answer, saying: "O thou rascal! Thou sayest to My ambassadors, 'I know not the strength and the power of your God'? Lo, I will make thee to stand, for to show thee My power, and that My Name may be declared throughout all the earth".

Having searched his list of the gods of the nations in vain for a mention of the God of the Hebrews, Pharaoh cited before him the wise men of Egypt, and he said to them: "Have ye ever heard the name of the God of these people"? They replied, "We have been told that He is a son of the wise, the son of ancient kings". Then spake God, saying, "O ye fools! Ye call yourselves wise men, but Me ye call only the son of the wise. Verily, I will set at naught all your wisdom and your understanding".

Pharaoh persisted in his obduracy, even after Moses and Aaron had performed the miracle of the rod. At the time when the two Hebrews succeeded in entering the palace, guarded as it was by lions, Pharaoh had sent for his magicians, at their head Balaam and his two sons Jannes and Jambres, and when they appeared before him, he told them of the extraordinary incident, how the lions had followed the two old men like dogs, and fawned upon them. It was Balaam's opinion that they were simply magicians like himself and his companions, and he prayed the king to have them come before him together with themselves, to test who were the master magicians, the Egyptians or the Hebrews.

Pharaoh called for Moses and Aaron, and he said to them: "Who will believe you when you say that you are the ambassadors of God, as you pretend to be, if you do not convince men by performing wonders"? Thereupon Aaron cast his rod to the ground, and it became a serpent. Pharaoh laughed aloud. "What", he exclaimed, "is this all your God can do?

It is the way of merchants to carry merchandise to a place if there is none of it there, but would anyone take brine to Spain or fish to Accho? It seems you do not know that I am an adept in all sorts of magic"! He ordered little school children to be brought, and they repeated the wonder done by Moses and Aaron; indeed, Pharaoh's own wife performed it. Jannes and Jambres, the sons of Balaam, derided Moses, saying, "Ye carry straw to Ephrain"! whereto Moses answered, "To the place of many vegetables, thither carry vegetables".

To show the Egyptians that Aaron could do something with his rod that their magicians could not imitate, God caused the serpent into which His rod had been changed to swallow up all the rods of the magicians. But Balaam and his associates said: "There is nothing marvellous or astonishing in this feat. Your serpent has but devoured our serpents, which is in accordance with a law of nature, one living being devours another. If thou wishest us to acknowledge that the spirit of God worketh in thee, then cast thy rod to the earth, and if, being wood, it swallows up our rods of wood, then we shall acknowledge that the spirit of God is in thee". Aaron stood the test. After his rod had resumed its original form, it swallowed up the rods of the Egyptians, and yet its bulk showed no increase. This caused Pharaoh to reflect, whether this wonderful rod of Aaron might not swallow up also him and his throne. Nevertheless he refused to obey the behest of God, to let Israel go, saying, "Had I Jacob-Israel himself here before me, I should put trowel and bucket on his shoulder". And to Moses and Aaron, he said, "Because ye, like all the rest of the tribe of Levi, are not compelled to labor, therefore do ye speak, 'Let us go and sacrifice to the Lord'. If you had asked for a thousand people, or two thousand, I should have fulfilled your request, but never will I consent to let six hundred thousand men go away".

The Suffering Increases

Beside refusing to dismiss the children of Israel, he ordered, on the very day of Moses and Aaron's audience with him, that the people be required to deliver the prescribed tale of bricks, though the taskmasters were not as heretofore to give them straw to make brick. Another decree was, that the children of Israel were not to be permitted to rest on the Sabbath, for Pharaoh knew that they used the leisure for reading the rolls that described their redemption. All this was a part of God's plan, the oppression of Israel was to be increased the closer the end approached. As they wandered up and down the land of Egypt gathering the straw they needed for the due tale of bricks, they were maltreated by the Egyptians if they caught them on their fields. Such unkind acts perpetrated by the whole people made it impossible for them to cast the entire blame for the bondage of Israel upon Pharaoh. All the Egyptians showed cruelty to the Israelites on their straw foraging expeditions, and therefore the Divine punishment descended upon all alike.

This frightful time of Israel's extreme suffering lasted six months. Meantime Moses went to Midian, leaving Aaron alone in Egypt. When Moses returned at the end of the reign of terror, two of the Israelitish officers accosted him and Aaron, and heaped abuse upon them for having increased the woes of their people rather than diminished them. They spake, saying, "If ye are truly the ambassadors of God, then may He judge between us and Pharaoh. But if you are seeking to bring about the redemption of Israel on your own account, then may God judge between you and Israel. You are responsible for the widespread stench now issuing from the Israelitish corpses used as bricks for building when our tale was not complete. The Egyptians had but a faint suspicion that we were waiting for our redemption. It is your fault if they are fully conscious of it now. We are in the quandary of the poor sheep that has been dragged away by a wolf. The shepherd pursues the robber, catches up with him, and tries to snatch the sheep from his jaws, and the wretched victim, pulled this way by the wolf and that way by the shepherd, is torn to pieces. Thus Israel fares between you and Pharaoh".

The two officers that spake these stinging words were Dathan and Abiram, and it was neither the first nor the last time they inflicted an injury upon Moses. The other Israelitish officers were gentle and kind; they permitted themselves to be beaten by the taskmasters rather than prod the laborers of their own people put under their surveillance.

The cruel suffering to which his people was exposed caused Moses to speak to God thus: "I have read the book of Genesis through, and I found the doom in it pronounced upon the generation of the deluge. It was a just judgment. I found also the punishments decreed against the generation of the confusion of tongues, and against the inhabitants of Sodom. These, too, were just. But what hath this nation of Israel done unto Thee, that it is oppressed more than any other nation in history? Is it because Abraham said, 'Whereby shall I know that I shall inherit the land?' and Thou didst rebuke him for his small faith, saying, 'Know of a surety that thy seed shall be a stranger in a land that is not theirs'? Why, then, are not the descendants of Esau and Ishmael held in bondage, too? Are they not likewise of the seed of Abraham? But if Thou wilt say, 'What concern is it of mine?' then I ask Thee, Why didst Thou send me hither as Thy messenger? Thy great, exalted, and terrible Name is feared in all the earth, yet Pharaoh heard me pronounce it, and he refuses obedience. I know Thou wilt redeem Israel in Thine own good time, and it is of little moment to Thee that now they are immuring living Israelites in these buildings".

Were He a God of justice only, the Lord would have slain Moses for the audacity of his last words, but in view of his having spoken as he had only out of compassion with Israel, the Lord dealt graciously with him. He answered Moses, saying, "Thou shalt see what I will do to Pharaoh", words conveying to Moses, that although he would be witness to the chastisement of Pharaoh, he would not be present at that of the thirty-one kings of Canaan. Thus he was rebuked for the unbecoming language he had used in addressing God. At the same time God's words were a rejoinder to another speech by Moses. He had said: "O Lord of the world, I know well that Thou wilt bring Thy children forth from Egypt. O that Thou wouldst make use of another instrument, for I am not worthy of being the redeemer of Thy children". God made answer thereto: "Yes, Moses, thou art worthy thereof. Through thee My children will be brought forth out of Egypt. Thou shalt see what I will do to Pharaoh".

At the same time God called him to account for having so little faith. He said: "O for the departed, their like cannot be found any more! I appeared unto Abraham, Isaac, and Jacob, as El Shaddai, God Almighty, but I was not known to them by My name Adonai, God All-Merciful, as I appeared unto thee. Nevertheless they did not cast aspersions upon My acts. I spake to Abraham, 'Unto thee will I give the land', but when he was about to bury Sarah, he had to pay out silver and buy a resting-place for her body; and yet he did not find fault with Me. I spake to Isaac, 'Unto thee, and unto thy seed, I will give all these lands', but when he desired water to drink, he had to strive with the herdsmen of Gerar; and yet he did not find fault with Me. I spake to Jacob, 'The land whereon thou liest, to thee will I give it, and to thy seed', but when he wanted to spread his tent, he had to acquire a parcel of ground for an hundred pieces of money; and yet he did not find fault with Me. None of them asked to know My Name. But thou didst demand to know it at the very first, when I desired to send thee down into Egypt, and after I revealed it to thee, thou didst speak, saying, 'Thou didst tell me that Thou art called Compassionate and Gracious, Longsuffering and Merciful, but as soon as I pronounced this Name before Pharaoh, misfortune descended upon the people of Israel'. Now I desire to fulfil My covenant with the three Patriarchs, and give their posterity the promised land, as a reward for the unquestioning faith of the Fathers, and also as a reward to the people, who, in spite of their suffering, did not find fault with My deeds. For this will I give them the land, which they do not deserve to possess for other reasons. I swear that I will do thus"! God pronounced this oath, to banish all fear from the mind of Moses, that He might act only in accordance with His attribute of justice, and thus delay the redemption of Israel for a time, on account of the sins of the people.

Now the redemption of Israel was a settled fact. But before Moses and Aaron could start on the work of delivering their people, God called various points to their attention, which He bade them consider in their undertaking. He spake to them, saying: "My children are perverse, passionate, and troublesome. You must be prepared to stand their abuse, to the length of being pelted with stones by them. I send you to Pharaoh, and although I will punish him according to his deserts, yet you must not fail in the respect due to him as a ruler. Furthermore, be careful to take the elders of the people into your counsel, and let your first step toward redemption be to make the people give up the worship of idols".

The last was a most difficult task, and the words of God concerning it wrung the exclamation from Moses: "See, the children of Israel will not hearken unto me. How, then, should Pharaoh hearken unto me"? It was the third time Moses declined to go on the errand of God. Now the Divine patience was exhausted, and Moses was subjected to punishment. At first God had revealed Himself only to Moses, and the original intention had been that he alone was to perform all the miracles, but henceforth the word of God was addressed to Aaron as well, and he was given a share in doing the wonders.

Measure for Measure

God divided the ten punishments decreed for Egypt into four parts, three of the plagues He committed to Aaron, three to Moses, one to the two brothers together, and three He reserved for Himself. Aaron was charged with those, that proceeded from the earth and the water, the elements that are composed of more or less solid parts, from which are fashioned all the corporeal, distinctive entities, while the three entrusted to Moses were those that proceeded from the air and the fire, the elements that are most prolific of life.The Lord is a man of war, and as a king of flesh and blood devises various stratagems against his enemy, so God attacked the Egyptians in various ways. He brought ten plagues down upon them. When a province rises up in rebellion, its sovereign lord first sends his army against it, to surround it and cut off the water supply. If the people are contrite, well and good; if not, he brings noise makers into the field against them. If the people are contrite, well and good; if not, he orders darts to be discharged against them. If the people are contrite, well and good; if not, he orders his legions to assault them. If the people are contrite, well and good; if not, he causes bloodshed and carnage among them. If the people are contrite, well and good; if not, he directs a stream of hot naphtha upon them. If the people are contrite, well and good; if not, he hurls projectiles at them from his ballistae. If the people are contrite, well and good; if not, he has scaling-ladders set up against their walls. If the people are contrite, well and good; if not, he casts them into dungeons. If the people are contrite, well and good; if not, he slays their magnates.

Thus did God proceed against the Egyptians. First He cut off their water supply by turning their rivers into blood. They refused to let the Israelites go, and He sent the noisy, croaking frogs into their entrails. They refused to let the Israelites go, and He brought lice against them, which pierced their flesh like darts. They refused to let the Israelites go, and He sent barbarian legions against them, mixed hordes of wild beasts. They refused to let the Israelites go, and He brought slaughter upon them, a very grievous pestilence. They refused to let the Israelites go, and He poured out naphtha over them, burning blains. They refused to let the Israelites go, and He caused His projectiles, the hail, to descend upon them. They refused to let the Israelites go, and He placed scaling-ladders against the wall for the locusts, which climbed them like men of war. They refused to let the Israelites go, and He cast them into dungeon darkness. They refused to let the Israelites go, and He slew their magnates, their first-born sons.

The plagues that God sent upon the Egyptians corresponded to the deeds they bad perpetrated against the children of Israel. Because they forced the Israelites to draw water for them, and also hindered them from the use of the ritual baths, He changed their water into blood.

Because they had said to the Israelites, "Go and catch fish for us", He brought frogs up against them, making them to swarm in their kneading-troughs and their bed- chambers and hop around croaking in their entrails. It was the severest of all the ten plagues.

Because they had said to the Israelites, "Go and sweep and clean our houses, our courtyards, and our streets", He changed the dust of the air into lice, so that the vermin lay piled up in heaps an ell high, and when the Egyptians put on fresh garments, they were at once infested with the insects.The fourth plague was an invasion of the land by hordes of all sorts of wild animals, lions, wolves, panthers, bears, and others. They overran the houses of the Egyptians, and when they closed their doors to keep them out, God caused a little animal to come forth from the ground, and it got in through the windows, and split open the doors, and made a way for the bears, panthers, lions, and wolves, which swarmed in and devoured the people down to the infants in their cradles. If an Egyptian entrusted his ten children to an Israelite, to take a walk with them, a lion would come and snatch away one of the children, a bear would carry off the second, a serpent the third, and so on, and in the end the Israelite returned home alone. This plague was brought upon them because they were in the habit of bidding the Israelites go and catch wolves and lions for their circuses, and they sent them on such errands, to make them take up their abode in distant deserts, where they would be separated from their wives, and could not propagate their race.

Then God brought a grievous murrain upon their cattle, because they had pressed the Israelites into their service as shepherds, and assigned remote pasturing places to them, to keep them away from their wives. Therefore the murrain came and carried off all the cattle in the flocks the Israelites were tending.

The sixth plague was a boil breaking forth with blains upon man and upon beast. This was the punishment of the Egyptians, because they would say to the children of Israel, "Go and prepare a bath for us unto the delight of our flesh and our bones". Therefore they were doomed to suffer with boils that inflamed their flesh, and on account of the itch they could not leave off scratching. While the Egyptians suffered thus, the children of Israel used their baths.

Because they had sent the Israelites forth into the fields, to plough and sow, hail was sent down upon them, and their trees and crops were destroyed.

They had been in the habit of saying to the Israelites, "Go forth, plant ye trees for us, and guard the fruit thereon". Therefore God brought the locusts into the Egyptian border, to eat the residue of that which was escaped, which remained unto them from the hail, for the teeth of the locust are the teeth of a lion, and he hath the jaw teeth of a great lion.

Because they would throw the Israelites into dungeons, God brought darkness upon them, the darkness of hell, so that they had to grope their way. He that sat could not rise up on his feet, and he that stood could not sit down. The infliction of darkness served another purpose. Among the Israelites there were many wicked men, who refused to leave Egypt, and God determined to put them out of the way. But that the Egyptians might not say they had succumbed to the plague like themselves, God slew them under cover of the darkness, and in the darkness they were buried by their fellow-Israelites, and the Egyptians knew nothing of what had happened. But the number of these wicked men had been very great, and the children of Israel spared to leave Egypt were but a small fraction of the original Israelitish population.

The tenth plague was the slaying of the first-born, and it came upon the Egyptians because of their intention to murder the men children of the Israelites at their birth, and, finally, Pharaoh and his host were drowned in the Red Sea, because the Egyptians had caused the men children of the Israelites to be exposed in the water.

Each, of the plagues inflicted upon Egypt had another parallel in the cruel treatment accorded to the Israelites. The first was a punishment for the arrogant words spoken by Pharaoh, "My Nile river is mine own, and I have made it for myself".

The plague of the frogs God brought down upon the Egyptians, "because", He said, "the frogs, which sometimes inhabit the water, shall take vengeance upon the Egyptians for having desired to destroy the nation destined to be the bearers of the Torah, and the Torah is likened unto water".

God sent vermin upon them, saying, "Let the lice made of the dust of the earth take vengeance upon the Egyptians for having desired to destroy the nation whose seed is like unto the dust of the earth".

Hordes of beasts, lions and wolves and swarms of serpents, came down upon them, "because", God said, "these animals shall take vengeance upon the Egyptians for having desired to destroy the nation that is likened unto lions, wolves, and serpents".

A fatal pestilence was brought upon them, "because", God said, "death shall take vengeance upon the Egyptians for having desired to destroy the nation that faces death for the glorification of the Name of God".

They were made to suffer with burning blains, "because", God said, "the boils coming from the ashes of the furnace shall take vengeance upon the Egyptians for having desired to destroy the nation whose ancestor Abraham walked into the fiery furnace for the glorification of the Name of God".

He made hail to descend upon them, "because", He said, "the white hail shall take vengeance upon the Egyptians for having desired to destroy a nation whose sins shall be white".

The locusts came upon them, "because", God said, "the locusts, which are My great army, shall take vengeance upon the Egyptians for having desired to destroy the nation that is called My hosts".

"Darkness", said God, "which is divided from the light, shall come and take vengeance upon the Egyptians for desiring to destroy the nation upon which shineth the light of the Lord, while gross darkness covers the other peoples".

The tenth plague, the slaying of the first-born, God inflicted, saying, "I will take vengeance upon the Egyptians for having desired to destroy the nation that is My first- born. As the night divided itself for Abraham, that his enemies might be vanquished, so I will pass through Egypt in the middle of the night, and as Abraham was proved by ten temptations, so I will send ten plagues upon Egypt, the enemy of his children".

The Plagues Brought Through Aaron

From the infliction of the first of the plagues until the passing of the last, after which the Egyptians yielded all that Moses and Aaron demanded, there elapsed a whole year, for twelve months is the term set by God for the expiation of sins. The deluge lasted one year; Job suffered one year; sinners must endure hell tortures for one year, and the judgment upon Gog at the end of time will be executed for the length of one year.

Moses announced the first plague to Pharaoh one morning when the king was walking by the river's brink. This morning walk enabled him to practice a deception. He called himself a god, and pretended that he felt no human needs. To keep up the illusion, he would repair to the edge of the river every morning, and ease nature there while alone and unobserved. At such a time it was that Moses appeared before him, and called out to him, "Is there a god that hath human needs"? "Verily, I am no god", replied Pharaoh, "I only pretend to be one before the Egyptians, who are such idiots, one should consider them asses rather than human beings".

Then Moses made known to him that God would turn the water into blood, if he refused to let Israel go. In the warning we can discern the difference between God and man. When a mortal harbors the intention to do an injury to an enemy, he lies in wait for the moment when he can strike an unexpected blow. But God is outspoken. He warned Pharaoh and the Egyptians in public whenever a plague was about to descend, and each warning was repeated by Moses for a period of three weeks, although the plague itself endured but a single week.

As Pharaoh would not lay the warning to heart, the plague announced by Moses was let loose upon him and his people--the waters were turned into blood. It is a well- known proverb, "Beat the idols, and the priests are in terror". God smote the river Nile, which the Egyptians worshipped as their god, in order to terrify Pharaoh and his people and force them to do the Divine will.

To produce the plague, Aaron took his rod, and stretched out his hand over the waters of Egypt. Moses had no part in performing the miracle, for God had said to him, "The water that watched over thy safety when thou wast exposed in the Nile, shall not suffer harm through thee".

Aaron had scarcely executed the Divine bidding, when all the water of Egypt became blood, even such as was kept in vessels of wood and in vessels of stone. The very spittle of an Egyptian turned into blood no sooner had he ejected it from his mouth, and blood dripped also from the idols of the Egyptians.

The transformation of the waters into blood was intended mainly as a punishment for the oppressors, but it was at the same time a source of profit for the oppressed. It gave the Israelites the opportunity of amassing great wealth. The Egyptians paid them large sums for their water, for if an Egyptian and an Israelite drew water from the same trough, the portion carried off by the Egyptian was bound to be useless, it turned into blood. To be sure, nothing helped the Egyptians in their distress, for though they drank water from the same cup as an Israelite, it became blood in their mouth.

However, this plague did not impress Pharaoh as a punishment inflicted in the name of God, because with the help of the Angels of Destruction the magicians of Egypt produced the same phenomenon of changing water into blood. Therefore he hearkened not unto the words of Moses.

The next was the plague of the frogs, and again it was Aaron that performed the wonder. He stretched forth his hand with his rod over the rivers, and caused frogs to come up upon the land of Egypt. Moses, whose life had been preserved by the water, was kept from poisoning his savior with the reptiles. At first only a single frog appeared, but he began to croak, summoning so many companions that the whole land of Egypt swarmed with them. Wherever an Egyptian took up his stand, frogs appeared, and in some mysterious way they were able to pierce the hardest of metals, and even the marble palaces of the Egyptian nobles afforded no protection against them. If a frog came close to them, the walls split asunder immediately. "Make way", the frogs would call out to the stone, "that I may do the will of my Creator", and at once the marble showed a rift, through which the frogs entered, and then they attacked the Egyptians bodily, and mutilated and overwhelmed them. In their ardor to fulfil the behest of God, the frogs cast themselves into the red-hot flames of the bake-ovens and devoured the bread. Centuries later, the three holy children, Hananiah, Mishael, and Azariah, were ordered by Nebuchadnezzar to pay worship to his idols on penalty of death in the burning furnace, and they said, "If the frogs, which were under no obligation to glorify the Name of God, nevertheless threw themselves into the fire in order to execute the Divine will concerning the punishment of the Egyptians, how much more should we be ready to expose our lives to the fire for the greater glory of His Name"! And the zealous frogs were not permitted to go unrewarded. While the others were destroyed from Pharaoh and the Egyptian houses at the moment appointed as the last of the plague, God saved those in the bake-ovens alive, the fire had no power to do them the least harm.

Now, although the Egyptian magicians also brought up frogs upon the land of Egypt through the help of demons, Pharaoh nevertheless declared himself ready to let the people go, to sacrifice unto the Lord. The difference between this plague and the first was, that water turned into blood had not caused him any personal inconvenience, while the swarms of frogs inflicted physical suffering, and he gave the promise to Moses to let Israel go, in the hope of ridding himself of the pain he experienced. And Moses in turn promised to entreat God for him on the following day. It could not be done at once, because the seven days' term had not yet elapsed. The prayer offered by Moses in behalf of Pharaoh was granted, all the frogs perished, and their destruction was too swift for them to retire to the water. Consequently the whole land was filled with the stench from the decaying frogs, for they had been so numerous that every man of the Egyptians gathered together four heaps of them. Although the frogs had filled all the market-places and stables and dwellings, they retreated before the Hebrews as if they had been able to distinguish between the two nations, and had known which of them it was proper to abuse, and which to treat with consideration. Beside sparing the Hebrews in the land of Egypt, the frogs kept within the limits of the land, in no wise trenching upon the territory of the neighboring nations. Indeed, they were the means of settling peaceably an old boundary dispute between Egypt and Ethiopia. Wherever they appeared, so far extended the Egyptian domain; all beyond their line belonged to Ethiopia.

Pharaoh was like the wicked that cry to God in their distress, and when their fortunes prosper slide back into their old, impious ways. No sooner had the frogs departed from him, his houses, his servants, and his people, than he hardened his heart again, and refused to let Israel go. Thereupon God sent the plague of the lice, the last of those brought upon Egypt through the mediation of Aaron. Moses could have no part in it, "for", said God, "the earth that afforded thee protection when she permitted thee to hide the slain Egyptian, shall not suffer through thine hand".

The Egyptian magicians having boasted that they were able to produce the first two plagues,--an empty boast it was, for they did not bring them about with their enchantments, but only because Moses willed them to do it,--God put them to shame with the third plague. They tried in vain to imitate it. The demons could not aid them, for their power is limited to the production of things larger than a barley grain, and lice are smaller. The magicians had to admit, "This is the finger of God". Their failure put an end once for all to their attempts to do as Moses did.

But Pharaoh's heart was hardened, and God spake to Moses, saying, "This wicked fellow remains hard of heart, in spite of the three plagues. The fourth shall be much worse than those which have preceded it. Go to him, therefore, and warn him, it would be well for him to let My people go, that the plague come not upon him".

The Plagues Brought Through Moses

The fourth plague was also announced to the king early in the morning by the river's brink. Pharaoh went thither regularly, for he was one of the magi, who need water for their enchantments. Moses' daily morning visits were beginning to annoy him, and he left the house early, in the hope of circumventing his monitor. But God, who knows the thoughts of man, sent Moses to Pharaoh at the very moment of his going forth.

The warning of the plague that was imminent not having had any effect upon Pharaoh, God sent the fourth plague upon Egypt, a mixed horde of wild animals, lions, bears, wolves, and panthers, and so many birds of prey of different kinds that the light of the sun and the moon was darkened as they circled through the air. These beasts came upon the Egyptians as a punishment for desiring to force the seed of Abraham to amalgamate with the other nations. God retaliated by bringing a mixture upon them that cost them their life.

As Pharaoh had been the first of the Egyptians to lay evil plans against the children of Israel, so he was the first upon whom descended punishment. Into his house the mixed horde of beasts came first of all, and then into the houses of the rest of the Egyptians. Goshen, the land inhabited by the Israelites, was spared entirely, for God put a division between the two peoples. It is true, the Israelites had committed sins enough to deserve punishment, but the Holy One, blessed be He, permitted the Egyptians to act as a ransom for Israel.

Again Pharaoh expressed his willingness to let the children of Israel sacrifice unto their God, but they were to stay in the land and do it, not go outside, into the wilderness. Moses pointed out to Pharaoh how unbecoming it would be for the Israelites to sacrifice, before the very eyes of his people, the animals that the Egyptians worshipped as gods. Then Pharaoh consented to let them go beyond the borders of his land, only they were not to go very far away, and Moses, to mislead him, asked for a three days' journey into the wilderness. But, again, when Moses had entreated God on Pharaoh's behalf, and the horde of wild beasts had vanished, the king hardened his heart, and did not let the people go.

The cessation of the fourth plague was as miraculous as the plague itself. The very animals that had been slain by the Egyptians in self-defense returned to life and departed from the land with the rest. This was ordained to prevent the wicked oppressors from profiting by the punishment even so much as the value of the hides and the flesh of the dead animals. It had not been so with the useless frogs, they had died on the spot, and their carcasses had remained where they fell.

The fifth plague inflicted by God upon the Egyptians was a grievous pestilence, which mowed down the cattle and beasts chiefly, yet it did not spare men altogether. This pestilence was a distinct plague, but it also accompanied all the other plagues, and the death of many Egyptians was due to it. The Israelites again came off unscathed. Indeed, if an Israelite had a just claim upon a beast held by an Egyptian, it, too, was spared, and the same good fortune waited upon such cattle as was the common property of Israelites and Egyptians.

The sixth plague, the plague of boils, was produced by Moses and Aaron together in a miraculous way. Each took a handful of ashes of the furnace, then Moses held the contents of the two heaps in the hollow of one of his hands, and sprinkled the ashes tip toward the heaven, and it flew so high that it reached the Divine throne. Returning earthward, it scattered over the whole land of Egypt, a space equal to four hundred square parasangs. The small dust of the ashes produced leprosy upon the skin of the Egyptians, and blains of a peculiar kind, soft within and dry on top.

The first five plagues the magicians had tried to imitate, and partly they had succeeded. But in this sixth plague they could not stand before Moses, and thenceforth they gave up the attempt to do as he did. Their craft had all along been harmful to themselves. Although they could produce the plagues, they could not imitate Moses in causing them to disappear. They would put their hands into their bosom, and draw them out white with leprosy, exactly like Moses, but their flesh remained leprous until the day of their death. And the same happened with all the other plagues that they imitated: until their dying day they were afflicted with the ills they produced.

As Pharaoh had wittingly hardened his heart with each of the first five plagues, and refused to turn from his sinful purpose, God punished him thereafter in such wise that he could not mend his ways if he would. God said, "Even though he should desire to do penance now, I will harden his heart until he pays off the whole of his debt".

Pharaoh had observed that whenever he walked on the brink of the Nile, Moses would intercept him. He therefore gave up his morning walk. But God bade Moses seek the king in his palace in the early hours of the day and urge him to repent of his evil ways. Therefore Moses spake to him as follows, in the name of God: "O thou villain! Thou thinkest that I cannot destroy thee from the world. Consider, if I had desired it, instead of smiting the cattle, I might have smitten thee and thy people with the pestilence, and thou wouldst have been cut off from the earth. I inflicted the plague only in such degree as was necessary to show thee My power, and that My Name may be declared throughout all the earth. But thou dost not leave off treading My people underfoot. Behold, to-morrow when the sun passes this point",--whereat

Moses made a stroke upon the wall-- "I will cause a very grievous hail to pour down, such as will be only once more, when I annihilate Gog with hail, fire, and brimstone".

But God's lovingkindness is so great that even in His wrath He has mercy upon the wicked, and as His chief object was not to injure men and beasts, but to damage the vegetation in the fields of the Egyptians, He bade Moses admonish Pharaoh to send and hasten in his cattle and all that he had in the field. But the warning fell on heedless ears. Job was the only one to take it to heart, while Pharaoh and his people regarded not the word of the Lord. Therefore the Lord let the hail smite both man and beast, instead of confining it to the herbs and the trees of the field, as He had intended from the first.

As a rule, fire and water are elements at war with each other, but in the hailstones that smote the land of Egypt they were reconciled. A fire rested in the hailstones as the burning wick swims in the oil of a lamp; the surrounding fluid cannot extinguish the flame. The Egyptians were smitten either by the hail or by the fire. In the one case as the other their flesh was seared, and the bodies of the many that were slain by the hail were consumed by the fire. The hailstones heaped themselves up like a wall, so that the carcasses of the slain beasts could not be removed, and if the people succeeded in dividing the dead animals and carrying their flesh off, the birds of prey would attack them on their way home, and snatch their prize away. But the vegetation in the field suffered even more than man and beast, for the hail came down like an axe upon the trees and broke them. That the wheat and the spelt were not crushed was a miracle.

Now, at last, Pharaoh acknowledged, and said, "The Lord is righteous, and I and my people are wicked. He was righteous when He bade us hasten in our cattle from before the hail, and I and my people were wicked, for we heeded not His warning, and men and beasts were found in the field by the hail, and slain". Again he begged Moses to supplicate God in his behalf, that He turn the plague away, and he promised to let the children of Israel go. Moses consented to do his will, saying, however: "Think not that I do not know what will happen after the plague is stayed. I know that thou and thy servants, ye will fear the Lord God, once His punishment is removed, as little as ye feared Him before. But to show His greatness, I will pray to Him to make the hail to cease".

Moses went a short distance out of the city from Pharaoh, and spread abroad his hands unto the Lord, for he did not desire to pray to God within, where there were many idols and images. At once the hail remained suspended in the air. Part of it dropped down while Joshua was engaged in battle with the Amorites, and the rest God will send down in His fury against Gog. Also the thunders ceased at Moses' intercession, and were stored up for a later time, for they were the noise which the Lord made the host of the Syrians to hear at the siege of Samaria, wherefore they arose and fled in the twilight.

As Moses had foreseen, so it happened. No sooner had the hail stopped than Pharaoh abandoned his resolve, and refused to let Israel go. Moses lost no time in announcing the eighth plague to him, the plague of the locusts. Observing that his words had made an impression upon the king's counsellors, he turned and went out from Pharaoh, to give them the opportunity of discussing the matter among themselves. And, indeed, his servants urged Pharaoh to let the Israelites go and serve the Lord their God. But, again, when Moses insisted that the whole people must go, the young and the old, the sons and the daughters, Pharaoh demurred, saying, "I know it to be customary for young men and old men to take part in sacrifices, but surely not little children, and when you demand their presence, too, you betray your evil purpose. It is but a pretense, your saying that you will go a three days' journey into the wilderness, and then return. You mean to escape and never come back. I will have nothing more to do with the matter. My god Baal-zephon will oppose you in the way, and hinder you on your journey". Pharaoh's last words were a dim presentiment. As a magician he foresaw that on their going forth from Egypt the children of Israel would find themselves in desperate straits before the sanctuary of Baal-zephon.

Pharaoh was not content with merely denying the request preferred by Moses and Aaron. He ordered them to be forcibly expelled from the palace. Then God sent the plague of the locusts announced by Moses before. They ate every herb of the land, and all the fruit of the trees that the hail had left, and there remained not any green thing. And again Pharaoh sent for Moses and Aaron, to ask their forgiveness, both for his sin against the Lord God, in not having hearkened unto His word, and for his sin against them, in having chased them forth and intended to curse them. Moses, as before, prayed to God in Pharaoh's behalf, and his petition was granted, the plague was taken away, and in a rather surprising manner. When the swarms of locusts began to darken the land, the Egyptians caught them and preserved them in brine as a dainty to be eaten. Now the Lord turned an exceeding strong west wind, which took up the locusts, and drove them into the Red Sea. Even those they were keeping in their pots flew up and away, and they had none of the expected profit.

The last plague but one, like those which had preceded it, endured seven days. All the time the land was enveloped in darkness, only it was not always of the same degree of density. During the first three days, it was not so thick but that the Egyptians could change their posture when they desired to do so. If they were sitting down, they could rise up, and if they were standing, they could sit down. On the fourth, fifth, and sixth days, the darkness was so dense that they could not stir from their place. They either sat the whole time, or stood; as they were at the beginning, so they remained until the end. The last day of darkness overtook the Egyptians, not in their own land, but at the Red Sea, on their pursuit of Israel. The darkness was not of the ordinary, earthly kind; it came from hell, and it could be felt. It was as thick as a dinar, and all the time it prevailed a celestial light brightened the dwellings of the children of Israel, whereby they could see what the Egyptians were doing under cover of the darkness. This was of great advantage to them, for when they were about to go forth from the land, and they asked their neighbors to lend them raiment, and jewels of gold and jewels of silver, for the journey, the Egyptians tried to deny having any in their possession. But the children of Israel, having spied out all their treasures during the days of darkness, could describe the objects they needed with accuracy, and designate their hiding-places. The Egyptians reasoned that the words of the Israelites could be taken implicitly as they spoke them, for if they had had any idea of deceiving them, asking for a loan when they intended to keep what they laid hands on, they might have taken unobserved during the days of darkness whatever: they desired. Hence the Egyptians felt no hesitation in lending the children of Israel all the treasures they asked for.

The darkness was of such a nature that it could not be dispelled by artificial means. The light of the fire kindled for household uses was either extinguished by the violence of the storm, or else it was made invisible and swallowed up in the density of the darkness. Sight, that most indispensable of all the external senses, though unimpaired, was deprived of its office, for nothing could be discerned, and all the other senses were overthrown like subjects whose leader has fallen. None was able to speak or to hear, nor could anyone venture to take food, but they lay themselves down in quiet and hunger, their outward senses in a trance. Thus they remained, overwhelmed by the affliction, until Moses had compassion on them again, and besought God in their behalf, who granted him the power of restoring fine weather, light instead of darkness and day instead of night.

Intimidated by this affliction, Pharaoh permitted the people to go, the little ones as well as the men and the women, only he asked that they let their flocks and their herds be stayed. But Moses said: "As thou livest, our cattle also shall go with us. Yea, if but the hoof of an animal belongs to an Israelite, the beast shall not be left behind in Egypt". This speech exasperated Pharaoh to such a degree that he threatened Moses with death in the day he should see his face again.

At this very moment the Lord appeared unto Moses, and bade him inform Pharaoh of the infliction of the last plague, the slaying of the first-born. It was the first and the last time that God revealed Himself in the royal palace. He chose the residence of Pharaoh on this occasion that Moses might not be branded as a liar, for he had replied to Pharaoh's threat of killing him if he saw his face again, with the words, "Thou hast spoken well; I will see thy face again no more".

With a loud voice Moses proclaimed the last plague, closing his announcement with the words: "And all these thy servants shall come down unto me and bow down themselves unto me, saying, Get thee out: and all the people that follow thee; and after that I will go out". Moses knew well enough that Pharaoh himself would come and urge him to lead Israel forth with as great haste as possible, but he mentioned only the servants of the king, and not the king himself, because he never forgot the respect due to a ruler.

The First Passover

When the time approached in which, according to the promise made to Abraham, his children would be redeemed, it was seen that they had no pious deeds to their credit for the sake of which they deserved release from bondage. God therefore gave them two commandments, one bidding them to sacrifice the paschal lamb and one to circumcise their sons. Along with the first they received the calendar in use among the Jews, for the Passover feast is to be celebrated on the fifteenth day of the month of Nisan, and with this month the year is to begin. But the computations for the calendar are so involved that Moses could not understand them until God showed him the movements of the moon plainly. There were three other things equally difficult, which Moses could comprehend only after God made him to see them plainly. They were the compounding of the holy anointing oil, the construction of the candlestick in the Tabernacle, and the animals the flesh of which is permitted or prohibited. Also the determination of the new moon was the subject of special Divine teaching. That Moses might know the exact procedure, God appeared to him in a garment with fringes upon its corners, bade Moses stand at His right hand and Aaron at His left, and then, citing Michael and Gabriel as witnesses, He addressed searching questions to the angels as to how the new moon had seemed to them. Then the Lord addressed Moses and Aaron, saying, "Thus shall My children proclaim the new moon, on the testimony of two witnesses and through the president of the court.

When Moses appeared before the children of Israel and delivered the Divine message to them, telling them that their redemption would come about in this month of Nisan, they said: "How is it possible that we should be redeemed? Is not the whole of Egypt full of our idols? And we have no pious deeds to show making us worthy of redemption". Moses made reply, and said: "As God desires your redemption, He pays no heed to your idols; He passes them by. Nor does He look upon your evil deeds, but only upon the good deeds of the pious among you".

God would not, indeed, have delivered Israel if they had not abandoned their idol worship. Unto this purpose He commanded them to sacrifice the paschal lamb. Thus they were to show that they had given up the idolatry of the Egyptians, consisting in the worship of the ram. The early law was different from the practice of later times, for they were bidden to select their sacrificial animal four days before the day appointed for the offering, and to designate it publicly as such, to show that they did not stand in awe of the Egyptians.

With a heavy heart the Egyptians watched the preparations of the Israelites for sacrificing the animals they worshipped. Yet they did not dare interpose an objection, and when the time came for the offering to be made, the children of Israel could perform the ceremonies without a tremor, seeing that they knew, through many days' experience, that the Egyptians feared to approach them with hostile intent. There was another practice connected with the slaughter of the paschal lamb that was to show the Egyptians how little the Israelites feared them. They took of the blood of the animal, and openly put it on the two side posts and on the lintel of the doors of their houses.

Moses communicated the laws regulating the Passover sacrifice to the elders, and they in turn made them known to the people at large. The elders were commended for having supported the leader at his first appearance, for their faith in Moses caused the whole people to adhere to him at once. Therefore God spake, saying: "I will reward the elders for inspiring the people with confidence in Moses. They shall have the honor of delivering Israel. They shall lead the people to the Passover sacrifice, and through this the redemption will be brought about".

The ceremonies connected with the Passover sacrifice had the purpose of conveying instruction to Israel about the past and the future alike. The blood put on the two side posts and on the lintel of their doors was to remind them of Abraham, Isaac, and Jacob; and the bunch of hyssop for sprinkling the blood on the doors was to imply that, although Israel's position among the peoples of the earth is as lowly as that of the hyssop among the plants, yet this little nation is bound together like the bunch of hyssop, for it is God's peculiar treasure.

The paschal sacrifice afforded Moses the opportunity for inducing the children of Israel to submit themselves to circumcision, which many had refused to do until then in spite of his urgent appeals. But God has means of persuasion. He caused a wind to blow that wafted the sweet scents of Paradise toward Moses' paschal lamb, and the fragrance penetrated to all parts of Egypt, to the distance of a forty days' journey. The people were attracted in crowds to Moses' lamb, and desired to partake of it. But he said, "This is the command of God, 'No uncircumcised person shall eat thereof', " and they all decided to undergo circumcision. When the Lord passed through the land of Egypt, He blessed every Israelite for his fulfilment of the two commands, the command of the paschal sacrifice and the command regarding circumcision".

The Lord performed a great miracle for the Israelites. As no sacrifice may be eaten beyond the borders of the Holy Land, all the children of Israel were transported thither on clouds, and after they had eaten of the sacrifice, they were carried back to Egypt in the same way.

The Smiting of the First-Born

When Moses announced the slaying of the first-born, the designated victims all repaired to their fathers, and said: "Whatever Moses hath foretold has been fulfilled. Let the Hebrews go, else we shall all die". But the fathers replied, "It is better for one of every ten of us to die, than the Hebrews should execute their purpose". Then the first-born repaired to Pharaoh, to induce him to dismiss the children of Israel. So far from granting their wish, he ordered his servants to fall upon the first-born and beat them, to punish them for their presumptuous demand. Seeing that they could not accomplish their end by gentle means, they attempted to bring it about by force.

Pharaoh and all that opposed the wishes of the first-born were of the opinion that the loss of so inconsiderable a percentage of the population was a matter of small moment. They were mistaken in their calculation, for the Divine decree included not only the first-born sons, but also the first-born daughters, and not only the first-born of the marriages then existing, but also the first-born issuing from previous alliances of the fathers and the mothers, and as the Egyptians led dissolute lives, it happened not rarely that each of the ten children of one woman was the first-born of its father. Finally, God decreed that death should smite the oldest member of every household, whether or not he was the first-born of his parents. What God resolves is executed. At the exact instant marking the middle of the night, so precise that only God Himself could determine and discern it, He appeared in Egypt, attended by nine thousand myriads of the Angels of Destruction who are fashioned some of hail and some of flames, and whose glances drive terror and trembling to the heart of the beholder. These angels were about to precipitate themselves into the work of annihilation, but God restrained them, saying, "My wrath will not be appeased until I Myself execute vengeance upon the enemies of Israel".

Those among the Egyptians who gave credence to Moses' words, and tried to shield their first-born children from death, sent them to their Hebrew neighbors, to spend the fateful night with them, in the hope that God would exempt the houses of the children of Israel from the plague. But in the morning, when the Israelites arose from their sleep, they found the corpses of the Egyptian fugitives next to them. That was the night in which the Israelites prayed before lying down to sleep: "Cause us, O Lord our God, to lie down in peace, remove Satan from before us and from behind us, and guard our going out and our coming in unto life and unto peace", for it was Satan that had caused frightful bloodshed among the Egyptians.

Among the slain there were, beside the Egyptian first- born, also the first-born of other nationalities residing in Egypt, as well as the Egyptian first-born dwelling outside of their own land. Even the long dead of the first-born were not spared. The dogs dragged their corpses out of their graves in the houses, for it was the Egyptian custom to inter the dead at home. At the appalling sight the Egyptians mourned as though the bereavement had befallen them but recently. The very monuments and statues erected to the memory of the first-born dead were changed into dust, which was scattered and flew out of sight. Moreover, their slaves had to share the fate of the Egyptians, and no less the first- born of the captive that was in the dungeon, for none was so low but he hated the Hebrews, and rejoiced when the Egyptians decreed their persecution. The female slaves that ground corn between mill-stones were in the habit of saying, "We do not regret our servitude, if only the Israelites are gagged, too.

In dealing out punishment to these aliens in the land of Egypt, God showed that He was at once the Master of the land and the Lord over all the gods of the nations, for if the slaves and the captives of war had not been smitten, they would have said, "Mighty is our god, who helped us in this plague". For the same reason all the idols of the Egyptians were swept out of existence in that night. The stone idols were ground into dust, the wooden idols rotted, and those made of metal melted away, and so the Egyptians were kept from ascribing their chastisement to the wrath of their own gods. Likewise the Lord God slew the first-born of the cattle, for the Egyptians paid worship to animals, and they would have attributed their misfortunes to them. In all these ways the Lord showed them that their gods were but vanity.

The Redemption of Israel from Egyptian Bondage

Pharaoh rose up in the night of the smiting of the first- born. He waited not for the third hour of the morning, when kings usually arise, nor did he wait to be awakened, but he himself roused his slaves from their slumber, and all the other Egyptians, and together they went forth to seek Moses and Aaron. He knew that Moses had never spoken an untruth, and as he had said, "I will see thy face again no more", he could not count upon Moses' coming to him. There remained nothing for him to do but go in search of the Israelitish leader. He did not know where Moses lived, and he had great difficulty and lost much time in looking for his house, for the Hebrew lads of whom he made inquiries when he met them in the street played practical jokes on him, misdirected him, and led him astray. Thus he wandered about a long time. all the while weeping and crying out, "O my friend Moses, pray for me to God"!

Meanwhile Moses and Aaron and all Israel beside were at the paschal meal, drinking wine as they sat and leaned to one side, and singing songs in praise of God, the Hallel, which they were the first to recite. When Pharaoh finally reached the door of the house wherein Moses abode, he called to him, and from Moses the question came back, "Who art thou, and what is thy name"?--"I am Pharaoh, who stands here humiliated".--Moses asked again: "Why dost thou come to me thyself? Is it the custom of kings to linger at the doors of common folk"?--"I pray thee, my lord", returned Pharaoh, "come forth and intercede for us, else there will not remain a single being in Egypt".--"I may not come forth, for God bath commanded us, 'None of you shall go out of the door of his house until the morning'. " --But Pharaoh continued to plead: "Do but step to the window, and speak with me", and when Moses yielded to his importunities, and appeared at the window, the king addressed these words to him: "Thou didst say yesterday, 'All the first-born in the land of Egypt will die', but now as many as nine-tenths of the inhabitants have perished".

Pharaoh was accompanied by his daughter Bithiah, Moses' foster-mother. She reproached him with ingratitude, in having brought down evil upon her and her countrymen. And Moses answered, and said: "Ten plagues the Lord brought upon Egypt. Hath evil accrued to thee from any of them? Did one of them affect thee"? And when Bithiah acknowledged that no harm had touched her, Moses continued to speak, "Although thou art thy mother's first-born, thou shalt not die, and no evil shall reach thee in the midst of Egypt". But Bithiah said, "Of what advantage is my security to me, when I see the king, my brother, and all his household, and his servants in this evil plight, and look upon their first-born perishing with all the first-born of Egypt"? And Moses returned, "Verily, thy brother and his household and the other Egyptians would not hearken to the words of the Lord, therefore did this evil come upon them.

Turning to Pharaoh, Moses said: "In spite of all that hath happened, I will teach thee something, if thou desirest to learn, and thou wilt be spared, and thou wilt not die. Raise thy voice, and say: 'Ye children of Israel, ye are your own masters. Prepare for your journey, and depart from among my people.

Hitherto ye were the slaves of Pharaoh, but henceforward ye are under the authority of God. Serve the Lord your God!' " Moses made him say these words three times, and God caused Pharaoh's voice to be heard throughout the land of Egypt, so that all the inhabitants, the home-born and the aliens, knew that Pharaoh had released the children of Israel from the bondage in which they had languished. And all Israel sang, "Hallelujah, praise, O ye servants of the Lord, praise the Name of the Lord", for they belonged to the Lord, and no more were the servants of Pharaoh.

Now the king of Egypt insisted upon their leaving the land without delay. But Moses objected, and said: "Are we thieves, that we should slink away under cover of the night? Wait until morning". Pharaoh, however, urged and begged Moses to depart, confessing that he was anxious about his own person, for he was a first-born son, and he was terrified that death would strike him down, too. Moses dissipated his alarm, though he substituted a new horror, with the words, "Fear not, there is worse in store for thee"! Dread seized upon the whole people; every one of the Egyptians was afraid of losing his life, and they all united their prayers with Pharaoh's, and begged Moses to take the Israelites hence. And God spake, Ye shall all find your end, not here, but in the Red Sea"!

The Exodus

Pharaoh and the Egyptians let their dead lie unburied, while they hastened to help the Israelites load their possessions on wagons, to get them out of the land with as little delay as possible. When they left, they took with them, beside their own cattle, the sheep and the oxen that Pharaoh had ordered his nobles to give them as presents. The king also forced his magnates to beg pardon of the Israelites for all they had suffered, knowing as he did that God forgives an injury done by man to his fellow only after the wrong- doer has recovered the good-will of his victim by confessing and regretting his fault. "Now, depart"! said Pharaoh to the Israelites, "I want nothing from you but that you should pray to God for me, that I may be saved from death".

The hatred of the Egyptians toward the Israelites changed now into its opposite. They conceived affection and friendship for them, and fairly forced raiment upon them, and jewels of silver and jewels of gold, to take along with them on their journey, although the children of Israel had not yet returned the articles they had borrowed from their neighbors at an earlier time. This action is in part to be explained by the vanity of Pharaoh and his people. They desired to pretend before the world that they were vastly rich, as everybody would conclude when this wealth of their mere slaves was displayed to observers. Indeed, the Israelites bore so much away from Egypt that one of them alone might have defrayed the expense of building and furnishing the Tabernacle.

On their leaving the land only the private wealth of the Egyptians was in their hands, but when they arrived at the Red Sea they came into possession of the public treasure, too, for Pharaoh, like all kings, carried the moneys of the state with him on his campaigns, in order to be prepared to hire a relay of mercenaries in case of defeat. Great as the other treasure was, the booty captured at the sea far exceeded it.

But if the Israelites loaded themselves down with goods and jewels and money, it was not to gratify love of riches, or, as any usurer might say, because they coveted their neighbors' possessions. In the first place they could look upon their plunder as wages due to them from those they had long served, and, secondly, they were entitled to retaliate on those at whose hands they had suffered wrong. Even then they were requiting them with an affliction far slighter than any one of all they had endured themselves.

The plagues did not stay the cruelty of the Egyptian oppressors toward the Hebrews. It continued unabated until the very end of their sojourn in the land. On the day of the exodus, Rachel the daughter of Shuthelah gave birth to a child, while she and her husband together were treading the clay for bricks. The babe dropped from her womb into the clay and sank out of sight. Gabriel appeared, moulded a brick out of the clay containing the child, and carried it to the highest of the heavens, where he made it a footstool before the Divine throne. In that night it was that God looked upon the suffering of Israel, and smote the first-born of the Egyptians, and it is one of the four nights that God has inscribed in the Book of Memorial. The first of the four is that in which God appeared to create the world; all was waste and void, and darkness brooded over the abyss, until the Lord came and spread light round about by His word. The second night is that in which God appeared unto Abraham at the covenant of the pieces. In the third night He appeared in Egypt, slaying the first-born of the Egyptians with His right hand, and protecting the first-born of the Israelites with His left. The fourth night recorded will be that in which the end of the redemption will be accomplished, when the iron yoke of the wicked kingdom will be broken, and the evil-doers will be destroyed. Then will Moses come from the desert, and the Messiah from Rome, each at the head of his flock, and the word of God will mediate between them, causing both to walk with one accord in the same direction.

Israel's redemption in future days will happen on the fifteenth of Nisan, the night of Israel's redemption from Egypt, for thus did Moses say, "In this night God protected Israel against the Angels of Destruction, and in this night He will also redeem the generations of the future".

Though the actual deliverance from Egypt took place in that night, the Hebrews did not leave the land until the following day.

During the same night God requited the Egyptians for their evil deeds in the sight of all the people, the night being as bright as day at the time of the summer solstice. Not one could escape the general chastisement, for by Divine dispensation none was absent from home at the time, so that none could fail to see the chastisement.

The angels in heaven learnt what was happening on earth. When they were about to begin their song of praise to God, He silenced them with the words, "My children on earth are singing now", and the celestial hosts had to stop and listen to the song of Israel.

Great as the joy of the Hebrews was at their deliverance from the Egyptian bondage, it was exceeded by that of Pharaoh's people at seeing their slaves depart, for with them went the dread of death that had obsessed them. They were like the portly gentleman riding an ass. The rider feels uncomfortable and longs for the moment of alighting, but his longing cannot compare in intensity with that of the ass groaning under the corpulent burden, and when their journey's end is reached, the ass rejoices more than his master. So the Egyptians were happier to be rid of the Hebrews than these were to be free.

In general, the Israelites were not in a joyous mood. The strength of men is readily exhausted, mentally and physically, by the strain of a sudden change from slavery to freedom. They did not recover vigor and force until they heard the angel hosts sing songs of praise and joy over the redemption of Israel and the redemption of the Shekinah, for so long as the chosen people is in exile, the Shekinah, who dwells among Israel, is also, as it were, in exile. At the same time, God caused the earth to exhale and send aloft a healing fragrance, which cured them of all their diseases.

The exodus of the Israelites began at Raamses, and although the distance from there to the city of Mizraim, where Moses abode, was a forty days' journey, yet they heard the voice of their leader urging them to leave the land. They covered the distance from Raamses to Succoth, a three days' march, in an instant. In Succoth God enveloped them in seven clouds of glory, four hovering in front, behind, and at the two sides of them, one suspended above them, to keep off rain, hail, and the rays of the sun, and one under them to protect them against thorns and snakes. The seventh cloud preceded them, and prepared the way for them, exalting the valleys and making low every mountain and hill. Thus they wandered through the wilderness for forty years. In all that time no artificial lighting was needed; a beam from the celestial cloud followed them into the darkest of chambers, and if one of the people had to go outside of the camp, even thither he was accompanied by a fold of the cloud, covering and protecting him. Only, that a difference might be made between day and night, a pillar of fire took the place of the cloud in the evening. Never for an instant were the people without the one or the other to guide them: the pillar of fire glowed in front of them before the pillar of cloud retired, and in the morning the cloud was there before the fire vanished. The clouds of glory and the pillar of fire were sent for the protection of Israel alone, for none beside, not for the heathen and not for the mixed multitude that went up with them; these had to walk outside of the cloud enclosure.

The cavalcade consisted of six hundred thousand heads of families afoot, each accompanied by five children on horseback, and to these must be added the mixed multitude, exceeding the Hebrews vastly in number.

So profound was Israel's trust in the Lord, that they followed Moses unmurmuringly into the wilderness, without supplying themselves with provisions. The only edibles they took were the remains of the unleavened bread and the bitter herbs, and these not to satisfy their hunger, but because they were unwilling to separate themselves from what they had prepared lovingly at the command of God. These possessions were so dear to them that they would not entrust them to the beasts of burden, they carried them on their own shoulders.

Other volumes in the series:

Kether Shem Tov – The Crown of the Good Name

by Avraham Ben Alexander of Cologne

Integral edition in English and Hebrew

Dealing specifically with the Divine Names and Sefirot, this is a deeply mystical text in the Jewish tradition written in the 13th century by the lay preacher Avraham of Cologne. Once it happened that Avraham walked into the synagogue of Shelomoh ibn Adret's father. While he was on the western side of the synagogue, a voice was coming out at the opposite side. They asked it every kind of question, and the voice also known as the "voice of Elijah" answered.

The Goraloth of Ahitophel – The Oracles of Ahitophel

English edition

In times of need, the authorities of Israel consulted an Oracle (Goral) to learn the will of HaShem (God) and to receive answers to their questions. Conceived by Ahitophel, special adviser of King David, the *Goraloth* elicit the intercession of 117 Angels in order to receive an answer directly from God concerning matters which we take at heart.

Tomer Devorah – Palm Tree of Devorah

by Moshe Cordovero

Integral edition in English

This is an introductory text to the study of Kabbalah that explains the moral virtues an apprentice needs to cultivate in order to become worthy of receiving kabbalistic secrets.

Brit Menucha – Covenant of Rest

by Avraham ben Yitzchak of Granada

Integral edition in English, Hebrew and Aramaic

Known only in restricted circles and closely guarded from unworthy hands, this is one of the most secret books of Kabbalah. It carefully describes the upper worlds in a very ethereal and symbolical language. It uses practical methods and pronunciations of the Divine Names that were employed by the High Priest in the Temple. It describes the names of Angels and Demons, and also explains how to summon them. This text is written for advanced readers who are at the conclusion of their kabbalistic formation.

Other volumes in the series:

Sheva Netivot Ha-Torah – The Seven Paths of Torah

by Avraham Abulafia

Integral edition in English and Hebrew

This book demonstrates the primacy of Kabbalah over every other branch of knowledge. It classifies seven levels of understanding of the Torah, showing what they are and how to reach them.

Or Ha-Sechel - Light of the Mind

by Avraham Abulafia

Integral edition in English and Hebrew

This book was written by Abulafia as a personal instruction for one of his disciples, learned in philosophy. By combining philosophy and kabbalah, the author uncovers in a logical way and by examples the keys and the techniques of Kabbalah. Thus, the access to the higher worlds is disclosed in a natural fashion.

Chaye Ha-Olam Ha-Ba – Life in the World to Come

by Avraham Abulafia

Integral edition in English and Hebrew

This major text by Abulafia concerns Prophetic Kabbalah. It is essentially a "book of names", of advanced Kabbalah. It is not written for beginners, but rather for those who are already on the path. There are not many explanations; the only important thing is the combinations of names to employ in meditation in order to open the holy gates and to reach the state of the restored Adam. Upon his return to Paradise, one can enjoy its fruits while still live physically on earth. The book investigates expecially the 72 Names of God.

Sefer Ha-Ot – The Book of the Sign

by Avraham Abulafia

Integral edition in English and Hebrew

This is one of the rare autobiographic books in Kabbalah. Abulafia relates his experiences and visions, some of which are really frightening. Most notable are his encounters with angels.

Other volumes in the series:

Sulam Aliyah – Ladder of Ascent

by Yehudah Albotini

Integral edition in English and Hebrew

This book explains in a very detailed manner the most secret kabbalistic techniques for attaining enlightenment and access to the higher realms of consciousness. Albotini summarizes very clearly the Abulafian system, while disclosing the paths for the sincere researchers. Thus, the gates of heaven will be open, making it possible to once again eat of the fruits of the Tree of Life.

Shaarei Kedusha – Gates of Holiness

by Chaim Vital

Integral edition in English, Hebrew and Aramaic

This text of prophetic Kabbalah teaches how to create the "external" and "internal" environment for successfully receiving the "Spirit of Propechy". It presents a clear, precise and revolutionary method for the one who feels the call but has gotten lost along the way and failed to reach the state of enlightenment.

Shaarei Tzedek - Gates of Justice

by Rabbi Shem Tov Sefardi of Leon

Integral edition in English

As Moshe Idel demonstrated, this book is incorrectly attributed to Rabbi Shem Tov Sefardi de Leon. Its apparently true author is a direct disciple of Avraham Abulafia, Natan ben Saadyah Harar. He describes instructions he received from his teacher, believed to be Aubulafia himself, along with his ecstatic experiences. This gives the book unparalleled importance, as auto-biographical works in Kabbalah are extremely rare. Additionally, he explains in detail many kabbalistic techniques, the very ones he employed to reach his prophetical states. The full text is a reconstruction based upon the four original known manuscripts, which in general have some notable differences or omissions.

Providence University:

Our University is affiliated to ULC (Universal Life Church), and operates in conjunction with the congregation ULC-ITALIA, an inter-faith and non-denominational church.

We sponsor the translation and promote the diffusion of kabbalistic texts, with particular attention to the teachings of Prophetic Kabbalah, while at the same time divulging the ways that permit a direct experience of God.

Most of our translations are of fundamental and often cited ancient Hebrew and Aramaic texts that have never before translated into English or any other language.

We do this, "for the earth shall be full of the knowledge of the Lord, as the waters cover the sea" (Isaiah 11:9). "And they shall teach no more every man his neighbor, and every man his brother, saying, Know the Lord: for they shall all know me, from the least of them unto the greatest of them". (Jeremiah 31:34)

Courses and lectures:

Providence University is persistently engaged in organizing courses, lectures, and seminars. We operate in many countries.

At our website, http://www.everburninglight.org/, you will find more information about our activities and agenda.

You may contact us by E-mail at info@everburninglight.org

If you cannot physically partecipate in our meetings, you may join us by videoconference; we have weekly meetings. If you have internet access, you can partecipate. Write us and we will send you further instructions.

For snail mail, we answer only if you contact us through our joint congregation in Italy. The address is:

ULC-ITALIA
via C.A. Colombo 20/F
34074 Monfalcone (GO)
ITALY

For urgent communications, you can contact our joint congregation in Italy at the following number:

+39-347-2295140

Printed in the United Kingdom
by Lightning Source UK Ltd.
136514UK00002B/8/A

9 781897 352120